ANNALS OF THE NEW YORK ACADEMY OF SCIENCES

Volume 270

PSYCHOLOGY IN PROGRESS

Edited by Kurt Salzinger

The New York Academy of Sciences
New York, New York
1976

Library of Congress Cataloging in Publication Data

New York Academy of Sciences. Section of Psychology.
  Psychology in progress.

  (Annals of the New York Academy of Sciences; v. 270)
  Papers presented during the 1974–1975 meetings of the
New York Academy of Sciences, Section of Psychology.
  1. Psychology—History—Congresses. 2. Psychology—
Congresses. I. Salzinger, Kurt. II. Title.
III. Series: New York Academy of Sciences. Annals;
v. 270. [DNLM: 1. Psychology. 2. Psychology—
History. W1 AN626L v. 270/ BF121 P9725]
Q11.N5 vol. 270 [BF95] 508'.1s [150'.9] 76-12789
ISBN 0-89072-024-X

WPC
Printed in the United States of America
ISBN 0-89072-024-X

ANNALS OF THE NEW YORK ACADEMY OF SCIENCES

VOLUME 270

April 28, 1976

PSYCHOLOGY IN PROGRESS: AN INTERIM REPORT*

Editor
KURT SALZINGER

CONTENTS

*This series of papers was presented during the 1974–1975 meetings of The New York Academy of Sciences, Section of Psychology. The editor gratefully acknowledges Dr. Virginia Staudt Sexton's work in arranging for the papers on the history of psychology and the advice given the The Psychology Section Advisory Committee: Helmut Adler; Leonore Adler; A. Appel; Joseph Church; George H. Collier; Florence Denmark, Vice-Chair; Cynthia Deutsch; Kay Estes; Elizabeth Fehrer; Robert Fried; Edward I. Gavurin; Louis J. Gerstman; Alberta Gilinsky; R. Rieber; Milton Schwebel; Sylvia Scribner; Jeri A. Sechzer; Virginia S. Sexton; Robert L. Thompson; Ethel Tobach; and Elizabeth Williams. Papers by Drs. A. Alland, W. J. McGill, and T. Verhave, although presented before the Psychology Section, unfortunately could not be prepared in time for the publication of this Annal.

INTRODUCTION:
WHAT'S IN A TITLE?

Kurt Salzinger

Biometrics Research Unit
New York State Psychiatric Institute
New York, New York 10032

Polytechnic Institute of New York
Brooklyn, New York 11201

I worried quite a bit about a title for this Annal. All the titles that were informative were entirely too long, and all the short ones, though desirable, seemed inaccurate. A large number of psychophysical judgments later and after a lot of paring down, I was finally left with a choice of two titles: "Progress in Psychology" and "Psychology in Progress." The choice reminded me of the importance of sequence in behavior and of the example a psychology teacher presented in class when I was an undergraduate student. He said, "There's a big difference between kicking a person, then saying 'excuse me,' and saying 'excuse me,' then kicking that person."

None of the papers in this volume requires an excuse. They are excellent examples of the progress we are making in the field of psychology. That is why the authors were invited to be speakers at The New York Academy of Sciences. But the notion of "work in progress" appealed to me much more than presenting the "progress in psychology." If there is anything that characterizes science, it is its ineluctable progress. No solution to a scientific problem is ever complete enough to forestall further progress in solving other problems. So it gives me great pleasure to be able to make these papers available to the reader for an overview of the field of psychology and to gain an intimate understanding of work in psychology as it progresses.

It is, of course, quite logical that consideration of psychology in progress today must begin with a view of its progress at an earlier time. The study of the history of psychology is only beginning to come into its own. Until fairly recently, the teaching of the history of psychology was relegated to the oldest member of the department, based on the notion that the oldest member, approaching his/her anecdotage and no longer engaged in empirical research, ought to be able to regale the interested graduate student with stories about the primitive apparatus constructed and used by the pioneering psychologists in fields now largely usurped by sophisticated electronic devices and on-line computers. Many psychologists still view history as a topic in which to feign interest because it sounds so much like an intellectual pursuit, rather than actually to partake of. In addition, the old saw that physical scientists stand on the shoulders of their scientific ancestors while social scientists step in their faces, well describes the attitude of many of those who *are* acquainted with the history of their predecessors. If you look for quotable remarks about history, you have no difficulty finding derogatory statements such as Henry Ford's "History is bunk" or Samuel Butler's ". . . although God cannot alter the past, historians can." Here, however, we are going to make the assumption along with Francis Bacon that "Histories make men wise" and with Abraham Lincoln that ". . . we cannot escape history."

Current culture and environment always structure both our methods and our theories, or, in the felicitous phrase of John Leonard, then editor of the New York Times Book Review section, "when the *Zeitgeist* sneezes, everybody catches cold." The study of history constitutes the only antihistamine we have to protect us against the cold of the present.

The delivery of the history papers here presented, happily coincided with the 100th year since the publication of Wilhelm Wundt's *Grundzuege der physiolo-gischen Psychologie,* the book which has strong claims to being the first truly psychological handbook, in contrast to the earlier, more physiological or philosophi-cal books, thus putting Wundt ahead of such notables as Helmholtz and Fechner. I realize that some psychologists would rather not open old Wundts, but I thought it might be a shot in the arm for us psychologists to consider ourselves as the descendants of Wilhelm Wundt, since that would automatically make us all Wundt-er Kinder.

But now to the substance of the introduction to the history papers. At first I thought I might give you my view on why the history of psychology should be studied; the only trouble is that Dr. Henle, who is far better equipped to cover this topic, will do so here. Then I thought I would trace the history of psychology in the Academy, only to come up against Dr. Tobach's paper. So what I will do instead, having tried quite hard to stick to the point of this volume but not being allowed to do so, is to ramble on, on a subject of interest to myself and only somewhat related to the subject matter of the papers that follow.

I happen to teach in a department of social sciences that consists, in addition to psychologists, of anthropologists, sociologists, economists, and, yes, historians. Because we take our cohabiting within one department seriously, we teach a course whose avowed purpose is the integration of all these fields. Having recently been inveigled into teaching that course, I have looked at what historians do, and viewing that activity from my Olympian psychological heights, I have concluded that *we* could do it better. Therefore, I hastened to review a nonrandom sample of the *Journal of the History of the Behavioral Sciences* for the better way. But once I got there, I found not much more of explicit methodology in those papers than in the more classical history journals.

True enough, the all-purpose rating scale reared its unattractive head with respect to prescriptive dimensions of various schools of psychology in one paper,[1] and the authors alerted the reader to an impending factor analysis; one investigator, by the name of Jones[2]—not Ernest—produced a kind of Urgraph, actually a cross between a table and a graph, to show the influence of Freud upon American sociology during the years 1909–1949; another author, Sulman,[3] using a calculating computer-clad contextual content analysis, demonstrated that Benjamin Spock's classic on baby care is actually a propaganda book for psychoanalysis. Finally, I came upon a methodological note. It did not describe the circuitry of a time machine—that would have been an apparatus note. It was a paper on the United States Patent Office as a source of historical material. This short paper describes how one obtains access to these documents either directly or through a law firm; it even discusses cost. What interested me, however, was the brief mention, in passing, of the discovery that in the recent past, inventors have taken out patents on some 34 different devices to prevent masturbation in stallions, and only 15 similar gadgets for human beings. The author, whose name, by the way, is Mountjoy,[4] makes some vague promise of separate and more detailed publication concerning these instruments. I could not help trying to integrate this information on antimasturbation devices with Sulman's computer-data finding that Spock viewed masturbation as "natural, harmless, and unless excessive, perfectly normal." Needless to say I was not successful in my integration.

All of which brings me to psychohistory and my plea for a different psychological approach. Historians today are being sold the bill of goods that psychoanalysis can make a contribution to the study of history. It is my belief that all aspects of psychology (by which I mean all aspects other than psychoanalysis) are relevant to the study of history. Whether we try to use psychophysics and our laws of perceptual constancy to explain primitive art and early structures, or social psychology to explain group behavior, or our knowledge of learning theory to explain various rates of acculturation, assimilation, and acquisition of knowledge, or our findings concerning the effect of pollutants to explain the downfall of Rome, or whether we contribute through our techniques of content analysis, reanalysis of old opinion polls, or use language traces to estimate contact among various groups, we can, I believe, make massive contributions to the field of history.

The papers in Part II of this volume, which treat of the history of psychology, trace the history of the Section of Psychology in The New York Academy of Sciences (Ethel Tobach), provide a cogent set of reasons for the importance of studying the history of psychology (Mary Henle), correct our current view of Wundt's place in psychology (Arthur L. Blumenthal), and reevaluate Louis William Stern's influence on current thinking in psychology (Francis P. Hardesty).

The papers gathered together in Part III, under the heading of **Current Psychology**, sample from among the activities of psychologists today.

The first paper of this section, by Gerard P. Smith, presents the research work characterizing one pole of the psychology axis, marking the nexus of biochemistry, neurophysiology, and behavior. The view I have of psychology, from the vantage point of planning a year's meetings covering the many different strands that in combination make up the rope tying all of psychology together, is that the rope is very thin and frayed. As psychologists we must work very hard to keep the strands together, for only thus will we be able to solve the problems that face us. The paper by Smith is certainly specialized in its attempt to explain the functioning of organisms, but the concept of arousal that it seeks to understand has implications for all areas of psychology.

The second paper in this section, by F. J. McGuigan, was invited for two reasons. It was the intent of the Advisory Committee of the Section of Psychology to honor Ralph Hefferline, who had died only a short time before, and to do so by recalling the kind of adventurous and original work that he had done in his lifetime. Ralph Hefferline's work encompassed pure science experiments on operant level and extinction as well as informal experiments on self-awareness. Between these extremes lies perhaps his most interesting work—his work on the avoidance-conditioned holding response and of course his most recent experiments on covert conditioning, using electromyographic recording. The name of F. J. McGuigan and his work on covert responses using the framework of behavior theory came immediately to mind. Unafraid to measure, he has gone inside the organism to follow behavior no matter where it occurs—as long as it is observable. Perhaps these experiments will be able, at last, to make clear that behaviorists must be classified by their behavior and not by the location of their measuring instruments.

The third paper, by Duane M. Rumbaugh and T. V. Gill, deals with the exciting new area of research in communication between human and nonhuman primates. There are now three different approaches in use to communicate with chimpanzees: one by the Gardners, who have trained their animals to use American sign language (I call it the Gardners' Gab); one by Premack, in which plastic chips are the stuff of which language is made (I call it Premack's Plastic Parlance); and the third, which is described in the paper in this Annal (I call it Rumbaugh's Reading and Writing). Having long ago convinced myself that language is not *the* feature that distinguishes the human species from other animals, I am particularly happy to be able to include this paper here.

But lest someone accuse me of believing that there is no difference at all between animals and human beings, I will quote Antonio the gardener in The Marriage of Figaro, because basically I agree with him: Antonio says to Countess Almaviva: "Drinking when we are not thirsty and making love at all seasons, madam: that is all there is to distinguish us from the other animals."

In order better to orient the reader to this paper, I would like to describe an earlier attempt at finding language behavior in animals. In 1960, I came across a statement to which both B. F. Skinner and J. P. Scott subscribed. Finding such an unlikely agreement, I was quite convinced that the statement had to be false. The statement to which both scientists subscribed was that barking in dogs was merely an emotional response that could not be the precursor of language and therefore could not be operantly conditioned. I managed to get myself a visiting investigatorship at the Jackson Memorial Laboratory in Bar Harbor and set right to work. Being a good Skinnerian, I placed my first subject, a wirehaired fox terrier, inside a box and waited for the first bark so that I could reinforce it by dropping food down a chute. My subject, however, had been trained to press a lever before I got to him, and, as a consequence, after establishing that the lever was not there, he simply spent his time circling inside the box. The dog wouldn't bark; I waited patiently as I had been taught in graduate school every good scientist must wait, but nothing happened. I then decided that maybe what I should do is to elicit the emotional response; maybe both Skinner and Scott were right. I therefore banged on the box, but that produced only faster circling. I was beginning to feel embarrassed. Having come out to Bar Harbor claiming that I would condition barking operantly, I found myself unable to evoke even the first bark, never mind condition it. There was only one thing left for me to do. I raised the one-way vision mirror and I barked at him. The dog's ears oriented toward me, and immediately, he barked back at me. Surprised as I was, I still managed to drop a piece of food into the box. Then I barked again, the dog followed suit, and I reinforced him. After a while, I barked and waited for the dog to bark several times before reinforcing him, and by the end of a few sessions, I found it possible to replace my presence altogether with a voice key that reacted to the dog's barks. Now at that time I really thought that I had accomplished something, but just as today, when the skeptics say about chimpanzee talk, "Yeah, yeah, she communicates after a fashion, but can she write poetry?" so was I criticized then for conditioning a dog to bark in a Viennese accent. "Could the dog bark in American?", they asked me.

The fourth paper, written by Bertram D. Cohen, also deals with communication, in this case with a problem of breakdown rather than one of acquisition. Working in an area—schizophrenia—where complexity of description appears to be the *sine qua non* of research, Cohen instead makes use of a simple but precise experimental technique that provides the kind of data on which sensible theories of schizophrenia can be built.

The last paper in this volume, by Joseph Church, provides us with the "other" pole of the psychology axis. Large in scope and scant of data, the paper seeks to explore a subject that few psychologists have dared to touch. While the rest of us have sought the refuge of the minimodel, Church has speculated about better ways of living. I leave to the reader to decide whether we know enough in psychology to speak about better ways of living or whether the greater danger lies in remaining silent. The fact is that precedents for such speculations exist, having been produced by such great psychologists as Koehler, Osgood, Skinner, and Tolman. What better note on which to end a volume on Psychology in Progress than one of constructive hopefulness!

REFERENCES

1. FUCHS, A. H. & G. F. KAWASH. 1974. Prescriptive dimensions for five schools of psychology. J. Hist. Behav. Sci. **10:** 352–366.
2. JONES, R. A. 1974. Freud and American sociology 1909–1949. J. Hist. Behav. Sci. **10:** 21–39.
3. SULMAN, A. M. 1973. The humanization of the American child: Benjamin Spock as a popularizer of psychoanalytic thought. J. Hist. Behav. Sci. **9:** 258–265.
4. MOUNTJOY, P. T. 1974. Methodological note: The United States Patent Office as a source of historical documents. J. Hist. Behav. Sci. **10:** 119–120.

A BRIEF HISTORY OF THE PSYCHOLOGY SECTION OF THE NEW YORK ACADEMY OF SCIENCES

Ethel Tobach

The American Museum of Natural History
New York, New York 10024

Today's celebration of "scientific psychology" suggests two historical issues that require investigation and deliberation. The first is the history of behavioral science in The New York Academy of Sciences. I am hopeful that my brief excursion into the history of the Psychology Section of the Academy will stimulate others to make a more definitive journey. As testified to by the letter inviting Titchener to talk on Wundt, there is sufficient historical material in the Archives of the Academy to make one or more dissertations.

A second issue is the categorization of the science of psychology among other sciences. It is hard to believe that even today, at the Academy and elsewhere, the epithet of "soft" is applied to psychology (as well as to anthropology and linguistics) as a science. Perhaps a review of the history and present modes of gathering, ordering, and using information in ways that may be defined as "scientific" is needed. Fresh insights are required into the societal processes in science and the social psychology of scientists. It is necessary to consider the hypothesis that the experience of psychologists in The New York Academy is not idiosyncratic. How psychologists interact with their colleagues of other disciplines is complex and the dynamics need to be understood, especially in an interdisciplinary world.

As I looked over the printed histories, the correspondence, and minutes, I saw a wealth of information relevant to a number of current matters confronting the Academy, the scientific community and society at large. As you know, the Academy is now examining its activities critically. One of the most important questions before it is: What should be the Academy's role in the scientific community and society at large? It is suggested by some that the national and international scope of the Academy's activities do not permit it to be more responsive to the needs of the city and state in which it is located without failing somewhat in its obligations to members outside the metropolitan area. As you will see from the following, the founding members of the Academy were only occasionally concerned with local or national matters; most frequently, at several stages of significant scientific advance, the Academy and its members were very much concerned with the latest developments and theories on the international scene. It is reasonable to propose that there is no contradiction between the responsibilities of the Academy to the local community and to the larger community in which it has long played a vital role. The recent decision to have affiliate chapters in other parts of the United States and in other countries attests to this proposal. Perhaps my brief review will give some historical perspective to this important issue. I will deal only with material from the first 130 years of the Academy, i.e., from 1817 (when it was The Lyceum of Natural History) to the end of World War II; only the last fifty of those years concern the Psychology Section specifically.

Much of the historical material comes from a volume printed in 500 copies at the author's expense: *A History of The New York Academy of Sciences Formerly the Lyceum of Natural History* by Herman Le Roy Fairchild, Recording Secretary, 1887.

The founding of the Academy is recorded as follows:

(Minutes of the Proceedings of the Lyceum of Natural History, New York, 1817.)

At a meeting of a number of Gentlemen favourable to the cultivation of *Natural Science*, held on Wednesday, the 29th January, 1817, at the Hall of the College of Physicians and Surgeons, in Barclay Street, New York, Doctor Samuel L. Mitchell was called to the chair, and Frederick C. Schaeffer appointed Secretary.

The object was stated to be the consideration and adoption of meaures for instituting a *Cabinet of Natural History*, in this city. After some discussion, Dr. A. W. Ives, Revd. F. C. Schaeffer and Dr. P. S. Townsend were appointed a Committee to report on the subject, to the meeting at some future day.—Adjourned.

Signed,   F. C. Schaeffer,

Secy.

CONSTITUTION

At a Meeting of a number of Gentlemen of the City of New York, on the 28th February, 1817, the following Preamble and Constitution were unanimously adopted:

Impressed with the importance of the study of Natural History as connected with the wants, the comforts, and the happiness of mankind, and particularly as it relates to the illustration of the physical character of the country we inhabit, We the subscribers do hereby agree to associate ourselves for the better cultivation and more extensive promotion of the same; and for our regulations as such Society, do adopt the following.

Space was a problem even then, and the following letter from General Swift indicates what the first home of the Academy was like:

Washington, 2d April, 1817

Dear Sir:

The room in the New York Institution which the Corporation destined for the use of the U.S. Military Philosophical Society is at the service of the Lyceum of Natural History upon the conditions mentioned in your interesting letter of 29th ult: I wish success to the Lyceum and that it may become a school for those who desire to contemplate the work of a beneficent creator.

Very respectfully yours, &c.,

J. G. Swift

To Caspar W. Eddy, M.D.,
1st Vice-Pres. Lyceum N.H.

The gentlemen who assembled to form the Lyceum in 1817 were mostly the friends, relatives, and students or former students of Samuel K. Mitchell, a physician who was teaching natural history at the College of Physicians and Surgeons. He was a true Renaissance Man of science, technology, law, literature, and the arts, and an elected member of the State Legislature as well as Congressman and United States Senator. Above all, he was noted for his ability to inspire students to scholarship and activity. The early members of the Lyceum ranged in age from 19 to 55, most of the members being in their early twenties and thirties. The occupations of these founders were also typical of the founders of the three older academies: The American Philosophical Society of Philadelphia (1769); The American Academy of Arts and Sciences (Boston, 1780); and The Academy of Natural Sciences of Philadelphia (1812).

They included several medical doctors, a minister, a Navy surgeon, a botanist, a veterinary surgeon, attorneys, shipmaster, flour merchant, carver and gilder. The members came from New York City and New York State, primarily, but there were some from Pennsylvania, South Carolina, and Tennessee. Honorary members came from Antwerp, London, Hamburg, Stockholm, and Odense, Denmark. They were truly a "lyceum"—a place of learning, offering public lectures as well as a museum with curators, specimens, and a library. But they were not destined to remain so. In a doctoral dissertation on the American Museum of Natural History by John Michael Kennedy in 1969,[1] the event is noted as follows:

> After 1810, the number of Americans interested in the study of natural history appears to have increased. Several societies devoted to these studies were formed between 1810 and 1830. In New York City some amateur naturalists founded the New York Lyceum of Natural Sciences in 1817. The members rented rooms, where they placed their collections, and met at regular intervals to read original papers. Many able American naturalists learned much of their science from the collections and libraries of these small societies. The very enthusiasm for natural history that brought these societies into existence, however, also limited their membership and the possibilities for their future growth. Only persons very interested in natural history would have cared to attend a meeting of the New York Lyceum of Sciences. Public support for and interest in the work of the natural history societies was therefore small. Often the members were obliged to store the collections in members' homes or barns, with the consequent large possibility of destruction by fire. . . .

> Several of the officers of the New York Lyceum were prominent members of the New York business community, but even after the Civil War, "when there was so much more money," they were unable to persuade most of their friends and colleagues to take any interest in the Lyceum. In April, 1865, the officers of the Lyceum sent a circular letter to many prominent business men, asking their aid in building a permanent home for the Lyceum. Their attempt failed; they raised only slightly more than seven hundred dollars. A little over a year later, on May 21, 1866, the Medical College Building, in which the Lyceum's collections had been placed, at the invitation of Columbia College, was burned to the ground. The Lyceum's collections were entirely destroyed. "Our difficulty always was," one of the officers of the Lyceum wrote a friend, "that the Lyceum did not look important enough. Too many of our friends, unfortunately, prefer to give their money only to successful institutions, with many wealthy supporters."

Dr. Kennedy, being much more concerned with the history of the Museum than with our Academy, then goes on to describe the role that Louis Agassiz played in the museology of the period. The history of the relationship between The New York Academy of Sciences and the American Museum of Natural History remains to be written, particularly in the period between 1860 and 1869, as does the special role of Albert Bickmore, a student of Agassiz in that relationship. One of the critical events in this history was the fire. Bickmore enlisted the help of William Haimes, D. Jackson Steward, and William E. Dodge, Jr., who reacted positively to the plan for a museum of natural history. Apparently this was a popular idea with other members of the Lyceum for Kennedy says:

> The widespread publicity given Agassiz' museum and the years of agitation by Andrew Haskell Green and the members of the New York Lyceum of Natural Sciences undoubtedly helped to persuade some of the other sponsors that such a museum would be a useful civic institution.

The American Museum of Natural History was officially chartered by New York State in 1869.

In the meantime, the word "lyceum" became more associated with concerts and musical and light entertainment. Here, too, the history needs filling in. In 1876 "The Lyceum of Natural History" became "The New York Academy of Sciences" under a charter of New York State. They organized themselves into four "Sections" of scientific work:

I., Biology; II., Chemistry and Technology; III., Geology and Mineralogy; IV., Physics, Astronomy and Mathematics.

The history written by Mr. Fairchild indicates that it was originally hoped that the Sections would take care of the collections and other business matters of running the Academy and be rather independent, but this proved too much, and he concludes:

It would seem as if the lesson of experience teaches that the simplest method is the best in the presentation of scientific papers, and that the meetings are most successfully conducted with the least formality.

Eight years after the charter, we find ten female members listed; also, a female patron, another woman as a contributor to the Publication Fund, and a Marchese from Italy as a corresponding member.

The original work of the Lyceum was continued; there were popular lectures, scientific meetings, and publications, and yearly exhibits of collections and instruments used in science were apparently begun sometime during the last decade of the century.

Thus, twenty years after the charter of the Academy, at the Third Annual Exhibit, we find a committee preparing an exhibit for Experimental Psychology of which J. McKeen Cattell is in charge. It is interesting to note that approximately ten years earlier, Cattell had been involved in trying to set up an "unofficial laboratory" at Cambridge. By 1887 he was successful and "made arrangements to start a laboratory in the building for physics."[2]

As to the actual founding of a Psychology Section, my information is still exceedingly incomplete. It appears from the correspondence so far unearthed that Franz Boas, who was then at the American Museum of Natural History, petitioned for and organized a subsection of the Biology Section to be composed of Anthropology, Psychology, and Philology sometime after 1895, and at the April 27, 1896 business meeting of the Academy, such a Section was formed. By 1899 there was a sufficient decrease in interest in philology (they preferred to meet elsewhere) to cause the subsection to drop the philologists and become "Anthropology and Psychology."

Perhaps the introduction of psychology to the Academy by an anthropologist at this comparatively late date in the history of American psychology is pertinent to the questions raised at the start of this paper. It is noteworthy that Benjamin Rush, the physician, revolutionist, philosopher, and father of American psychiatry, introduced the concepts of psychology during the American Revolution to such men as John Adams and Thomas Jefferson.[3] Rush was deeply impressed by Hartley's "associationism."[4] Rush thought that a people who had just changed their form of government should "effect a revolution in our principles, opinions, and manners so as to accomodate them to the forms of government we have adopted."[3] He believed Hartley's concepts would be helpful in this respect.

It is to be noted that Rush was a medical man and a Philadelphian, primarily, and so his papers were mainly addressed to the audiences of the American Philosophical Society. Rush died in 1813, before The New York Academy was founded. Perhaps an investigation of the possible relationship between the founders of the Lyceum and Rush would be instructive.

The partnership between anthropology and psychology was apparently quite strained, and much of the correspondence in the files concerns efforts on the part of the Recording Secretary of the Academy to obtain on time the minutes, notices of meetings, nominations, and so on, from the subsection. There is much confusion as to whether Anthropology or Psychology was responsible for giving the information to the Academy.

The names of Cattell, Woodworth, Thorndike, Judd, Lough and Hollingsworth are featured prominently in the years from 1896 through 1920. However, there then appears a letter in 1923 to R. W. Tower at the Museum from Boas at Columbia, saying that there were "no nominations for selection of a chairman who is to be a psychologist this year. We therefore voted to refer the selection of a chairman to the Council of the Academy." Penciled on the letter in another handwriting are the names of Hollingsworth and Poffenberger, with the word "Fellows" under them. It appears that neither of them accepted the nominations, and so from 1923 to 1929 there was no Psychology Section.

In February 1929 there is a letter from a psychiatrist (!), Dr. Lowell Selling of New York University, inquiring about the Biology meeting. Apparently, either in a letter that is lost, or in conversation, Dr. Selling and a Dr. Gilbert Rich, also a physician, indicated interest in reviving the Psychology Section. There then appears a draft of an invitation by Dr. Elaine Kinder of New York University inviting people to participate in the reorganization of the Psychology Section. The people invited are of interest: Emily Burr, Helen Montague and William Montague (both psychiatrists, he didn't join, she did), A. T. Poffenberger, P. D. Scott, Hans Syz, Leta Hollingsworth, Grace O'Neill, Gladys Tullman, and "Crafts, Jenkins, and Fisher" of New York University (referred to in a letter from Selling). The activity of Dr. Kinder was apparent in the correspondence that followed, and by April 8, 1930, the Section was established. As one might expect, Elaine Kinder became secretary and A. T. Poffenberger became chairman (possibly because only fellows could be officers at that time).

The "active members" list, for Oct. 21, 1930, showing only last names, was as follows:

Cattell	Selling
Woodworth	Kinder
Poffenberger	Garrett
Montague	Worden
Hayes	P. D. Stout
Fryer	Syz
Burr	Thorndike
O'Neill	

There were also listed some names under "Section"

Korn	Birdsall
Sharp	Taylor
Word	

Responding to invitations to the first organization meeting in October 1930 were Woodworth: No; Thorndike: No; Fryer: had a class to teach; Cattell: No, but would come later (unsigned note).

According to notes relating to the establishment of the Psychology Section, those signing the petition for the Section as of February, 1930 were as follows.

Cattell: kept membership	E. T. Burr: joined
Woodworth: kept membership	Helen Montague, M.D.: joined NYAS
Thorndike: kept membership	Syz
Poffenberger: joined NYAS	Selling: was a member (he actually
C. J. Warden: kept membership	wrote to psychologists at
Garrett	Columbia inviting them to join)

Stout   Mary W. S. Hayes: joined
Douglas Fryer: joined   O'Neill: joined
                                                    Kinder: joined

On April 8, 1930, the Psychology Section was established. Dr. Selling left New York University in May, 1930 and turned the Section over to Elaine Kinder in a letter. However, A. T. Poffenberger became Chairman *pro tem,* and E. Kinder became Secretary by October, 1930.

This is some of the organization history of the Section. What were the scientific activities of the Academy—how did psychology contribute? Unfortunately, the records before 1876 are either not readily available or have been lost. Most of them were lost because of fires, frequent moving, and so on. The following data, therefore, came primarily from the publication lists after the Academy was chartered in 1876. By 1877 (Vol. I, NYAS Annals) the impress of Darwin was clear, and an analysis of the papers given and published testifies to this. Papers in evolutionary theory, paleontology, and geology, as well as in chemistry, zoology, and ecology, were most frequent. There were occasional but regular papers in astronomy and physics.

Some of those early papers are a little poignant; one in 1893-95:

> A study of the New York Obelisk as a decayed
> boulder by Alexis A. Julien;

and another:

> On certain bacteria from the air of New York City
> Harrison G. Dyan

In 1887 we see two papers by women: one on the osteology of the shad and the other (done collaboratively with a husband or brother) on taxonomy.[5,6]

The number of papers describing the characteristics of the "country we inhabit" was usually low, from zero to three a year, the last one in 1929. There were slightly more on the flora and fauna of other parts of the United States. With the separation of the botanists from the Academy toward the end of the nineteenth century, the botanical papers ceased to appear. In 1911-12, T. H. Morgan, the great geneticist, published a paper on mouse-coat color, and thereafter papers in genetics appeared from time to time. In 1915-16 the first paper in biochemistry appeared, but it was another 15 years (1930) before papers in various aspects of biomedical science were presented and published fairly regularly.

Anthropology papers appear sporadically, the earliest in the first volume in 1877-1880; a philology paper appears in 1899-1900. Boas himself did not publish in the Academy until 1911. One of his papers sold as an "individual," for ten cents.

Where are the psychological papers? At the time of the Academy Charter (1876), William James was an assistant professor of physiology at Harvard, and G. Stanley Hall was studying for his Ph.D. with him. J. McKeen Cattell was still in college. G. T. Ladd was shortly to be at Bowdoin, teaching "mental and moral philosophy." Scripture finished his degree with Wundt fifteen years later.

Yet, the first paper, even after the formation of the Anthropology-Psychology subsection is one, in 1931: "The tetrad-difference criterion and the measurement of mental traits," by Garrett and Anastasi.

Why the low representation of psychologists in the Academy publications? Was it because psychologists tended to write books rather than give papers—a tradition among zoologists and geologists? Was it because the psychologists already had a journal, the American Journal of Psychology, founded by G. Stanley Hall in 1887? Was it that more journals were appearing in the early twentieth century? The psychologists gave papers regularly at the Academy, often in conjunction with the

New York Division of the American Psychological Association (founded by Hall in 1892). Abstracts of these papers appeared in the *Journal of Philosophy,* although given under the auspices of the Academy when it was housed at the American Museum or at Columbia University. Could the tie to philosophy have been responsible, in part, for the relationship between psychology and the other sciences at the Academy?

During the period that the Academy's ties with the Museum were strong, there were many papers on animal behavior, beginning with one by C. Lloyd Morgan on "The Origin of Instinct" on January 31, 1896, to which James McKeen Cattell was invited as a discussant. The session was sponsored by the Biology Section!

Despite the interest in animal behavior evidenced by the earliest psychologists and although zoologists were publishing papers in animal behavior in Academy journals, there is no readily apparent indication that there was much communication between the two groups.

There are many questions raised by this rather limited look at the Academy's records. Nonetheless, some interesting research is suggested. Boas and Cattell were both at Columbia University. What was their relationship? What was the effect of Cattell's difficulties with Columbia concerning the relationship, if there was one? Boas left the Museum after a disagreement with Morris K. Jessup, President of the American Museum of Natural History in 1903. How did this affect the relationship between the Academy, Columbia, and the Museum? Did Boas' sensitivity to racism affect his relationship with the individuals and institutions involved in the activities of the proponents of eugenics? Did this play a role in the Academy and his eventual withdrawal from the Museum and the Academy? What was the Academy's role and activity in World War I and the period thereafter, when great changes in the political world were taking place? One might guess that the Academy itself was quite withdrawn and uninvolved. During World War II, the first two papers having any relevance to the war appeared in 1943 (Vol. 44). One was on parasitic diseases and the other was on personnel selection by L. S. Kubie, Gardner Murphy, and others.

A list of publications (Annals) dealing with Psychology, Psychiatry, and Related Fields during the period of 1941–1950 shows the following distribution of topics:

Chemistry	9
Behavioral Theory	3
Human Engineering	1
Physiology	6
Psychopharmacology	5
Experimental Psychology	2
Physiological Psychology	3
Conditioning Phenomena	2
Social Psychology	2
Behavior Genetics	1

I have been able only to increase the number of questions I had. The reader can certainly think of many more. I think some fascinating answers are for the finding in the history of the Academy.

ACKNOWLEDGMENTS

I wish to thank Svetlana Kostic-Stone for her help in going through the archives of the Academy.

REFERENCES

1. KENNEDY, J. M. 1969. Philanthropy and Science in New York City: The American Museum: 277. University Microfilms. Ann Arbor, Mich.
2. SOKAL, M. M. 1972. Psychology at Victorian Cambridge—the unofficial laboratory of 1887–1888. Proc. Amer. Philos. Soc. **116** (2): 145–147.
3. D'ELIA, D. J. 1970. Benjamin Rush, David Hartly, and the revolutionary uses of psychology. Proc. Amer. Philos. Soc. **114** (2): 109–118.
4. BORING, E. G. 1929. A History of Experimental Psychology. Second edit.: 777. Appleton-Century-Crofts. New York, N.Y.
5. HITCHCOCK, F. R. M. 1887. Further notes on the osteology of the Shad (*Alosa sapidissima*) Ann. N. Y. Acad. Sci. IV. 1887–1889.
6. EIGENMANN, C. H. & R. S. EIGENMANN. 1887. A revision of the ederhilous genera of Curimatinae. Ann. N. Y. Acad. Sci. IV. 1887–1889.

WHY STUDY THE HISTORY OF PSYCHOLOGY?

Mary Henle

Graduate Faculty
New School for Social Research
New York, New York 10011

We are tired of hearing that those who do not know their history are forced to repeat it. But I would like to give the aphorism more concrete meaning by way of examples from the contemporary psychological scene and its history. The examples I select will, of course, be taken from the problems and the sources I know best, but others will find no shortage of instances in their own special fields of interest.

What have we to fear from repeating history? Clearly, the errors of earlier psychologies. "I have been told," Titchener once wrote, "that in philosophy errors never die, and it may be that they die hard in psychology because that earlier habit of immortality is still strong upon them." I wonder if that is the reason. It may be that we repeat the errors of our predecessors because we have not examined them in the context of that earlier thinking. I am not now talking about methodological errors—here the picture is one of progress—nor about factual errors, which will correct themselves through the use of the scientific method. I am concerned with theoretical or conceptual errors.

But why do we need history to show us our errors? I would like to suggest that it is because of the nature of cognitive processes. For reasons inherent in the thought processes themselves, it is most difficult to see the errors in our own thinking. For one thing, it is perhaps impossible for anyone to make fully explicit all of his own assumptions. In this respect the formal disciplines of mathematics and logic have an enormous advantage over the empirical sciences. In psychology, we come to our work with assumptions about the world, about people, about science, that we have picked up informally or learned explicitly, many of which we no longer question as mature thinkers. The phenomenologists have attempted to deal with this problem by stripping away such assumptions one by one, but I believe it is fair to say that no full-scale scientific psychology has come out of these efforts. We have to bear the weight of the hidden assumptions of the language we use. What would become of behaviorism, as a single example, if its adherents were to sit down and examine the meanings of the key terms "stimulus" and "response"?

Of course, where differences of opinion exist in psychology, our opponents can explicate some of our assumptions and meanings for us. On two occasions Chomsky has, in part, performed this service for Skinner. Skinner, however, was not impressed, and this for a good reason, which brings us to a second factor that makes it so difficult for us to see the errors in our own thinking.

Our thinking does not work with a set of isolated and unrelated propositions, but with a structure of ideas, usually much more consistent than we realize. In an earlier day, we used to speak of systems of psychology: thus perception, learning, memory, thinking, and other psychological processes were treated in terms consistent with one another. Now we have become specialists, and a perceptionist, for example (once he has passed his examinations), is not expected to know anything about, say, verbal learning or personality. But what he says about perception has implications for these other fields. Thus he makes assumptions about neural processes corresponding to perceptual events; he is not likely to alter this largely assumptive nervous system if he were to approach verbal learning or personality. The same nervous system must get us through all our varied activities. I would be willing to make predictions about what kinds of learning theories or theories of personality would appeal to variously oriented perceptionists. Whether we like it or not, we tend to be cryptosystematists.

I am suggesting, then, that our thought in psychology (and elsewhere) constitutes a structure, even where this system is largely implicit. This structure easily absorbs criticism from outside. It can do so because the meaning of an item is determined by the context in which it appears. We can see this on the simplest perceptual level. Line up three black circles on a white ground; one of them will be the center circle. Now add circles to the line; this is easily done so as to give a different circle the property of center. And so, too, in our thinking. A fact or an idea has one meaning in one context, a different meaning in a different structure of ideas. The word *man* has a different meaning depending on whether you are a paleontologist, a zoologist, an adolescent boy, a women's libber, etc. The facts of transposition have one meaning if you are a behaviorist, another if you are a Gestalt psychologist. To multiply examples is unnecessary. The effects of context are commonplace, and we have only to apply them to the case in which a criticism is leveled against us. Such criticism may be viewed as irrelevant or unimportant, or it may be reinterpreted—all because, while it makes sense in the context of our opponent's thinking, it does not make sense in the context of our own. No wonder Skinner was not impressed by the critical articles of Chomsky. In the confrontation between a particular criticism and a structure of thought, the structure—by far the more powerful creature—usually has an easy victory.

If such structures of ideas possess to a marked degree a tendency toward self-preservation, making them highly resistant to criticism, it should be added that there are also very valuable influences of context. We could not have a coherent view of our subject matter—or of the world—if our ideas did not constitute just the kind of structure of which I have been speaking.

I hope it is clear that I am speaking of strictly cognitive matters. It may be, as some have emphasized, that considerations of egoism enter into the difficulty of changing one's mind in the face of criticism. But quite apart from such considerations, the effects of context are sufficient to make our thinking resist the intrusion of even good criticism. To the extent that the system is implicit, the difficulties, we have seen, are compounded.

Still a third aspect of thinking makes it difficult to apply criticisms to ourselves. It seems to be well established that the differences we see depend upon where we stand on a continuum of opinion. Small differences in the neighborhood of our own views are easily seen, but at the opposite end of the opinion spectrum we tend to lump together divergent positions. It would be easy to find examples in political opinion. Here is a single instance in psychology: I was once criticizing a family of approaches to a particular problem, not just a specific theory. Psychologist X held a theory similar to the one I was using for illustration, although not the same theory. He whispered to his neighbor: "She's talking about Y." It was easy for him to see the difference between his own and Y's positions, while I, from a very different vantage point, find it difficult to distinguish between them (though I know what X thinks the differences are).

Now one more point about cognitive processes, and then we can return to the question of how the study of history can help us to avoid certain errors. It is sometimes difficult to solve a problem simply because the objective is too near. An animal, for example, has previously solved a particular detour problem; on another trial this same animal is helpless in the face of the same problem situation because now the objective is too close to him. Concentration on the goal makes it impossible to take the necessary detour. It is easy to transpose this finding to human thinking.

For a number of reasons, in summary, it is difficult to see our own errors. Our assumptions are not fully explicit; our thinking provides a context in which criticism from another point of view is absorbed and its power lost; our ability to see differences over the whole spectrum of thinking is reduced; and we are so near to our own concerns as to impede problem solving.

History gives us the distance necessary for problem solving. Critical examination of the implicit assumptions of our predecessors is much easier than such examination of our own assumptions. In this connection, Köhler once remarked that it is the obligation of each scientific generation to make explicit the implicit assumptions of its predecessors. And examination of errors in the history of a problem eliminates the unequal struggle between a criticism and our own opposing structure of explicit and implicit assumptions. The study of history, in short, gives us distance not only from our immediate objective, but from our own thinking. It enables us to examine a criticism in the context of somebody else's point of view.

This is perhaps the time to make the distinction between reading history of psychology and reading the historians of psychology. If history is to save us from some of the errors of the past, we must not allow it to plunge us into the errors of our historians. Fortunately, historians of psychology are today learning their craft, and, as Robert I. Watson documented impressively at the most recent meeting of the Cheiron Society, the field is becoming professionalized. But this is a continuing process, and we have much to learn. Although history may be taken ad lib, historians are to be used only as directed, which is to say, with great care.

Since it is difficult today in psychology to distinguish between errors and differences in psychological theory, may I start with a few instances in which old errors retarded the progress of other sciences. Then we may move cautiously back to psychology.

Köhler has pointed out that it took generations of physicists to discard anthropomorphism in physics and thus to make possible a science of physics as we know it.[1] Ancient and erroneous ideas persisted in Kepler's notion that stars are animate because they move, as Jaynes has discussed.[2] Opposition to the recognition of Harvey's discoveries came largely from the Galenists; that is, it derived from a body of doctrine, wrong in the critical respects, nearly fifteen hundred years old. Why did Galileo trouble to answer an argument based on a biblical story in the famous controversy of the comets of 1618? I can only guess it was because such ideas were not ones he could entirely dismiss from his own thinking.

If such ancient errors can so greatly influence the course of other sciences, it is hardly reasonable to suppose that psychology is immune to them. Köhler comments:

> There are moments when we interrupt our own scientific operations and begin to wonder whether, without our knowledge, there are not strange remnants of the past also in our own thinking which calmly determine its course as much as do our most advanced principles.[3]

How can we detect such strange remnants of the past that doubtless figure in our thinking? Clearly by the study of our history.

It is now no easier than it was a few minutes ago to decide what an error is in contemporary psychological theory. Nobody would like to define error by its difference from his own point of view. But it is not difficult to identify remnants of the past, perhaps even strange ones. Thus I will choose as my examples cases with the following characteristics: 1) the historical prototype is pretty generally agreed to be wrong, or else criticisms of it have been ignored or gone unanswered; 2) there is a clear historical continuity; and 3) alternatives to the conception in question are now available or are beginning to become available. Some of my instances will be ones in which, by and large, we have not learned the lesson from history.

My first example represented a very old tradition in 1726, where I shall begin the story. I do not understand how anyone who has read *Gulliver's Travels* can seriously hold an associationistic theory of creativity. Gulliver, it will be recalled, encountered a professor whose ambition it was to create a complete body of knowledge by the random combination of all the words of his language. And yet just this conception of the chance combination of elements, which Swift makes so patently ridiculous, constitutes the foundation of contemporary associationistic and behavioristic theories of creativity. I think it is no exaggeration to say that this kind of thinking is the mainstream of academic thought about creativity today. And yet nobody in the eighteenth century, except perhaps Helvétius, could take it seriously after reading Swift.[4] We would not need to trivialize so important a subject matter if we had learned the lesson that history presented so palatably in *Gulliver's Travels*.

I would have more to say about the associationistic tradition, and about specific problems treated in its terms, except that it does not yet fully meet the criteria of error set forth. True, the criticisms of it have largely been ignored or gone unanswered, but there is not yet general agreement that it is wrong. I hope that, some years from now, somebody who discusses the value of studying history will feel freer than I do to take many examples from associationistic theory.

My next example concerns the relation between logic and actual thinking. How Aristotle thought about this problem is the subject of speculation. But it is apparent that, at least from the middle of the sixteenth century, scholars believed that logic deals with the nature of thinking; they held that logic is not the exclusive possession of a few cloistered monks. This view prevailed for three centuries thereafter. The nineteenth century, after Boole, reversed this view, strictly separating logic from actual thinking processes. The reasons for this reversal are not altogether clear, but one thing is certain: it was not based on empirical evidence. It is doubtless related to the development of symbolic logic and the corresponding decline in interest in Aristotelian logic. Psychologists, of course, went along with the logicians in viewing logic as irrelevant to thinking as it actually occurs. Perhaps for them it was another symptom of philosophobia; and other influences doubtless contributed, for example the influence of the irrationalism that we have inherited from that rationalist, Freud. In quite recent years the problem has come under empirical investigation with methods that do not prejudice the answer. It is now beginning to look as if the sixteenth century view of the relation of logic and thinking is right. If this is the case, we have been living with an error that has arisen because we tend to trace back the history of our problems seven years or so, not—in this case—the required four hundred. Indeed, a knowledge of the literature of scarcely more than a century would have alerted us to the fact that a problem existed the solution of which we had been taking for granted.

I hope that I may now be permitted a more technical example. Through the first two decades or more of the present century, psychologists interested in perception simply assumed a one-to-one correspondence between local stimulation of receptors and local sensations. This assumption Köhler called the constancy hypothesis. Unfortunately for this hypothesis, the facts of perception do not bear it out. Facts of contrast, of color, brightness, shape, and size constancy, stroboscopic motion, illusions, and so on, failed to show the required correspondence with local retinal stimulation. Therefore the constancy hypothesis, the very foundation of the traditional theory of perception, was bolstered up by means of supporting assumptions. Of these auxiliary assumptions, Helmholtz's theory of unconscious inferences is still today the best known. It was held that perception really conforms to the constancy hypothesis, but that our judgment alters it. Since observers could not detect such judgments in their consciousness, these were assumed to be unconscious. Thus if a dark object in bright illumination continues to look dark, even though it reflects as much light to the eye as a white object, this was put down to unconscious inference from the known color of the object. Other assumptions, too, were devised to support the constancy hypothesis; for example, that the required sensations are present but just not noticed.

Since the constancy hypothesis could not be examined directly, protected as it was by these auxiliary assumptions, Köhler in 1913 examined the supporting assumptions.[5] Most of them were, by definition, untestable: what is unnoticed or unconscious cannot be tested—a situation most uncongenial to the scientist; but Köhler pointed to cases where even conscious judgments could not account for the discrepancy between the observed facts and predictions from the constancy hypothesis. His 1913 paper contains other equally compelling arguments.

The argument was later extended by the Gestalt psychologists to the production theory of the Graz school, to the "complex theory" of G. E. Müller, and more and more to empiristic hypotheses—explanations in terms of past experience—all of them formally similar in that they started with local sensory data which had to be worked over by higher mental processes to produce the organized forms we perceive. In America, we had E. B. Titchener's context theory, in which a sensory core is endowed with meaning by a context of images and other processes associated with it in the past.

Without any attempt to refute the arguments against them, the criticized theories still survive. A study of a history of only sixty years would have saved such theorists from what must be regarded as a fundamental error in the absence of refutation of the arguments against this position.

As final examples, I should like merely to refer to two important areas in which strange remnants of the past continue to determine our thinking. Cartesian views have had a virtual monopoly on our thinking about how the nervous system functions. Even in the face of much psychological and physiological evidence to the contrary, a machine theory of the nervous system prevails. We have substituted nerve fibers for Descartes's system of tubes and threads, and we have replaced his animal spirits by nerve impulses; but we continue to view nervous activity in terms of the constraints provided by these fibers. We are interested in tracing nerve pathways, while neglecting what goes on outside and around the nerve fibers. Although we regard the specific formulations of Descartes as quaint, it is ironic that we have merely modified his system of constraints and do our thinking, very largely, without considering the free dynamics that must occur in the brain as it does elsewhere in the natural world.[6]

Once again: if we do not want to believe the arguments of the philosophers, we will have to take it from physics that naive realism—the identification of the percept with the physical object—is wrong. Even physics required generations to free itself of this doctrine altogether. In psychology this hardy position has persisted, not only among the behaviorists (who mainly take perception for granted and so do not even see the problem), but among others, too. A little reading of history (or philosophy, which is also our history) would spare us this philosophical embarrassment.

I have been suggesting that the study of the history of psychology would save us from needless errors in contemporary thinking, errors that are not exclusive to us, but have been made before us and, in the cases mentioned, presumably put to rest. But it seems that if we cling to our ignorance of history, error, crushed to earth, will rise again, and we will have to go on solving the same old problems again and again.

There are, of course, other reasons for studying the history of our discipline, and I would like to mention a few. First, history contains forgotten treasures. In some ways our ancestors knew more than we do. This is partly because, as already mentioned, we have become specialists and have sacrificed the broader view as we pursue our specialties. Partly, we tend to take our problems from the laboratory, not from life as they did. There is today a marked reaction against this tendency of ours, but we have not yet learned well how to formulate specific problems out of practical necessity.

It is easy to find in our ancestors anticipations of contemporary theories and even of contemporary findings. A few examples: Solomon Diamond has recently pointed out many contemporary theories foreshadowed and even formulated by Alexander Bain.[7] Paul Mountjoy has shown that Frederick II, the Holy Roman Emperor, was, about 1250, already familiar with the technology of operant conditioning.[8] This he wisely confined to the training of falcons, not trying to use it as a comprehensive approach to human beings.

My final example concerns an author who did not realize that he had been anticipated. A recent issue of the *Psychological Review* contains an article the theme of which is that behavior is not a function of the environment alone, but of the person and the environment. The name of Kurt Lewin, whose work has been available in English since 1935, and whose central formulation is B = f (P,E), does not even appear in the bibliography of more than a hundred titles. Not much in the way of historical research would have been needed to show the author and the editors that they had been "scooped." I do not want, of course, to make Lewin the originator of this idea, either. It is only that he stated it so clearly, and was so widely known, that one would have thought it could not easily have been lost. I can conclude only that history does not start at *t* minus seven years.

If our ancestors knew things that we have since discovered for ourselves, perhaps they knew things that we have not yet discovered. Anatole France has said everything that needs to be said about this use of history:

> I have studied at length the history and habits of dragons, not to satisfy an idle curiosity, but to discover examples to follow in the present circumstances. And such, Samuel, my son, is the use of history.[9]

There is another way in which the insights of our forebears can be useful to us. Jerome Bruner has made the distinction between knowing, as he puts it, with the right hand and that with the left.[10] "Reaching for knowledge with the right hand is science." This hand is skilled, orderly, exacting. From the awkward left hand we have the gifts of intuition. Both science and art require the inspiration of the left hand and the discipline of the right. Psychological science is today markedly right-handed. But our prescientific history is a gold mine of left-handed psychology. Who would think, as a single example, that a student could design a series of experiments to test a casual paragraph of Montaigne on our ability to find extenuating circumstances for an action of our own, while condemning the same action by another? I know a student who did. Our history is in this sense a largely untapped source of psychological knowledge.

Another reason for the study of the history of psychology: the specialization in our field has been sufficiently mentioned; with specialization has come fragmentation. Sensory psychologists, I have said, do not know what personality psychologists are doing, and vice versa. There even seems to be the feeling that it is better never to find out. Indeed, these categories are still too crude to describe the current fragmentation of psychology. Every broad area has its specialists: in social psychology, for example, attribution theorists, interpersonal attraction theorists, cognitive dissonance theorists, specialists in person perception, in nonverbal communication, in the risky shift, in dyads or simulated dyads, in small groups, etc., etc. The subject matter is rich, but who is going to put together these many approaches? It seems to me that by looking to our history we can hope to do so. For it is a sad fact that it is mainly our predecessors who viewed the phenomena, say, of social life in an integrated manner.

If we do not find a broader perspective—and where but in history can we look for guidance?—we will have not only a one-sided and narrow view of our subject matter, we may actually have a wrong view. Wertheimer and Köhler, in particular, have shown that a perfectly true proposition, torn out of context, may be misleading and, in this larger sense, wrong. We are very busy, all over psychology, unearthing facts that are undoubtedly true for the most part. But what do they mean? Only when we are able to place them in context can we know. We find ourselves once more forced to the study of history.

I am not suggesting that history will provide us, readymade, a framework, a larger perspective, in which to hang all the facts in our scrap pile. But I am suggesting that the example of scholars struggling for an integrated view of human beings as human beings might provide the model we need.

Our specialists of today not only have the techniques and the knowledge of their small area; they also offer what we now call minitheories: theories intended to explain their own special findings without much regard for the larger world of psychology. But I have suggested above that we tend to be cryptosystematists. Such minitheories often have systematic relations to the more comprehensive theories of the recent and more distant past. Is the interpersonal attraction theorist only that? We may, for example, find that reinforcement plays a central role in explaining interpersonal attraction in a given minitheory, and then we cannot help noticing the relation to behaviorism. Not all our examples will be so transparent, but all deserve comparison with the systems of the past. In this way a knowledge of history may do more than provide a model of scholarship: it may help us to overcome the theoretical fragmentation in our field, thus to see where we are in psychology and whether we like being there.

If further urging is needed, I have a final and most important reason for studying the history of psychology: it is fascinating. It not only, if properly used, helps keep our thinking straight, serves as a source of problems and of knowledge, gives us perspective, but it is intrinsically interesting. It is not just something to be taken because it is good for you—like vitamin pills—although it *is* very good for you . It is a gourmet dish to be enjoyed for itself. It is high adventure, like the history of all man's intellectual pursuits—perhaps the highest adventure of all, because it is the story of man himself.

NOTES AND REFERENCES

1. KÖHLER, W. 1938. The Place of Value in a World of Facts: 372. Liveright. New York, N.Y.
2. JAYNES, J. 1970. The problem of animate motion in the seventeenth century. J. History of Ideas: 219–234.
3. KÖHLER, W. 1958. The nature of the organism. Gifford Lectures. Second series, Lecture 2. Library of the American Philosophical Society. Philadelphia, Pa. Quoted by permission.
4. I owe this reference to Helvétius to Robert G. Weyant. Cf. Weyant, R. G. 1973. Helvétius and Jefferson: Studies of human nature and government in the eighteenth century. J. History Behav. Sciences. 9: 29–41.
5. KÖHLER, W. 1971. On unnoticed sensations and errors of judgment. In M. Henle, Ed. The Selected Papers of Wolfgang Köhler. Liveright. New York, N.Y.
6. Cf. KÖHLER, W. 1969. The Task of Gestalt Psychology. Princeton University Press. Princeton, N.J.
7. DIAMOND, S. 1974. The greatness of Alexander Bain. Invited address, Sixth ann. mtg. Cheiron Society. Durham, N.H.
8. MOUNTJOY, P. T., J. H. BOS, M. O. DUNCAN, & R. B. VERPLANCK. 1969. Falconry: Neglected aspect of the history of psychology. J. History Behav. Sciences 5: 59–67.
9. FRANCE, A. Penguin Island. Book II. Chap. 8.
10. BRUNER, J. S. 1962. On Knowing. Essays for the Left Hand. Harvard University Press. Cambridge, Mass. The reader will not be surprised to learn that this is not the first use of this metaphor.

WUNDT—REVISIONS AND REAPPRAISALS

Arthur L. Blumenthal

University of Massachusetts at Boston
Boston, Massachusetts 02125

Among the few current scholars who give serious study to the writings of Wilhelm Wundt, there is fair agreement that the Wundt described in most modern texts as the first patron of experimental psychology is something of a mythical character, one who may have little semblance to the historical Wundt. The mythical Wundt has emerged, it seems, through a series of legends, of doubtful accuracy, that developed and descended from author to author without serious recourse to original sources. This problem in historical awareness might seem a paradox when you consider Wundt's importance as putative founding father and still, as of today, history's most prolific psychologist.

Nevertheless, there are several reasons for this situation that are not difficult to discover. But rather than recount them in detail, one can summarize by observing that psychologists, in contrast to historians, are usually "presentists" in their approach to history. That is, they use history to find support for the direction of current research whenever a history can be found that cooperates with immediate needs. Thus, there is little effort to replace original sources in their historical contexts, or to unravel distortions that may have come about over the years.

One strong tradition of interpreting psychology's past became firmly established (particularly by Boring[2]) when the behaviorist and positivist movements were at their pinnacles. There was then little motivation for the sympathetic study of the old Wundtian psychology, for in the dramatic promotion of behaviorism Wundt was the primary scapegoat. Accordingly, the habit soon developed of citing only isolated passages (and peculiar translations) that would support the popular negative views of his work. And although he may have been widely referenced, Wundt was thereafter seldom read in the original.

It is a commonplace in intellectual history that later schools of thought foster distortions and misinterpretations of earlier ones. The history of psychology offers numerous examples, and I believe that the case of Wundt stands out today as its most notable example.

But the intellectual mood of the second half of the twentieth century has changed. It is my thesis that sometime after midcentury there began a steadily growing reconstruction of Wundtian psychology, although the connection between the "new" and the "old" Wundtian psychology remains largely unrecognized. Later, I will propose several specific examples of these recent reconstructions, but more important, I would like to portray here some fundamentals of Wundt's psychology that have, for better or worse, been disguised or lost in the course of historical machination.

Wundt's system of thought stems from one primitive premise, namely, that the only certain reality is that of immediate experience. From that assertion Wundt goes on to a twofold goal for all of science: (1) the construction of explanations of experience, and (2) the development of techniques for objectifying experience, which meant techniques for communicating experience and replicating it in others in standardized ways. With this latter goal, it becomes possible to perform tests that may lead to public agreement about phenomena and their explanations. In the natural sciences it is the attributes of experience derived from external objects and energies that are subjected to tests, explanations, and public agreement. But in the case of psychology, it is the attributes of experience derived from the processes of the experiencing subject that are made the object of tests, explanations, and public agreement. These psychological entities include experienced memory and perceptual capacities, fluctuations of attention or alertness, ranges of our sensitivities, and so on. In the modern jargon, we would say "human information-processing capacities."

Now it is this subtle division between the physical and the psychological sciences that led to many descriptions of Wundt as a mind-body dualist. But if you read Wundt, you will discover that his rejection of mind-body dualism was consistent and emphatic. It led him to say that psychology cannot be defined as the science of the mind because there are no objects called "minds" that are distinct from objects called "bodies," a scenario that appears repeatedly in his works.

At the same time, however, Wundt was an ardent opponent of reductionism in science in general, and most particularly with regard to psychology. If we should restrict observations to neurophysiology, then, he argued, we shall always miss the essential phenomena of psychology. Although physiologists and psychologists study one and the same organism, in Wundt's view they analyze and objectify different aspects of experience; i.e., they observe the same phenomenon but from different vantage points. As a rule, this is now called the "double-aspect" resolution of the mind-body separation. Wundt's use of the phrase "psychophysical parallelism" referred to this same view, but unfortunately, it led many later reviewers to the misinterpretation of classical mind-body dualism. Rather, it referred to the separate orientations of physiology and psychology; that is, it is separate *methodologies* that run in parallel.

Another serious problem in Wundt interpretation concerns *introspection*. It was Wundt's claim that progress in psychology had been slow because of reliance on subjective introspection, which led invariably to acrimonious and unresolvable debates. In several books and monographs [24,29] he argued that armchair introspection could never succeed, being a logical impossibility as a scientific technique. One influential monograph [29] was his severe critique of the Wurzburg psychologists for their return to uncontrolled introspection.

But Wundt often used the phrase "experimental self-observation" to describe his own approach, and years later this was often taken to mean simple introspection in what is actually a pre-Wundtian sense. Nevertheless, Wundt's intention here came from his discussion of techniques that all experimental sciences are to use—what he described as making public our private experience by arranging conditions in standardized ways so that other individuals can have the same experience on other occasions.

Wundt's adherence to these canons of experimental procedure were in fact so strict as to limit sharply his use of experiments in psychology. Thus, in the case of most "higher" mental processes such as language or concept formation, he felt that workable experiments were not feasible. Instead, he argued that these subjects must be approached through techniques of naturalistic observation and logic. This he did primarily by examining the social-cultural products of human mental activities in order to make inferences about the underlying mental processes. In the case of language, for example, he was led deeply into the technical study of linguistics. It seems a little-appreciated fact that the greater part of Wundt's psychological work falls in this latter category, i.e., outside the range of his experimental psychology.

Let us now turn abruptly from Wundt's methodology to his psychological theory. What emerged as "the paradigm psychological phenomenon" in Wundt's system would now be described as selective volitional attention. Hence he described his psychology as "voluntaristic," to distinguish it from other schools. He did not use the label "structuralist," which was proffered and perpetuated by Titchener and James.

Mischel[12] has recently analyzed in detail Wundt's basic commitment to volitional processes, or in more modern terms, motivational processes.

But with a strong impact on early historical interpretation, Titchener[19] had repudiated this theme, the very heart of Wundtian psychology, because of its overtones of continental Idealist philosophy. Titchener's longest period of formal education came at Oxford, and, not surprisingly, he favored a psychology based on the British Empiricist-Associationist tradition. That tradition was anathema to Wundt's views, and more than any other topic, the brunt of his polemical writings. Also, perhaps by giving a heavily slanted account of Wundt, Titchener may have wished to render him more palatable to noncontinental audiences, which have traditionally had less sympathy for the voluntarist philosophies.

The strong influence of Titchener over later interpretations of Wundt may thus account for the general lack of attention to "volitionism" in the historical accounts of Wundtian psychology. Without giving citation, Boring[2] states that Wundt had opposed the implication of an active volitional agent in psychology. But now Mischel,[12] with very extensive citation, has shown, on the contrary, how central this is to Wundt's system. And it is with this orientation that Wundt claimed another point of separation between psychology and physics—a difference between psychological and physical causality: in physics actions are *made* by an active agent with reference to rule systems.

Thus, the physical sciences may describe the act of greeting a friend, driving a car, or eating an apple in terms of the laws of mechanics, or in terms of physiology; yet no matter how complicated we make such descriptions, they are insufficient to describe psychological events. Those events must be described in terms of intentions and goals, according to Wundt, because the actions, or physical forces, for a given psychological event may take an infinite variety of physical forms. For example, Wundt argued that human language cannot be fully described in terms of its physical shape or of the segmentation of utterances, but rather must be described also in terms of the rules and intentions underlying speech. The ways of expressing a thought in language are infinitely variable because language is governed by creative rules rather than by fixed laws.

These distinctions lead to a related and consistent theme in Wundt's writings. It is what he called "the false materialization of mental processes," which he saw occurring in other schools of psychology; in particular, associationism. Wundt's reactions against associationism were directed especially against the form it assumed in midnineteenth century Germany in Herbart's psychology. Herbart had atomized mental processes into elemental ideas that became associated into compounds according to the classical associationist descriptions. That approach, Wundt felt, was merely a primitive analogy to physics and chemistry, or to systems of simple physical mechanics. "No such system can ever teach anything about the interrelations of psychological processes," said Wundt.[25] For those systems were oblivious to what he felt was the essential distinction between psychological and physical causality; they portrayed the mind as if it were a "mere field of billiard balls" colliding and interacting with each other.

Boring's statement that "Wundt turned to chemistry for his model" seems clearly inaccurate to the serious reader of Wundt (see also Mischel[12]). But unfortunately, the mental chemistry cliché became popular among psychology historians. For the sake of brevity, I would like to quote a rebuttal comment made by Wundt's son, Max Wundt, in a book published in 1944 (my own translation):

> One may follow the methodologically obvious principle of advancing from the simple to the complicated, indeed even employing the approach that would construct the mind from primitive mechanicial elements (the so-called psychology of mental elements). In this case,

however, method and phenomena can become grossly confused. . . . Whoever in particular ascribes to my father such a conception could not have read his books. In fact, he had formed his scientific views of mental processes in reaction against a true elementistic psychology, namely against that of Herbart, which was dominant in those days. (M. Wundt[22])

Wundt did, of course, postulate elementary sensory-perceptual processes and elemental affective processes (with the emphasis on *process*) because he acknowledged that a major part of any scientific methodology involves analysis of a system into components. But then he stressed that these elements were hypothetical constructs to be used as tools in the description of experience. Such elemental processes would never actually be observed in pure isolation, but would always be aspects or features of larger images or configurations. Here Wundt used the German word *Gebilde*. For a translation, the dictionary (*Cassell's*) gives us the following choices: either "structure," or "formation," or "system," or "image," or "creation." But in the few English translations of Wundt, we find the word "compound," a divergent choice, one that unfortunately again suggests the analogy to chemistry. Another example: Wundt's "whole or unified mental impression" (*Gesamtvorstellung*) is translated as "aggregate ideas."

The later movement toward holism in Gestalt psychology placed Wundt in a contrastive position and again portrayed him as an elementalist in ways not characteristic of his intentions. Reacting to this, the later Wundtians, such as Sander, Krueger, and Volkelt, renamed their school *Ganzheit* psychology or roughly "holistic psychology," and throughout the 1920s and 1930s the old Wundtian institute at Leipzig was a center for theorists with a holistic bent. Wundt's journal, the *Psychologische Studien,* which had ceased publication upon Wundt's retirement, was now reactivated by his students. This journal, the *Neue Psychologische Studien,* was then the central organ of *Ganzheit* psychology. Its articles primarily followed Wundt's interests in the "higher" mental processes and hence were mostly nonexperimental investigations.

Werner[21] has written that Wundt represented the halfway mark in the transition from Herbart's atomism to the Gestaltist's holism. But from Wundt's point of view, the essential central control-processes, which he summarized under the term "apperception," were of no more primacy to the Gestaltists than to Herbart—both conceived a rather passive organism, one to be pushed and pulled by external or independent forces.

It was a curiosity about the process of central selective attention that may have stimulated Wundt's earliest interests in psychology.[23] In the late 1850s, with simple reaction-time experiments he attempted to demonstrate the central and controlling function of attention. The experiment had descended from the "personal equation" problem that had vexed astronomers roughly a generation earlier. Astronomers once had considerable trouble in obtaining agreement from the observers who estimated the precise time that a star passes a meridian grid line in a telescope. In Wundt's test, subjects observed a pointer moving over a calibrated arc where at a certain instant an auditory click sounded, and observers then indicated the pointer's position at the time of the click. The reported position was displaced away from the true position of physical coincidence by a fraction of a second. The direction of displacement, ahead or behind, depends on whether observers anticipate the sound or the pointer. When not expecting the sound, it is experienced as later in time than its true occurrence. Thus experience depends on an act of selective attention.

Regarding this early work of Wundt's, Titchener[20] once noted:

There is no more remarkable incident in the history of experimental psychology than Wundt's attempt, by way of a single critical experiment, to overturn the whole of Herbartian psychology.

Some thirty years after Wundt's initial work in experimental psychology, his student Külpe[11] wrote of Wundt as follows:

> It is one of Wundt's services to modern psychology that he has recognised the unique nature and the general and fundamental importance of attention, and has given expression to both in his doctrine of *apperception*. The English *association* psychology, with the German and French schools which have adopted its tenets, refers all the phenomena of conscious mental life to the mechanics of sensations and ideas, and more or less completely ignores the significance of the attentive state. Wundt has realised that the "having" of an idea is not identical with its attentive experience, and that the conditions of attention are not given with the internal and external stimuli which we regard as the physical counter-parts of centrally and peripherally excited sensations.

Now I want to suggest, in brief, some six current trends that may be viewed as modern reconstructions of Wundtian psychology.

First, Wundt's studies of the volitional processes of "apperception" bear notewor-thy resemblance to the modern work on "cognitive control" as found, for one example, in extensive researches by Gardner *et al.* and their associates.[7] Both traditions used notions of different styles of attention-deployment to explain a variety of perceptual and thought processes (sometimes involving the same materials, e.g. the Muller-Lyer illusion).

A dominant theme in the recent research stems from the delineation through factor analysis of two independent variables of cognitive control, which Gardner calls "field-articulation" and "scanning." These can be defined fairly well simply by substituting a similar description found in most of Wundt's psychology texts, as follows: First, in corresponding order, is Wundt's mental "clearness" process that concerns the focusing or emphasizing of a single item of experience. Wundt also described this as "apperceptive synthesis," where variations from broad to narrow mental syntheses may occur. The second variable is a mental "distinctiveness" process that is the marking off of an item of experience from all others. This Wundt also called "apperceptive analysis," a relating and comparing function. The discovery and testing of nearly identical attention deployment factors in recent times occurred independently of the old Wundtian psychology. And the more recent work has made frequent use of elaborate personality theory that was unavailable to Wundt.

Second, detailed comparisons have been made recently between the development of psycholinguistics in the 1960s and that of Wundtian psycholinguistics at the turn of the century.[1] Both the modern transformational grammarians after Chomsky and the Wundtian psycholinguists at the turn of the century trace their notions of language back to the same historical sources (e.g. to Humboldt). And the psycholin-guistics issues debated in the 1960s often parallel those at the turn of the century, such as the opposition between taxonomic and generative descriptions of language. Very briefly, Wundt's analysis of language usage depicted the transformation of simultaneous configurations of thought into a sequential representation in language symbols by means of the scanning activities of attention.

A *third* reconstruction concerns abnormal psychology. The one student of Wundt's who maintained the longest intellectual association with him was the psychiatrist Emil Kraepelin.[6] Kraepelin's attentional theory of schizophrenia[10] is an application of Wundtian psychology, an explanation of schizophrenias as abnormali-ties of the attention-deployment process (apperception). It conceives the abnormal behavior as resulting from a flaw in the central control process that may take the form of highly reduced attentional scanning, or highly erratic scanning, or extremes of attentional focusing; and it was proposed that abnormalities in simple perceptual tests should show up in schizophrenic individuals that correspond to these particular control-process distortions. The modern attentional theory of schizophrenia is a direct revival of the Kraepelin-Wundt analysis, as has been shown in an extensive review by Silverman.[17]

Fourth is Wundt's three-factor theory of affect, which was developed by analogy to his formulations of multidimensional descriptions of certain areas of sensory experience. However, Wundt's attempt to relate each of his three bipolar dimensions of affect* to patterns of physiological response was never widely accepted. Still, with the invention of factor analysis years later, statistical studies of affective and attitudinal states have again yielded factors that parallel Wundt's rather closely (cf. Burt,[5] Schlosberg,[16] and Osgood, et al.[14]).

Emotions and affects held an important place in Wundt's system because volition was explained as emerging from these processes. Further, Wundt suggested that almost every experience (perception, thought, or memory) has an effective component. This component, in turn, became the basis for Wundt's theory of pattern recognition. A melody, for instance, produces a very similar emotional configuration as it is transformed to other keys or played on other instruments. Wundt speculated that affect is a by-product of the act of apperceptive synthesis (discussed above), and as such it is always on the periphery of consciousness. That is, we can never focus our attention upon an emotion, but can focus only on objects or memories that produce an emotional aura in immediate experience.

Fifth, the study of selective attention has been at the heart of most recent work on human information-processing (e.g., Broadbent,[4] Moray,[13] Kahneman[9]). It isn't possible here to relate this highly complex field to the early Wundtian psychology other than to note the prominence of attention in both, and that the time variable is central to both. Consider one specific example: the seminal investigations of Sperling[18] concerning perceptual masking. In these studies Sperling took inspiration directly from Wundt's 1900 monograph[27] on the use of tachistoscopes in psychological research where Wundt came to the following three conclusions about the perception of extremely brief stimuli: (1) the effective stimulus duration is not identical with the duration of the stimulus source, but rather reflects the duration of a psychological process; (2) the relation between accuracy of a perception and stimulus duration depends on pre- and postexposure fields (which may induce what we now call masking), and (3) central processes determine these delays, rather than peripheral sense-organ aftereffects. Wundt's observations resulted in a body of early research, and those same observations are now relevant to a large body of modern research.

For a *sixth* and final comparison, I would refer to what Wundt called his deepest interest, which motivated a ten-volume work that in English translation could be titled, *Cultural Psychology: An Investigation of the Developmental Laws of Language, Myth, and Morality.*[28] This series, which appeared between 1900 and 1920, contains two books on language, three books on myth and religion, one book on art, two books on society, one book on law, and one book on culture and history. If there is a later work by another author that is conceptually close to this work of Wundt's, it is Heinz Werner's *Comparative Psychology of Mental Development,*[21] today read by many students of developmental psychology. Werner describes an *organismic* psychology that is in opposition to *mechanistic* psychologies. This indeed is the essence of Wundt's thought. Werner also draws parallels, as did Wundt, between the development of an individual and of societies; and Werner acknowledges his indebtedness to Wundt at the outset of the book. But in Wundt's *Cultural Psychol-*

---

*These may be described approximately as *pleasant-unpleasant, active-passive, concentrated attention-relaxed attention.*

ogy there is, again, greater emphasis on volitional and attentional processes in the analysis of the development of human culture. He theorized that those central processes had emerged as the highest evolutionary development, and that they are the capacities that set men above other animals. It is the highly developed selective-attention capacities that, as he claimed, enabled mankind to make a consistent mental advance, and to develop human culture. For without these capacities men would forever be at the mercy of sporadic thoughts, memories, and perceptions.

Wundt was not a mere encyclopedist or compiler of volumes, contrary to many descriptions. It was typical of him, however, always to compare and to contrast his system with other psychological systems, ancient and modern. Perhaps in that sense he could be considered an encyclopedist. True, most of his works begin with a long recital of his philosophical antecedents and the antecedent of rival positions. Wundt's productivity is not surprising, considering the strong family traditions that lay behind him. Recent scholars (Bringmann, *et al.*[3]) have claimed that no other German intellectual has a family tree containing as many ancestors engaged in intellectual pursuits. On his father's side were historians, theologians, economists, and geographers. On his mother's side were natural scientists and physicians. Two of his ancestors had been rectors of the University of Heidelberg.

To conclude, I wish to draw an outline of the streams of history in which Wundt lived. Historians usually define a few broad, alternating cultural fluctuations in the nineteenth century. These periods begin with the dominant Romanticism and Idealism early in the century, largely a German-inspired Zeitgeist shared by Kant, Humboldt, Schopenhauer, Goethe, Hegel, and Fichte, to mention a few. In that era, philosophy, science, religion, and art were often combined into something called nature-philosophy. Such an integration was exemplified in the pantheistic writings of Gustav Fechner, an exotic latecomer to the Romantic movement and an important source of inspiration for Wundt. (In several ways Wundt's ten-volume *Cultural Psychology* reflects the spirit of the old nature philosophy).

Around the midnineteenth century, positivist and materialist philosophies grew dominant by vigorously rejecting the old Idealism. For instance, there was the influential Berlin Physical Society, the mechanistic psychology of Herbart, the behavioristic linguistics of the so-called *Junggrammatiker* linguists, and many other examples across the disciplines. At the peak of this movement academicians became methodology-conscious to an extreme degree. Taxonomic methods of biologists were imported into the social sciences. There was a general downgrading of "mentalism" in favor of "physicalism" and environmentalism.

Then, toward the end of the nineteenth century, there came a resurgence of the Romantic-Idealist mood, particularly in continental Europe. It has been described either as neo-Romanticism, neo-Idealism, or neo-Kantianism. H. Stuart Hughes summarized this revival in an influential book, *Consciousness and Society: The Reorientation of European Social Thought 1890–1930.*[8] At around the time of the First World War, this movement went into sharp decline, being displaced by a rebirth and rise in popularity of positivism and behaviorism, which subsequently dominated many intellectual circles well into the twentieth century.

Wundt's psychology rose and fell with the late nineteenth century neo-Idealism. His core emphasis on volition and apperception comes straight out of classical German Idealist philosophy. It is not surprising that this should be so, for as a youth Wundt had been deeply affected by the Romantic-Idealist literature and nature philosophy. Later, he was obviously influenced by the midnineteenth century positivism, especially in his promotion of experimental psychology. But during that positivist period he had remained largely unrecognized as a psychological theorist. It was not until the change in the Zeitgeist back toward Idealism that he blossomed intellectually, and his psychological system became fully formed in the *Grundriss*[26] of 1896 and later editions.

But unfortunately for Wundt, his Zeitgeist support disappeared rapidly early in the twentieth century, so that his works were soon meaningless to a newer generation of psychologists. Then few, especially those outside Germany, understood any more what the old term "apperception" had once referred to.

This concludes a brief review of a massive intellectual epoch. Much of the story of Wundt remains to be told. However, I hope to have shown that serious consideration should be given to the revision of most current accounts of Wundt's psychology. In turn, that may force a broad revision of our understanding of the history of psychology over the past century. In any case, the serious study of Wundt leads to the conclusion that he is now relevant for our time.

REFERENCES

1. BLUMENTHAL, A. 1970. Language and Psychology: Historical Aspects of Psycholinguistics. John Wiley & Sons Inc. New York, N.Y.
2. BORING, E. G. 1950. A History of Experimental Psychology. Appleton-Century-Crofts. New York, N.Y.
3. BRINGMANN, W., W. BALANCE & R. EVANS. 1975. Wilhelm Wundt 1832-1920: a biographical sketch. J. Hist. Behav. Sci. 11: 287-297.
4. BROADBENT, D. 1958. Perception and Communication. Pergamon Press. New York, N.Y.
5. BURT, C. 1950. The factorial study of emotions. In Feelings and Emotions. M. Reymert, Ed. McGraw-Hill Inc. New York, N.Y.
6. FISCHEL, W. 1959. Wilhelm Wundt and Emil Kraepelin. Karl-Marx Universität Beiträge zur Universität Geschichte. Vol. 1. Karl Marx University. Leipzig, Germany.
7. GARDINER, R., G. HOLZMAN, H. KLEIN & SPENCE. D. 1959. Cognitive Control. Psychological Issues. 4. International Universities Press. New York, N.Y.
8. HUGHES, H. S. 1958. Consciousness and Society: The Reorientation of European Social Thought 1890-1930. Alfred A. Knopf Inc. New York, N.Y.
9. KAHNEMAN, D. 1974. Attention and Effort. Prentice-Hall Inc. Englewood Cliffs, N.J.
10. KRAEPELIN, E. 1919. Dementia Praecox and Paraphrenia. (Translated by M. Barclay from selected writings of Kraepelin.) Chicago Medical Book Co. Chicago, Ill.
11. KULPE, O. 1893. Gründriss der Psychologie. Engelmann. Leipzig, Germany. (Translated by E. Titchener as Outlines of Psychology. 1895. Macmillan Inc. New York, N.Y.)
12. MISCHEL, T. 1970. Wundt and the conceptual foundations of psychology. Philos. Phenomenol. Res. 31: 1-26.
13. MORAY, N. 1970. Attention. Academic Press. New York, N.Y.
14. OSGOOD, C., G. SUCI & P. TANNENBAUM. 1957. The Measurement of Meaning. University of Illinois Press. Urbana, Ill.
15. RINGER, F. 1969. The Decline of the German Mandarins: The German Academic Community 1890-1893. Harvard University Press. Cambridge, Mass.
16. SCHLOSBERG. H. 1953. Three dimensions of emotion. Psychol. Rev. 61: 81-88.
17. SILVERMAN, J. 1964. The problem of attention in research and theory in schizophrenia. Psychol. Rev. 71: 352-379.
18. SPERLING, G. 1960. The information available in brief visual presentations. Psychol. Monogr. 74. no. 11.
19. TITCHENER, E. 1908. The Psychology of Feeling and Attention. Macmillan Inc. New York, N.Y.
20. TITCHENER, E. 1923. Wundt's address at Speyer. 1861. Amer. J. Psychol. 34: 341.
21. WERNER, H. 1948. The Comparative Psychology of Mental Development. Science Editions. New York, N.Y.
22. WUNDT, M. 1944. Die Wurzeln der deutschen Philosophie in Stamm und Rasse. Junker und Dünnhaupt. Berlin, Germany.

23. WUNDT, W. 1862. Beiträge zur Theorie der Sinneswahrnehmung. Winter. Leipzig, Germany.
24. WUNDT, W. 1888. Selbstbeoachtung und innere Wahrnehmung. Philosophische Studien. 4: 292–309.
25. WUNDT, W. 1896. Ueber die Definition der Psychologie. Philosophische Studien. 7: 1–66.
26. WUNDT, W. 1896. Grundriss der Psychologie. Engelmann. Leipzig, Germany. (English translations as Outlines of Psychology, 1896 and 1907 edits, by C. Judd. Stechert. New York, N.Y.)
27. WUNDT, W. 1900. Zur Kritik tachistokopischer Versuche. Philosophische Studien. 15: 287–315; 16: 61–71.
28. WUNDT, W. 1900–1920. Völkerpsychologie: Eine Untersuchung der Entwicklungsgesetze von Sprache, Mythus, und Sitte. Engelmann. Leipzig, Germany.
29. WUNDT, W. 1907. Ueber Ausfragenexperimente und Methoden zur Psychologie des Denkens. Psychologische Studien. 3: 301–360.

William Stern.

LOUIS WILLIAM STERN:
A NEW VIEW OF THE HAMBURG YEARS*

Francis P. Hardesty

Department of Psychology
The City College of the City University of New York
New York, New York 10031

William Stern, *ausserordentlicher* professor of philosophy in the University of Breslau; pioneer in the study of individual psychology; a leader among European students of child life; known and honored wherever psychology itself is honored, doctor of laws.

The foregoing citation appeared in *The Worcester Telegram* on September 11, 1909.[1] With this award Clark University in Worcester, Massachusetts, became the first of two American institutions of higher learning to confer an honorary degree upon Louis William Stern in recognition of his accomplishments. The occasion was the now well-known conference commemorating the twentieth anniversary of the founding of the University.† At the time of the conference and accompanying ceremonies, William Stern was 38 years old; it was ten years before his appointment to his first university *Ordinariat*.

Today, reference to the activities and contributions of Stern (1871–1938) relevant to the current status of psychology is likely to evoke an array of mixed images and impressions. To some extent this is due to the way our histories have been compiled. On the other hand, such mixed display is in part a function of the extent to which interests have been invested in one or another contemporary subspecializations of the field. Specialists in experimental and physiological psychology are likely to associate the name of Stern with a series of investigations done early in his academic career, dealing with the perception and apperception of difference and change in the various sensory modalities,[6-9] with his invention of the tone variator,[10] and then with a set of interests leading away from the laboratory and into the realm of metaphysics. Psychometricians are likely to recall that Stern originated the concept of the intelligence quotient to provide an age-independent index of intellective adaptation,‡ only later to renounce its heuristic value when applied in isolation or without regard

---

*This paper was partially supported by a Fulbright-Hays Research Award for the academic year 1973–74.

†Hermann Ebbinghaus, Ernst Meumann, and Wilhelm Wundt had been invited to present lectures before the departments of psychology and pedagogy. Ebbinghaus accepted, but died before the meetings took place; Meumann and Wundt declined (cf. Munroe,[1] Ross,[2] and Titchener[3]). Stern, one of the most active participants in the phase dealing with psychology and psychiatry, presented four lectures and conducted three separate sessions of demonstrations. Freud delivered five lectures. Leo Burgerstein, Carl G. Jung, and E. B. Titchener were similarly active, as were Franz Boas, Herbert S. Jennings, and Adolf Meyer. In addition to these eight, thirteen other internationally known scholars received honorary doctorates on the evening of September 10. Among the latter were the physicists Vito Voterra of the University of Rome, and the Nobel prize winners Albert Michelson and Ernest Rutherford of the Universities of Chicago and Manchester (cf. Clark University,[4] Ross,[2] and Stern[5]).

‡A different account is offered by Boring[11] and by Herrnstein and Boring[12] with respect to authorship of the concept of IQ. Boring, for example, asserts that "Stern in 1911 suggested that the mental age of a child can be divided by its chronological age to give a 'mental quotient' . . . [and] Terman and his associates renamed this ratio the intelligence quotient (IQ) when they issued the Stanford Revision of the Binet Scale in 1916 . . ." (Ref. 11, p. 574). A survey of primary sources will disclose, however, that while Stern lectured and published several works

to other facets of personality in an effort to appraise the intelligence of a given individual.§ Specialists pursuing cross blends of psychology with other disciplines are likely to remember Stern's contributions[17-19] in securing the establishment of forensic psychology in the first years of this century. For others, more familiar will be Stern's role in the early application of quantitative techniques to analyses of linguistic and personal components in the emergence of language in the infant and young child.[20] For workers focusing on comparative treatments of the great schools and systems of psychology, Stern's name is likely to evoke such catch statements as "Individuality, the problem of the twentieth century,"[21] "the concept of the person as an *unitas multiplex*," and "no gestalt without a gestalter."[22]

Along with others handling developments in psychology immediately following the first world war, Misiak and Sexton inform us that Stern ". . . was the most influential psychologist in Germany at that time." (Ref. 23, p. 108) The period coincides with Stern's activities based in Hamburg from 1916 through 1933, first with his appointment to a full professorship in that city-state's Program for General Lectures and then later, in 1919, with his appointment in the newly founded University of Hamburg as *Ordinarius* for philosophy, psychology, and pedagogy.

From the perspective of today, assay of these years acquires importance from several standpoints. First, the Hamburg years represented for Stern the long-awaited opportunity finally to implement a curriculum of research, teaching, and application consistent with the claim of psychology to be not only a theoretical and empirically based science, but also an applied discipline capable of serving in the affairs of the world. In similar vein, the facilities and conditions accorded by his Hamburg years enabled Stern to promote and bring to fruition another facet of his penchant for synthesis, that of transforming his philosophically articulated doctrine of personalism into tenets and terms consistent with a scientifically researchable personalistic psychology.

Finally, scrutiny of Stern's Hamburg years has implications for the historiography of the behavioral and social sciences. Events attended by those years demonstrate how surrounding milieu and changing distributions of forces of a social, economic, and political order—external to an activity—can serve not only to determine the selection of topics for investigative concentration but also to determine the course and fate of that activity. Such items are generally sidelined in immanent and in problem- or issue-centered approaches to the history of psychology. For contextualistic or transcendental historiography, however, identification and compilation of such items remains central.¶

---

on mental tests in 1911 no mention is made of a mental quotient or ratio. The concept of IQ was indeed first used by Stern in his 1912 treatise[13] where he described its usefulness and applied it to a reanalysis of data originally generated by Chotzen. Boring's reference probably stems from the 1914 English translation of the volume[14] where the terms, mental quotient and mental ratio, were interchangeably treated as equivalent to Stern's term *Intelligenzquotient* and his abbreviation of it as *IQ*.

§This view, implied in several of Stern's publications after 1918, is perhaps nowhere more forthrightly formulated than in the 1938 English version of his *Allgemeine Psychologie auf personalistischer Grundlage*.[15,16] Here, in referring to the meaning of a computed IQ, Stern states "whoever imagines that in determining this quantity he has summed up 'the' intelligence of an individual once and for all, so that he may dispense with the more intensive qualitative study, leaves off where psychology should begin." (Ref. 16, p. 60)

¶Historical approaches to psychology can be conceptualized along a continuum of events internal to the field (immanent) and events surrounding and external to the field (transcendental).[24] Boring's approach[11] is illustrative of the former, Holzkamp's[25] of the latter. Intermediate between these extremes is the problem- or issue-centered position such as that of Pongratz[26] and Mueller-Freienfels[27] and the contextural approach of Van Hoorn.[28]

Prior to his move to Hamburg, Stern had distinguished himself through a number of accomplishments during his 19-year span in Breslau. Forming the basis for his inauguration there as *Privat Dozent* at the invitation of Ebbinghaus in 1897, the series of experiments making up his *venia legendi* (Habilitation) was put into book form the following year under the title *Psychologie der Veraenderungsauffassung*.[8] In 1898, together with several colleagues in medicine, law, education, and other disciplines, Stern founded in Breslau a division of the German Society for Psychological Research complementing those already existing in Munich and Berlin.

It was a series of activities and publications appearing from 1900 to 1907, however, which was to bring Stern to early international distinction. For some, like Gordon Allport, it is a period that can be marked off as one "of pure genius within which Stern manifested his originality to its fullest extent." (Ref. 29, p. 273) The evaluation is not without warrant, inasmuch as the span of years in Breslau was richly productive; for during this period, Stern forged new perspectives and fresh methods for the then virgin domains of differential, child, applied, and forensic psychology. His 1900 volume on differential psychology[21] structured with the sweep of broad and articulate outlines the founding of the field of the psychology of individual differences as a legitimate area of systematic inquiry. His first monograph on the psychology of testimony,[17] a topic of renewed interest today, appeared two years later and contributed relevance to principles derived from the psychology of the laboratory for the discipline of law, legal proceedings, and the events of the courtroom. Other investigations ensued in this area, and the first journal Stern was to edit, *Beitraege zur Psychologie der Aussage,* was established in 1903.

Die Kindersprache,[20] the first of several works developed in collaboration with his wife, née Clara Joseephy, was published in 1907. Employing a comparative statistically manipulative approach to describe linguistic and personal components in the emergence of language in their three young children, this pioneering classic was followed the next year by a less quantitatively detailed monograph[30] demonstrating the theoretical and practical implications that the convergence of personal experience and maturational limits impose on the individual's memory, verbal reconstruction and fabrication in early childhood. Together with a monograph on Helen Keller,[31] the views underlying these two works were subsequently extended to other investigations of the varieties of perception and expression in childhood.[32-35] The effort and activities of Stern and his students in the small psychological seminary in Breslau resulted in a number of subsequent publications, two of which may be singled out for special comment. The first[13] was issued in 1912 and was translated into English two years later by Guy Whipple as *Psychological Methods for Testing Intelligence*.[14] Reflecting broad concern for exact methods for the establishment of data, this interpretative survey of existing methodology sought to place the testing movement in Germany on a sound footing, and, in this context, introduced the concept of IQ for the first time. The second work[36] appeared in 1914 in the form of a comprehensive text outlining the principles of individual psychological development through the preschool years. Both volumes were destined to command international attention and were subject to repeated revisions and translation into several foreign languages.

Still other distinctions were to characterize Stern's Breslau years. His 1903 call for a centralized agency to serve as a clearing house for scientific information, consultation, and special-topic workshops for the rapidly differentiating new psychology had not gone unheard.[18] In 1906, just two years after the formal founding of the German Society for Experimental Psychology in Giessen, the Institute for Applied Psychology and Cumulative Research was secured in Wilmersdorf-Berlin with the codirectorship of Otto Lipmann, a former student of Ebbinghaus and Stern in Breslau. Under their joint editorship, Stern and Lipmann were also to begin publication in 1907 of a new journal, *Die Zeitschrift fuer angewandte Psychologie und Sammelforschung,* as an official organ of the German Society and the new institute. Replacing the earlier *Beitraege,* the establishment of the new journal represented a major broadening of publication outlet and coverage of ideas and research relative to the application of psychology. This editorship and still another yet to come were to place Stern close to the heart of communication and knowledge with respect to the multifaceted aspects of the rapidly developing area of applied psychology in Germany for the next quarter of a century.

Joining this manifold of early attainments, still another was to manifest itself early in Stern's career, which, like those already mentioned, was to be carried over and find continuity of commitment in his Hamburg years. In 1906, a year before his elevation to the associate professorship in Breslau, the first of what was to become a three-volume work detailing Stern's more global views and philosophical system, *Person und Sache,*[37] was published. Laid out and made bare were the derivatives and foundations of his critical personalism and method of radical synthesis. The second and third volumes dealing with his conceptions of the nature of human personality and the structure of values and judgment were to be completed during the first phase of his Hamburg years.

At the time of Stern's move to Hamburg, the founding of a university in that city-state had been a topic of public debate for decades but still was far from a reality. By the turn of the century, a series of scientific, medical, and scholarly installations existed, and the municipality supported a Program of General Lectures (*Allgemeines Vorlesungswesen*) embracing an array of subjects in the social and political sciences as well as in the humanities. A long-standing interest had been maintained by Hamburg's mercantile and importing-exporting community in matters pertaining to scientific and medical questions associated with tropical exploration and colonial ventures. An institute for colonial matters was finally organized in 1908, funded largely by ministries of the central government in Berlin. With the *Kolonialinstitut* established, a plan rapidly emerged to extend the system of general lectures and to combine its enlarged program with the new institute to form the core of a full-fledged, new German university. The plan, however, was not to be realized for another eleven years.[38]

It was in the context of these movements that Ernst Meumann, in 1911, relinquished his post at the University of Leipzig and accepted a newly created professorship in Hamburg. Mandated with the position was the setting up of a department of philosophy, including a psychological laboratory. Both facilities were housed in a three-story building on Domstrasse that formerly had served as a residence for professors in the old section of the city near its cluster of municipal buildings and city hall. Budget allocations for personnel, space, demonstration materials, and experimental equipment had been relatively generous, as had been moneys for the development of a specialized library.[39,40] Along with philosophy and psychology, an experimentally oriented research program had been projected as central to the facilities's mission. By 1915 several publications[41-44] in general and educational psychology had issued from activities of the department, including the completion of Meumann's three-volume introduction to experimental pedagogy and its psychological foundations.[45] In April of that year, however, the chronically ailing Meumann died at the age of 53. Stern was immediately selected to replace him as coeditor of the *Zeitschrift fuer Paedagogische Psychologie und experimentelle Paedagogik.* After a year of provisional administration of the department and laboratory, first by George Anschutz and then by Theodor Kehr, Stern accepted the chair in philosophy, psychology, and pedagogy. It entailed membership in the faculty council of the *Vorlesungswesen* and the combined council of it and the *Kolonialinstitut.*

Despite the restrictions and stress imposed by a nation lockstepped in war and the unexpected death of Kehr, his principal research assistant, Stern was able to effect several important administrative changes during the next three years.[40] These came first in the form of gaining for the laboratory a degree of budgetary autonomy, and of finally establishing and placing under the supervision of Walter Classen a special unit devoted to matters of child care that had been projected but only partially realized during Meumann's tenure. In the fall of 1917, the services of 27-year-old Heinz Werner, fresh from the completion of his doctorate at the University of Vienna, were secured to replace those vacated by Kehr. That same year, two public school instructors, Rudolf Peter and Hans Roloff, were placed on leave and assigned full-time to Stern's staff by the Hamburg school board. At the same time, two other public school teachers, Martha Muchow and Otto Wiegmann, became active participants in projects and activities of the Laboratory.

With these beginnings, Stern was not only to implement the program charted by Meumann, but to extend it into new spheres. While experimental work in attention, perception, and other facets of general psychology continued, a number of projects of a more practical order were introduced that tied the laboratory to pressing social needs of the time. An intensive long-range program of intelligence-test construction was set into motion as well as a large program of aptitude testing to assist in the selection of pupils for the newly created foreign language courses in the public schools. Short- and long-term faculty-student workshops (*Arbeitsgemeinschaften*)— a curriculum device advocated and utilized by Stern throughout his years in Breslau to accomplish research and teaching goals simultaneously[46]—were convened to deal with various phases of problems associated with vocational selection and counseling and child life.[40]

The ongoing war generated its own variety of direct and indirect requirements, and the Psychological Laboratory was also bent to meet these through providing assistance not only for the evaluation and guidance of handicapped veterans and their supporting services, but for other public agencies as well. For example, at the instigation of the command of the pilot-training school in Hamburg-Fuhlsbuettel, Stern devised procedures, first in collaboration with Kehr and then with Wilhelm Benary[47,40] for the evaluation of trainee competencies in flight observations, attention, spatial perception, and orientation. Similarly, using modifications of equipment and techniques developed by Kehr[48] for the measurement of conditions affecting continuous attention, Stern assisted the Altona office for vocational counseling in its selection of women street-car operators.[40] In 1918, the latter project led to several long-term special municipal appropriations in support of additional laboratory personnel for the investigation, development, and validation of procedures and apparatus to assist in the determination of psychological proficiencies of street-car motormen in general and in the selection of operators for the city's subway and its electric elevated and suburban commuter trains.[40] Subsequent involvement in the development of equipment for the measurement of a wide variety of aptitudes related to vocational counseling and selection for public agencies and schools was soon to make the Hamburg Laboratory an important center in northern Germany. To furnish a consistent outlet for reports related to the laboratory's projects, in 1919 Stern began to publish a separate series of one-volume supplements to his journal for applied psychology, the *Hamburger Arbeiten zur Begabungsforschung*.

The Armistice and the collapse of the *Kaiserreich* were to play a significant role for the academic community of Hamburg, the Psychology Laboratory, and, person-ally, for Stern. On November 13, 1918 after a reportedly sleepless night, Stern proposed to the faculty council of the Hamburg *Vorlesungswesen* that an emergency university be formed consisting of private courses to meet the needs of the stream of veterans returning home. Stern's suggestion was accepted, and on January 1 of the following year the first private university courses were offered.** The unanticipated success of the venture suddenly brought to an abrupt close the long debate as to whether Hamburg should have a university. The University of Hamburg was formally founded in the spring of 1919, with the Psychology Laboratory and the Department of Philosophy as two of its original institutes.[38]

The advent of the university and its continuous flow of regular students in pursuit of degrees and certification fostered expansion of the department and the laboratory's physical plant and the eventual acquisition of two three-story structures on each side of the Domstrasse building.[40] Inasmuch as he was the only representative for the disciplines of philosophy, psychology, and pedagogy when the university was founded, Stern was instrumental in securing the faculty appointment of Ernst Cassirer as professor of philosophy in early 1919 to share in the joint administration of the Department of Philosophy, while Stern retained directorship of the laboratory. In 1920 Werner satisfied the requirements for his Habilitation, enabling a broader coverage of a psychological subject matter through formal lectures and seminars and the supervision of laboratory activities. By 1922 Stern's program for the laboratory had taken on a rather stable structure of course offerings, research commitment, and instruction consisting of three major divisions: general psychology, including theoretical and experimental; industrial psychology, including vocational selection, counseling, and investigation of man-machine interface; and educational and child psychology, including the psychology of teaching, child study, development, and assessment.[40]

In addition to those already discussed, another external event in the early 1920s was to contribute to the shaping of the laboratory's program. Representing an innovation in traditional organizations of higher education in Germany, the decision was made in Hamburg to affiliate a teachers' college with the newly founded university. A new section, partially derived from the department and laboratory, was subsequently created, and in 1923 it was finally organized as a department for educational science (Erziehungswissenschaft) under Gustav Deuchler,[51,40] a former student of Max Wundt. To it were assigned courses more specifically related to comparative education, to the psychologies of the school, instruction, administration, and remedial practices, as well as the previously established unit for child care.[52] One effect this differentiated realignment had on Sterns's laboratory was to enable the concentration more fully on the investigation of invariant characteristics of the psychological world of the child and adolescent, the conditions affecting growth and development, and the identification of giftedness in children for which the center was to achieve international recognition.

A wealth of rich contributions to psychology, theoretical and applied, were to flow from the pens of Stern and his coworkers over the next ten years. In addition to his completion of the final volume of *Person und Sache*[37] (Person and Thing), Stern wrote a number of new works dealing with the problems of puberty and adolescence[53-56] and with issues having meaning for the psychology of legal proceedings.[57,58] In one of these dealing with personal components in the onset of puberty and maturity,[54] Stern inadvertently furnished psychologists with an exceptionally creative example of the use of personal documents as a method by providing a psychological

---

**This event, mentioned in several of Stern's publications,[40,49] did not go unnoticed by his colleagues. In an address commemorating the 100th anniversary of Stern's birth, Curt Bondy quoted the following passage of a letter from Professor Heinrich Sieverking, Rektor of Hamburg University, sent to Stern on February 12, 1928: "Tomorrow it will be ten years since you first spoke of university lectures. You can be assured that historians will always remember this fact. We shall always be grateful to you." (Ref. 50, p. 2.)

analysis based on disguised excerpts taken from his own diary kept during boyhood. This period of publication was also earmarked by Stern's revisions and updating of his earlier volumes on the development of language[20] and other psychological characteristics of the young child,[30] as well as his work on the nature and measurement of intelligence in children and adolescents.[59] In 1930, the sixth edition of his *Psychology of Early Childhood*[36] appeared, incorporating supplementary chapters on principles underlying magical behavior and the use of film in studying expressive movements, by Werner and Kurt Lewin, respectively. With more than 20,000 copies sold since its publication in 1914, this edition, the second to be made available in English, was translated by Anna Barwell.[60] In order to provide additional outlet for the laboratory's investigations into child and adolescent behavior, in 1929 Stern began to edit still another set of special supplements to his journal for applied psychology, the *Hamburger Untersuchungen zur Sozial-und Jugendpsychologie.*

During the interval, Stern and his coworkers were regular participants in the meetings of numerous professional societies both at home and abroad. In 1927, Stern's autobiography was published in the prestigious series edited by Schmidt,[61] furnishing the basis for that to be published in English, edited by Murchison, three years later.[49] That same year, already elected to the national psychology societies of France and England, Stern was awarded *in absentia* his second honorary doctorate in the United States in the course of proceedings of the International Symposium on Feelings and Emotions at Wittenberg College, Springfield, Ohio, when it opened its new psychological laboratory.

Accompanied by Lipmann, Stern made his second trip to America in the autumn of 1929 to participate in the Ninth International Congress of Psychology in New Haven, Conn. The trip was an eventful one, for it enabled Stern not only to renew old friendships but to visit several new centers[62] and make new friends. After a conversation with Lawrence K. Frank, Stern applied the following December to the trustees of the Rockefeller Foundation requesting support for the extention of the Laboratory's investigations in child psychology to stimulate the international discussion of problems related to child-care, and for a travel grant for a member of his staff to visit America and study methods of research such as those associated with the Yale Clinic, the Judge Baker Foundation, and the institutes for juvenile and child research in Chicago and Detroit. The former request was rejected, but the latter was accepted, and with the assistance of the Laura Spelman Fund of New York, Martha Muchow visited American installations for a three-month period during the fall and winter of the following year.[63]

Viewed with respect to the full span of years between 1916 and 1933, the program of the Psychology Laboratory seems to have reached its zenith of activity and excitement in the eventful month of April 1931, coinciding with the meeting of the 12th Congress of the German Society for Psychology in Hamburg. A member of its executive committee for more than a decade, Stern was the Society's vice-president. The Laboratory, now renamed the Psychological Institute and housed since 1929 in more spacious quarters in a large, recently acquired university building on Bornplatz, was host for the meetings.[64,65] In addition to Werner and Martha Muchow, among those who had taught in the institute over the interval and who were eventually to become even more familiar to American psychologists were Curt Bondy, Fritz Heider, Heinrich Kluever, Martin Scheerer, and others. Now, more richly endowed with staff and equipment, the curriculum of the institute had expanded enormously. ‡

‡ The institute occupied the entire second floor of the Bornplatz building; some 41 rooms, including three large lecture halls; a library of some 7,000 works; an adjoining reading room for 60 persons; 25 rooms set aside for offices and research; special rooms for the observation of

Integrated with the earlier established divisions in general psychology, child and adolescent psychology, and industrial psychology, a specialization encompassing legal, criminal and forensic psychology was now in full swing.[65] That semester the institute offered a total of 23 courses, some cosponsored by von Uexkuell's Institute for Environmental Research (Umweltforschung), and others by departments of the university's schools of medicine and law.[66]

Festivities honoring Stern's 60th birthday and the presentation of a *Festschrift*[67] also took place that April. Included in the commemorative volume were articles by present and past coworkers in the University and institute and by colleagues in Germany and from abroad: Alfred Adler, Jonas Cohn, Fritz Giese, Erich Jaensch, David and Rosa Katz, Phillip Kohnstamm, Geza Revèsz, and others.

In addition to bringing about a fusion of theoretical and applied psychology, William Stern devoted an important segment of the second half of his seventeen years in Hamburg to a synthesis of his critical personalism and his personalistic psychology. A significant portion of the more formal stipulations derived from his view of how the world works had already been brought to fruition with the publication of the final two volumes of *Person und Sache*: *Die menschliche Persoenlichkeit* 1917 and *Wertphilosophie* 1924.[37] Stemming from a desire early in his academic career to bring together and fully integrate his affection for empirical research on the one hand and his love for speculative venture on the other,[49] Stern's effort had as its goal the programmatic transformation of the latter into terms receptive to the methods of a rapidly advancing objective psychology. As in his generation and the academic generation preceding him, psychology was to remain a science focused upon experience as dependent upon an experiencing person. The implementation of this lifelong endeavor resulted in two final major works,[68,15] both of which incorporated in varying degrees of completeness his perception of the differential interrelatedness of major movements in psychology in Germany—the Berlin Gestalt school, the developmental-structural psychology of Felix Krueger, and the typological approach of Erich Jaensch. The first monograph of his *Studien zur Personwissenschaft* dealing with personalistics as science was issued in 1930 after presentation a year earlier before the German psychological society, where he entertained criticisms by Narzis Ach, Theodor Erismann, Kurt Lewin, Arthur Wreschner, and others.[69] Other monographs originally projected for this series were to remain undone, due to the intervention of forces which lay beyond his control.[70] Stern's larger introductory text to general psychology[15] was completed in 1935, but not in Germany.

Conditions of the German national economy began to affect the program in higher education, first in the turmoil of the 1920s and then in the catastrophe of the early 1930s. In the context of social unrest and progressive problems of employment, overcrowding of the universities recurred, bringing about a shift of policy in professorial roles away from research to those emphasing teaching.[71] From the onset of the new psychology up to the 20s, an increasing number of "chairs" in philosophy had been allocated to individuals whose background had included laboratory method and research orientation. The effect of the gradual change in policy was that philosophers and educators without scientific training were appointed to chairs vacated by psychologists. Troubled by the rapidly shrinking support of the needs of psychology, Stern joined other members of the executive committee of the German Society for Psychology in a formal proclamation of protest which was sent to all

---

children and group behavior; and storage rooms, a workshop, and a dark room for the construction of apparatus and custom equipment.[65] Designed according to the specifications of Stern and his coworkers, the facility was one of the largest in Germany at that time.

German institutions of higher learning, appropriate ministries, legislatures, psychologists, and representatives of related disciplines as well as to professional journals and the daily newspapers.[69]

As troubles deepened, Stern became increasingly the advocate of the academic status and continuing needs of the field of psychology. For example, in October of 1930, addressing himself publicly to the position of psychology in the university and, viewing problems confronting it in broad perspectives, he asserted:

> ". . . it should be . . . emphatically pointed out that in the way in which psychology is currently being treated, the great international reputation of German science is at stake. Earlier Germany was the world master in the field of psychology; today it is on equal footing with other modern societies. . . . In my judgment . . . we in Germany are just on the road to resisting overemphasis on any one point of view and to developing a new type of psychology which perhaps could also point the way for those abroad. For this we need the full means for unfolding our unique potentiality. Were this not to be accorded us, then it is indeed to be feared that we forfeit one of the more important assets with which we take part in international intellectual life. (Ref. 72, p. 11–12)

But the trends in the economic situation continued to deteriorate, and the transcending national crisis entered dark and even more chaotic days early in 1933. On March 24 the National Socialist regime in Berlin was empowered by a new enabling act to govern without a constitution for a period of approximately four years. Fourteen days later, the law for the reconstruction of the German professional civil service came into effect on April 7, suddenly bringing about the virtual collapse of the Psychological Institute that William Stern and his coworkers had built.‡‡ Stern, Cassirer, and Werner, as well as many of their long-time associates, were abruptly prohibited even to set foot in the institute. Stern was barred from conducting lectures, his books were removed from the libraries, and his students were warned that he was a *Schaedling* (noxious person).[50]

Stern was the duly elected president of the German Society for Psychology that year, and he was scheduled to preside over its meeting in April. Instead the date and location of the thirteenth *Kongress* were shifted, and in mid-October, in Leipzig, Felix Krueger presided.

To his three earlier reports[40,51,65] Stern added a fourth[70] and final accounting of his beloved institute before his several editorships were terminated. In early autumn of that same year, two of Stern's closest associates, Martha Muchow and Otto Lipmann, died, alleged political suicides.[29] It fell to Stern to publish notices of their passing in the last issue of the journal of applied psychology he was to edit.[73,74]

Before immigration to the United States in 1934, William and Clara Stern secured a brief period of residence in the Netherlands. There he was able to complete his general psychology from a personalistic standpoint[15] and obtain a publisher for its appearance in German, a feat he is reported to have regarded as a triumph over the prevailing circumstances.[75] Professor Phillip Kohnstamm initiated efforts to get a professorship for Stern in the Netherlands, but these efforts failed.[24] With the assistance of William MacDougall he gained a position and eventually a professor-

---

‡‡ The law of April 7, 1933 provided four grounds for the mandated dismissal of all tenured members of the university and higher education civil service system: having insufficient training; being of non-Aryan status; political unreliability; and for the purpose of simplifying administration. Although the law required full enforcement of its main provisions by the end of the following September, it had run through a dozen or more supplementary regulations and amendments by April 1935. For the effects of this law on professorial ranks and other details, see Hartshorne.[71]

ship at Duke University, Durham, North Carolina, in 1934. Already known and honored in the United States, Stern was an occasional lecturer at Brown, Columbia, Harvard, and other eastern universities. He was reportedly deeply gratified with the publication of the American edition of his comprehensive text in general psychology.[29] Approximately one month after its completion, William Stern died suddenly at 67, the night of March 27, 1938 in Durham. §§

With this overview in hand, Stern emerges as a totally committed individual—in today's terms a humanist—who, with a mode of synthesis characteristic of him throughout his career, sought a fusion of theory and practice, attempting to apply the best to both. His work, especially that associated with his years in Hamburg, attests not only to his belief that a basic unity underlies all facets of the field of psychology but to his complete faith in psychology as essentially a tool for the enlightenment of man and for providing a basis for social reform. For Stern, psychology as an institution existed not as a unit in the fraternity of sciences but as an instrument for confronting and contributing to the solution of the social problems of his day. By the early 1930s and under his guidance, the investigative activities and curriculum of his Psychological Institute were deeply interwoven in collaboration with Hamburg's public school system, child and juvenile authorities, vocational and counseling centers, and law-enforcement agencies and courts. To Stern it was inconceivable that psychology as an institution could exist divorced from its obligations to society and its relevance to societal issues as they affect individual behavior.

Putting the contributions of Stern into a larger perspective, it may be noted that a full century has now passed since Wilhelm Wundt completed the final segment of his *Grundzuege*[77] and made his historic move to Leipzig. Since that time, differentiations within psychology have been rapid, and great strides have been made in achieving the status it enjoys today as a science, discipline, and applied art. Although progress has been steady, development of the field has hardly been programmatically linear; it has been characterized by many starts, stops, crises, and deviations. In an article in the *American Psychologist,* Forrest Tyler[78] has recently made the telling point that psychology, like any other science, is shaped by a dynamic interaction of internal and external forces distributed over time. Viewing psychology as an institutionalized form of behavior, Tyler notes that it can be seen from three interrelated aspects of science: first as a search for truth; then as a role for which individuals are educated; and finally as an array of expert skills used in the service of society. Hence, today's struggles in finding appropriate institutionalization of the roles of the psychologist can be seen as evolving from the original institutionalization of the psychologist as professor-scholar-scientist toward the end of the nineteenth century.

Tyler's differentiations are not lacking in validity. In this context, Stern can be classified as a frequently neglected but highly salient transitional figure centrally located in the series of role shifts leading from the initial one as professor-scholar-scientist to today's institutionalization of the psychologist as scientist-professional

---

§§The story, however, does not end here. A William Stern archive was established at Harvard University and is now on loan to Hebrew University, in Jerusalem. Since World War II, new editions of three of Stern's books[15,20,36] have been reissued in West Germany. Curt Bondy returned to Germany in 1950 and reestablished the Hamburg Psychological Institute. In October 1971 ceremonies were held at the University of Hamburg commemorating the hundredth anniversary of Stern's birth, and a bronze bust of him was installed outside Kokoschka Hall beside that of Ernst Cassirer. A similar tribute was paid in Israel in April 1972.[76]

and flexible problem-solver. The classification acquires more meaning when one notes that Stern shared in common with Wundt the view that psychology should never be allowed to develop as a science independent of philosophy.¶¶

Although his critical personalism and corresponding personalistic psychology failed to achieve immediate popularity, Stern firmly believed they would eventually gain favor and be recognized as his most outstanding contribution. While it is to be noted that his personalistic system is today nowhere to be found intact, its influence upon Gardner Murphy's biosocial approach to personality is acknowledged.[80,81] Wolman[82] has pointed out that Gordon Allport adopted Stern's personalistic content and that Stern's philosophical position became basic to the psychology of Kurt Lewin.

At less global levels, Stern's influence, modified and made over, is still to be found in many facets of today's psychology. With the rise of a reemphasis on cognition and psycholinguistics and the emergence of a vigorous humanistic psychology, the range and scope of Stern's contributions once again come to the forefront.

ACKNOWLEDGMENTS

The assistance of Dr. Horst Gundlach and Miss Erika Nostadt (University of Heidelberg) and of Diplom Psych. Burisch and Mr. Volker Jordan (University of Hamburg) in gathering some of the materials forming the basis for this paper is most gratefully acknowledged. The encouragement of the CUNY Committee for Transnational Research and Exchange in Psychology is also appreciated.

REFERENCES

1. MUNROE, H. 1972. The 1909 Conference at Clark University. Psychology Department, The City College. New York, N.Y. Unpublished manuscript.
2. ROSS, D. 1972. G. Stanley Hall: The Psychologist as Prophet. University of Chicago Press. Chicago, Ill.
3. TITCHENER, E. B. 1910. The past decade in experimental psychology. Am. J. Psychol. 21: 404–421.
4. CLARK UNIVERSITY. 1910. Lectures and addresses delivered before the Departments of Psychology and Pedagogy in celebration of the twentieth anniversary of the opening of Clark University. Clark Univ. Press. Worcester, Mass.
5. STERN, W. 1910. Der Betrieb der reinen und angewandten Psychologie in Amerika: Auf Grund persoenlicher Eindruecke. Z. Angew. Psychol. 3: 449–459.
6. STERN, L. W. 1894. Die Wahrnehmung von Helligkeitsveraenderungen. Z. Psychol. 7: 249–278; 395–397.
7. STERN, L. W. 1896. Die Wahrnehmungen von Tonveraenderungen. Z. Psychol. 11: 1–30, 449–459.
8. STERN, L. W. 1898. Psychologie der Veraenderungsauffassung. Preuss & Juenger. Breslau, Germany. 2nd rev. edit., 1906.

¶¶ During the last years of his career, Wundt became increasingly concerned with the role of psychology in the organization and the curriculum of the university. In a significant but infrequently cited work during these years,[79] he stressed the relationship of the new psychology to the concerns of philosophy rather than to the natural sciences, urging that special chairs in the discipline be set aside for individuals trained in empirical and experimental methods.

For Stern's position in relation to this issue, see his paper presented before the meetings of the national organization of teachers and instructors in Leipzig in October 1930.[72]

9. STERN, L. W. 1899. Die Wahrnehmung von Tonveraenderungen. Z. Psychol. 21: 360-387; 22: 1-12.
10. STERN, L. W. 1903. Der Tonvariator. Z. Psychol. 30: 422-432.
11. BORING, E. G. 1950. A History of Experimental Psychology. Appleton-Century-Crofts, Inc. New York, N.Y.
12. HERRNSTEIN, R. J. & E. G. BORING, Eds. 1965. A Source Book in the History of Psychology. Harvard University Press. Cambridge, Mass.
13. STERN, L. W. 1912. Die psychologischen Methoden der Intelligenzpruefung. In Bericht ueber den V. Kongress fuer experimentelle Psychologie. F. Schulmann, Ed. 1-102. J. A. Barth. Leipzig, Germany.
14. STERN, L. W. 1914. The Psychological Methods of Testing Intelligence. Translated by G. M. Whipple. Warwick and York, Inc. Baltimore, Md.
15. STERN, L. W. 1935. Allgemeine Psychologie auf personalistischer Grundlage. Martinus Nijhoff. The Hague, The Netherlands. 2nd edit., 1950.
16. STERN, W. 1938. General Psychology from the Personalistic Standpoint. Translated by H. D. Spoerl. MacMillan Co. New York, N.Y.
17. STERN L. W. 1902. Zur Psychologie der Aussage. Z. Ges. Strafrechtswiss. 22.
18. STERN, L. W. 1903. Angewandte Psychologie. Beitr. Psychol. Aussage. 1: 4-45.
19. STERN, L. W. 1904. Die Aussage als geistige Leistung und als Verhoersprodukt. J. A. Barth. Leipzig, Germany.
20. STERN, C. & W. STERN. 1907. Die Kindersprache. J. A. Barth. Leipzig, Germany. 2nd edit., 1920; 3rd edit., 1922; 4th edit., 1928, 1965, 1975.
21. STERN, L. W. 1900. Ueber Psychologie der individuellen Differenzen. J. A. Barth. Leipzig, Germany.
22. STERN, W. 1927. Personalistische Psychologie. In Einfuhrung in die neuere Psychologie. E. Saupe, Ed.: 187-197. A. W. Zickfeldt. Osterwieck-Hartz, Germany.
23. MISIAK, H. & V. S. SEXTON, 1966. History of Psychology: An Overview. Grune & Stratton. New York, N.Y.
24. VAN HOORN, W. Personal Communication.
25. HOLZKAMP, K. 1973. Sinnliche Erkenntnis: Historischer Ursprung and gesellschaftliche Funktion der Wahrnehmung. Athenaeum Fischer. Frankfurt am Main, Germany.
26. PONGRATZ, L. J. 1967. Problemgeschichte der Psychologie. Francke. Bern, Switzerland.
27. MUELLER-FREIENFELS, R. 1935. The Evolution of Modern Psychology. Yale University Press. New Haven, Conn.
28. VAN HOORN, W. 1972. As Images Unwind: Ancient and Modern Theories of Perception. University Press Amsterdam. Amsterdam, The Netherlands.
29. ALLPORT, G. 1968. The Personalistic Psychology of William Stern. In The Person in Psychology: Selected Essays. G. Allport, Ed. 271-297 Beacon Press, Boston. Mass.
30. STERN, C. &. W. STERN. 1908. Erinnerung, Aussage, und Luege in der ersten Kindheit. J. A. Barth. Leipzig, Germany. 2nd edit., 1920; 3rd edit., 1922; 4th edit., 1931.
31. STERN, W. 1905. Helen Keller. Die Entwicklung und Erziehung einer Taubstummblinden als psychologisches, paedagogisches und sprachtheoretisches Problem. Reuther & Reichard. Berlin, Germany.
32. KRAMER, F. & W. STERN. 1906. Selbstverrat durch Assoziation. Beitr. Psychol. Aussage 4: 1-32.
33. STERN, W. 1908. Sammlung freier Kinderzeichnungen. Z. Angew. Psychol. 1: 179-187.
34. STERN, W. & F. KRAMER. 1908. Psychologische Preufung eines elfjaehrigen Maedchens mit besonderer mnemotechnischer Faehigkeit. Z. Angew. Psychol. 1: 291-312.
35. STERN, W. 1909. Die Entwicklung der Raumwahrnehmung in der ersten Kindheit. Z. Angew. Psychol. 2: 412-423.
36. STERN, W. 1914. Psychologie der fruehen Kindheit bis zum sechsten Lebensjahre. Quelle & Meyer. Leipzig, Germany. 2nd edit., 1921; 3rd edit., 1923; 4th edit., 1927; 5th edit., 1928; 6th edit., 1930.; 7th edit., 1952; 8th edit., 1965; 9th edit., 1967; 10th edit., 1971.
37. STERN, W. 1906; 1917; 1924. Person und Sache: Vol. 1. Ableitung and Grundlehre; Vol. 2. Die menschliche Persoenlichkeit; Vol. 3. Wertphilosophie. J. A. Barth. Leipzig, Germany.
38. UNIVERSITAET HAMBURG. 1969. Universitaet Hamburg 1919-1969. Selbstverlag der Universitaet Hamburg. Hamburg, Germany.

39. HASSERODT, W. 1912 Das Institut fuer experimentelle Psychologie in Hamburg. Z. Paed. Psychol. Exp. Paed. **13**: 587–589.
40. STERN, W. 1922. Das Psychologische Laboratorium der Hamburgischen Universitaet. Z. Paed. Psychol. Exp. Paed. **23**: 161–196.
41. MEUMANN, E. 1912. Beobachtungen ueber differenzierte Einstellungen bei Gedaechtnisversuchen. Z. Paed. Psychol. Exp. Paed. **8**: 456–472.
42. HASSERODT, W. 1913. Gesichtspunkte zu einer experimentellen Analyse geometrisch-optischer Taeuschungen. Arch. Ges. Psychol. **28**: 336–347.
43. PETER, R. 1914. Beitraege zur Analyse der zeichnerischen Begabung. Z. Paed. Psychol. Exp. Paed. **15**: 96–104.
44. PETER, R. 1915. Untersuchungen ueber die Beziehungen zwischen primaeren und sekundaeren Faktoren der Tiefenwahrnehmung. Arch. Ges. Psychol. **34**: 515–564.
45. MEUMANN, E. 1914. Vorlesungen zur Einfuehrung in der experimentelle Paedagogik und ihre psychologischen Grundlagen. Vol. 3. Engelmann. Leipzig, Germany.
46. STERN, W. 1901. Ueber Arbeitsgemeinschaft in der Psychologie. *In* C. R. IVe Cong. int. de Psychol. 435–438. Alcan. Paris, France.
47. STAATSARCHIV HAMBURG. Documents in Hochschulwesen II. Hamburg, Germany.
48. KEHR, T. 1916. Versuchsanordnung zur experimentellen Untersuchung einer kontinuierlichen Aufmerksamkeitsleistung. Z. Angew. Psychol. **11**.
49. STERN, W. 1930. William Stern. *In* History of Psychology in Autobiography. C. Murchison, Ed. Vol. 1: 335–388. Clark University Press. Worcester, Mass.
50. BONDY, C. 1973. Festvortrag zum 100. Geburtstag von William Louis Stern. Paper presented Oct. 29, 1971. Kokoschka Hall. Hamburg University. Hamburg, Germany. Mimeographed.
51. STERN, W. 1925. Aus dreijaehriger Arbeit des Hamburger Psychologischen Laboratoriums. Z. Paed. Psychol. Exp. Paed. **26**: 289–307.
52. DEUCHLER, G. 1925. Das Seminar fuer Erziehungswissenschaft der Hamburgischen Universitaet. Z. Paed. Psychol. Exp. Paed. **26**: 379–381.
53. STERN, W. 1924. Das Ernstspiel der Jugendzeit. Z. Paed. Psychol. Exp. Paed. **25**: 241–252.
54. STERN, W. 1925. Anfaenge der Reifezeit. Quelle & Meyer. Leipzig, Germany. 2nd edit., 1929.
55. STERN, W. 1925. Freundschafte-und Feindschafts-Erlebnisse in der fruehen Pubertaet. Z. Paed. Psychol. Exp. Paed. **26**: 81–97.
56. STERN, W. 1927. Zur Psychologie der reifenden Jugend. Z. Paed. Psychol. Exp. Paed. **28**: 1–10.
57. STERN, W. 1926. Sittlichkeitsvergehen an Kindern und Jugendlichen. Z. Paed Psychol. Exp. Paed. **27**: 45–51; 73–80.
58. STERN, W. 1926. Jugendliche Zeugen in Sittlichkeitsprozessen. Quelle & Meyer. Leipzig, Germany.
59. STERN, W. & O. WIEGMANN. 1920. Die Intelligenz der Kinder und Jugendliche und die Methoden ihrer Untersuchung. J. A. Barth. Leipzig, Germany. 2nd edit., 1922; 3rd edit., 1926; 4th edit., 1928.
60. STERN, W. 1924. The Psychology of Childhood up to the Sixth Year of Age. Translated by A. Barwell. Henry Holt & Co. New York, N.Y. 2nd rev. edit., 1930.
61. STERN, W. 1927. William Stern. *In* Philosophie der Gegenwart in Selbstdarstellungen. R. Schmidt, Ed. Vol. 6: 129–184. Felix Meiner. Leipzig, Germany.
62. STERN, W. 1930. Eindruecke von amerikanischer Psychologie. Z. Paed. Psychol. Exp. Paed. **31**.
63. STAATSARCHIV HAMBURG. Documents in Hochschulwesen II. Hamburg, Germany.
64. KAFKA, G., Ed. 1932. Bericht ueber den XII. Kongress der Deutschen Gesellschaft fuer Psychologie. G. Fischer. Jena, Germany.
65. STERN, W. 1931. Das Psychologische Institut der Hamburgischen Universitaet in seiner gegenwaertigen Gestalt. Z. Angew. Psychol. **39**: 181–227.
66. HAMBURGISCHE UNIVERSITÄT. 1931. Verzeichnis der Vorlesungen. Sommer-Semester: 30–31. Hamburg, Germany.
67. PSYCHOLOGISCHES INSTITUT HAMBURG. 1931. William Stern. Festschrift zum 60. Geburtstag. Beihefte Z. Angew. Psychol. **59**.
68. STERN, W. 1930. Studien zur Personwissenschaft. I. Personalistik als Wissenschaft. J. A.

Barth. Leipzig, Germany.
69. VOLKELT, H. Ed. 1930. Bericht ueber den XI. Kongress fuer experimentelle Psychologie in Wien. G. Fischer. Jena, Germany.
70. STERN, W. 1933. Aus dem letzsten Arbeiten des Psychologischen Instituts der Hamburgischen Universitaet 1931–33. Z. Angew. Psychol. **45**: 397–418.
71. HARTSHORNE, E. Y. 1937. The German Universities and National Socialism. Harvard University Press. Cambridge, Mass.
72. STERN, W. 1931. Die Stellung der Psychologie an den deutschen Universitaeten. Die Deutsche Schule **2**: 3–12.
73. STERN, W. 1933. Martha Muchow. Z. Angew. Psychol. **45**: 418.
74. STERN, W. 1933 Otto Lipmann. Z. Angew. Psychol. **45**: 420.
75. CASSIRER, E. 1941. William Stern. Acta Psychol. **5**: 1–15.
76. MICHAELIS-STERN, E. 1972. William Stern 1871–1938. The man and his accomplishments. *In* Year Book XVII of the Leo Baeck Institute: 143–154. Secker & Warburg. London, England.
77. WUNDT, W. 1874. Grundzuege der physiologischen Psychologie. Engelmann. Leipzig, Germany.
78. TYLER, F. B. 1970. Shaping of the science. Am. Psychol. **25**: 219–226.
79. WUNDT, W. 1913. Die Psychologie im Kampf ums Dasein. Leipzig, Germany.
80. EVANS, R. Ed. 1966. Dr. Gardner Murphy speaks. Part II. NSF Notable Contributors to the Psychology of Personality Series. University of Houston. Houston, Texas.
81. MURPHY, G. 1947. Personality. A Biosocial Approach to Origins and Structure. Harper & Brothers. New York, N.Y.
82. WOLMAN, B. 1960. Contemporary Theories and Systems in Psychology. Harper & Row. New York, N.Y.

PART III.   CURRENT PSYCHOLOGY

THE AROUSAL FUNCTION OF CENTRAL
CATECHOLAMINE NEURONS*

Gerard P. Smith

Department of Psychiatry
Cornell University Medical College
New York, New York 10021

The Edward W. Bourne Behavioral Research Laboratory
The New York Hospital, Westchester Division
White Plains, New York 10605

Between primary sensory receptors and final motor neurons lies the great mass of interneurons that embodies the strategies, decisions, and retrievals that structure behavior. In the past decade one group of interneurons has been well characterized by a convergence of histochemical and neurochemical techniques.[1] These are the catecholamine (CA) neurons. They are specified by their ability to synthesize, store, and release the catecholamines norepinephrine and dopamine. Their anatomy is unusual. All the cell bodies are in the brainstem except for several clusters of cells in the medial sector of the ventral diencephalon. The CA axons and terminals are distributed throughout the neuraxis from the cerebral cortex to the lumbar spinal cord. Their extensive distribution can be appreciated by considering that the individual CA cells of the locus coeruleus lying beneath the cerebellum have terminal projections to the cerebellum, the hippocampus, and the neocortex as well as numerous synapses *en passant* in the midbrain and hypothalamus. Although CA neurons are distributed widely throughout the brain, they do not provide a dense projection to any particular region. For example, in the rat striatum (n. caudatus-putamen) where CA terminals are most dense, they account for about 10% of synaptic boutons.[2] In the rat neocortex, CA boutons account for about 1% of the total.[3]

The behavioral importance of the diffuse CA network was uncovered by pharmacological research that demonstrated that the powerful psychological and behavioral effects of reserpine, amphetamine, chlorpromazine, iproniazid, and imipramine depended on altering the function of central CA neurons. On the basis of these drug actions Kety[4] suggested that CA neurons were involved in behavioral arousal. That hypothesis spurred investigation of the function of CA neurons in normal behavior.

Ablation is a traditional way of analyzing the behavioral function of neural tissue, but the usual lesion techniques are not well suited for removing such a diffuse network. Such ablation experiments were made possible by the discovery of Thoenen and Tranzer[5] that 6-hydroxydopamine destroys CA neurons selectively. The mechanism of toxicity is not understood, but the selective destruction is.[1] The selectivity depends on the fact that 6-OHDA satisfies the structural requirements of the active transport system located in the cellular membrane of CA neurons. This membrane pump is arranged so that the catecholamine transmitters, norepinephrine and dopamine, are transported from outside the neuron back into the CA axon or

*The research was supported by National Institutes of Health Grant NS08402 and was performed during the tenure of Career Development Award NS38601.

45

terminal. (This recapture of released CA transmitter is a major mechanism for limiting the duration of the normal synaptic action of norepinephrine and dopamine.) Since 6-OHDA resembles dopamine so closely, it is pumped into CA neurons. This vectorial transport results in a concentration of 6-OHDA that is much higher inside the CA neuron than in the extracellular fluid or in other neurons that lack the membrane pump. Since the toxicity of 6-OHDA is directly related to its concentration, it is possible to give a dose of 6-OHDA that produces a nontoxic concentration of 6-OHDA in extracellular fluid, but a toxic concentration in CA neurons. Ablation of peripheral CA neurons is easily accomplished with systemic injections. For lesioning central CA terminals, systemic injections of 6-OHDA cannot be used because 6-OHDA does not cross the blood-brain barrier effectively. A number of investigators have gone around the blood-brain barrier by injecting 6-OHDA intraventricularly or intracisternally. Such injections produced widespread lesions of CA neurons, judged by loss of histofluorescence, loss of norepinephrine and dopamine, and loss of other parameters of CA neuronal function.[6,7] The damage appeared selective for CA: the central acetycholine and serotonin neurons were not affected significantly. Finally, the CA damage appeared permanent, at least up to 6 months.

The behavioral effects of such widespread, long-lasting CA damage were extremely variable. Transient disturbances in activity and shock avoidance,[8] prolonged aphagia and adipsia,[9] apparently permanent loss of the ability to acquire or perform an active avoidance response,[10] increased responsiveness to handling,[11] and decreased exploratory activity[12] were all reported. It appeared that behavior was most disrupted when catecholamines, particularly dopamine, were most depleted.[10]

In considering these results it is important to understand that the diffuse application of 6-OHDA by CSF injections has little potential for neurological localization of behavioral function. The results can only be interpreted in terms of a mass action effect of central CA neurons. To search for localization of function, 6-OHDA must be restricted to small regions of the brain. In 1968, Ungerstedt[13] accomplished this by microinjecting 6-OHDA into the pars compacta of the substantia nigra and destroying the dopamine cell bodies and their axons, which make up the nigrostriatal tract. Except for some nonspecific damage at the tip of the injection cannula, the 6-OHDA lesion seemed to involve only CA neurons.[14,15] Since such specificity is not always obtained,[16] histological control of the technique is essential. When the 6-OHDA microinjection technique works optimally, it provides a much more informative lesion than can be obtained with electrolysis or radiofrequency (TABLE 1).

The 6-OHDA microinjection technique has now been used extensively to study the behavioral effects of lesions of the nigrostriatal system.[17,18] The most complete bilateral nigrostriatal lesions produce rats that move very little.[17] Such rats are, of course, behaviorally impoverished and fail to eat, drink, explore, or actively avoid electric shock.[17,18] Incomplete lesions appear to fractionate this syndrome. Iversen and her colleagues have produced several permutations while attempting the same nigral lesion.[18]

To attempt to produce CA-lesioned rats that were more competent behaviorally, we began to microinject 6-OHDA bilaterally along the medial forebrain bundle (MFB). Rats injected in the posterolateral hypothalamus appeared as crippled as nigral lesioned rats. This is consistent with the trajectory of the nigrostriatal tract through this region. Injections into the anterolateral hypothalamus cephalad to the point where most of the nigrostriatal tract has left the lateral hypothalamus produced rats that looked normal after a brief period of aphagia and adipsia.[19] Extensive testing of these rats demonstrated a group of behavioral deficits that we believe depends on the loss of the arousal function of forebrain CA terminals. This paper describes those deficits and discusses them in relation to the pattern of loss of CA neurons in the forebrain.

MATERIALS AND METHODS

Sprague Dawley male rats (Hormone Assays, Chicago, Illinois), weighing between 200 and 400 g at the time of operation, were used in these experiments. Stereotactic microinjections were made in rats anesthetized with chloral hydrate and barbpurate ("Equi-Thesin," 3 ml/kg, i.p.; Jensen Salsbery Laboratories, Kansas City). Each microinjection was $4\,\mu$l of distilled water containing 6-hydroxydopamine hydrobromide (6.5 μg of base/μl) and ascorbic acid (0.4 or 0.8 μg/μl). Vehicle injections were injections of 4 μl of distilled water containing ascorbic acid (0.4 or 0.8 μg/μl). Injection solutions were mixed just prior to operation and chilled until loaded into a Hamilton syringe (50 μl) equipped with an automatic dispenser. The Hamilton syringe was connected by polyethylene tubing (PE 10) to a cannula of stainless steel hypodermic tubing (30 gauge). After the cannula was lowered to the desired brain coordinates, 4 μl of fluid was injected over 30 seconds. The cannula was left in place for 30 to 60 seconds longer and then withdrawn.

TABLE 1

COMPARISON OF 6-OHDA AND ELECTROLYTIC LESIONS*

	6-OHDA	Electrolytic
Neuronal specificity	*Catecholamine*	none
Direction of lesioned fibers	*ascending*	multidirectional
Transmitter systems lost	*catecholamines*	unknown

*The comparison assumes optimum use of 6-OHDA so that only catecholamine damage is obtained. How closely an experiment approaches this ideal must be decided on the relevant evidence presented.

Bilateral microinjections of 6-OHDA or vehicle alone were made into the anterolateral (AL) or anteromedial (AM) hypothalamus. The AL site was in the head of the medial forebrain bundle just above the caudal edge of the optic chiasm, 2.0 mm from the sagittal midline (A7.0, RL2.0, and H8.0 down from the dural surface according to the atlas of De Groot [20]; all distances are mm). The AM site was 1.0 — 1.25 mm medial to the AL site (A7.0, RL0.75, or 1.0, H8.0 down).

Rats were housed individually on a 12-hour light cycle (7 A.M. to 7 P.M.). Food pellets and tap water were available ad libidum except when constrained by experimental design.

Statistical comparisons were made with the Mann-Whitney U test unless otherwise indicated.

RESULTS

Visual Placing Deficit

After bilateral 6-OHDA microinjections into the anterolateral hypothalamus (AL) (n = 37), rats were examined neurologically at frequent intervals (sometimes daily) for up to 6 months. [21] The neurological examination tested forelimb placing responses to the touch of vibrissae, chin, or the dorsum of the forepaws, and to the sight of a covered surface (visual placing). Other tests were hindlimb placing responses to the touch of the dorsum of the hindpaws, hopping reactions, and righting responses. All 37 rats injected with 6-OHDA failed to place their forelimbs in response to visual stimuli. The defect was present on the first postinjection day and it persisted for 6 months. The defect in placing was restricted to visual stimuli; vibrissae, chin, and tactile placing were normal. Righting and hopping reactions were also normal in the 6-OHDA rats.

The visual placing deficit was not observed in 11 rats that received vehicle microinjections into the AL, or in 10 rats that received 6-OHDA in the AM. Thus the defect was linked to the effect of 6-OHDA at the AL site.

The deficit in visual placing was not the result of blindness produced by microinjection of 6-OHDA. The 6-OHDA rats did not show increased exploration characteristic of blinded rats[22] (see *Open Field Deficit*) and the microinjection did not damage the optic tract (see *Histological Analysis* and SECHZER et al.[21])

I wish to emphasize how normal the 6-OHDA rats appeared in their home cages or while being handled. It was always surprising to demonstrate such a profound and permanent visual placing deficit in these animals.

There was one way in which the 6-OHDA rats did appear abnormal to casual observation: they did not move much when left alone on a table during the daily maintenance routine. This observation led us to test AL 6-OHDA rats in an open field.

Open Field Deficit

Methods

Nine rats received AL injections of 6-OHDA and eight rats received AL vehicle injections given as described above. All rats were tested in the open field (OF) on postinjection days 1, 3, 5, and 7.

Four unoperated rats and two sham-operated rats (skull holes drilled) were tested in the OF on four alternate days to define the normal range of OF behavior under our conditions.

Open field testing was performed in a rectangular area (76 cm × 93 cm) enclosed by brown cardboard walls 60 cm high. The floor was covered with white contact paper and was divided into 8 cm squares by brown lines. Fluorescent ceiling lights 2.6 m above the floor provided 20μ W/cm^2 in the center of the OF.

Each rat was tested in the OF by being placed in a corner of the OF with its head toward the wall. Latency period before moving into the OF, number of squares traversed, number of rears and fecal boluses were counted during a 6-minute test. Then the rat was immediately returned to its home cage. On each test day, a rat was given two 6-minute tests separated by an interval of 55 minutes.

In addition to OF testing, the home cage activity of all 6-OHDA and vehicle rats was measured by counting the interruptions of a photocell beam mounted in the middle of the long axis of the Plexiglas cage (21 × 44 × 20 cm) in which each rat was housed. Beginning 3 days prior to the microinjection procedure and continuing through the first postinjection week, cumulative photocell counts were recorded daily for each rat at 0700 and 1900 hours. These times bounded the light phase of the daily cycle. Counts that occurred within 30 minutes after OF tests, feeding or weighing were subtracted from daytime photocell counts (0700 to 1900).

TABLE 2

OPEN FIELD ACTIVITY AFTER ANTEROLATERAL HYPOTHALAMIC
INJECTIONS OF 6-OHDA OR VEHICLE*

Postinjection Day	Median Number of Squares Traversed		
	6-OHDA	Vehicle	No Injection
1	0‡	62‡	491
3	0†‡	113	514
5	0†‡	121‡	576
7	0†‡	180	609
30	0†‡	510	
31	0†‡	481	
32	0†‡	357	
33	0†‡	477	
34	0†‡	409	

*There were 9 6-OHDA and 8 vehicle rats tested on days 1, 3, 5, and 7; 7 6-OHDA and 7
vehicle rats were tested on days 30 through 34. Six rats received no injection.
†Significantly different from vehicle, $p < .05$.
‡Significantly different from control, $p < .02$.

Results

The 6-OHDA rats moved significantly less in the OF than vehicle-injected rats
(TABLE 2).[23,24] The 6-OHDA rats also reared less and had significantly longer latency
periods, but they did not defecate more (unpublished data of R. C. Young, G. N.
Ervin, and G. P. Smith). Despite this global deficit in OF behavior, home cage
activity of 6-OHDA rats was normal and not different from that of vehicle-injected
rats by the third postinjection day (TABLE 3).

Although 6-OHDA rats were clearly less active in the OF than vehicle rats,
vehicle rats were frequently less active than control rats (TABLE 2). To eliminate this

TABLE 3

HOME CAGE ACTIVITY AFTER ANTEROLATERAL HYPOTHALAMIC
6-OHDA OR VEHICLE*

Experimental Day	6-OHDA (n = 9)	Vehicle (n = 8)
-1	646	637
Microinjection		
1	237†	369†
3	678	810
5	803	741
7	735	891

*Data are median photocell interruptions per 24 hours.
†Significantly different from day -1, $p < .05$

nonspecific effect of microinjection, we tested seven 6-OHDA and seven vehicle rats in the OF for 5 consecutive days beginning on postinjection day 30 (TABLE 2). Now the vehicle injected rats moved normally in the OF, but 6-OHDA rats did not. Furthermore, these 6-OHDA rats also had the very prolonged latency periods and decreased rearing observed in 6-OHDA rats in the first postinjection week (unpublished data, R. C. Young, G. N. Ervin, and G. P. Smith). The failure of 6-OHDA rats to move in the OF could have been the result of increased reactivity to novel stimuli that manifested itself in freezing behavior. We rejected this possibility for the following reasons: (1) we did not observe a tense crouching posture or other evidence of freezing; (2) 6-OHDA rats did not react excessively to handling; (3) 6-OHDA rats showed a smaller adrenocortical response to the OF than did vehicle rats (unpublished data); and (4) 6-OHDA rats did not defecate more often in the OF than vehicle rats (unpublished data).

We conclude that the failure to move in the OF is a failure of the distant, unfamiliar stimuli of the OF to control the sequence for forward movement. The failure to move in the OF contrasts sharply with the normal activity in the home cage and suggests that 6-OHDA rats react less to distant, unfamiliar stimuli. This is maladaptive and it suggested the 6-OHDA rats would have difficulty using distant, unfamiliar stimuli as cues for an instrumental response. To test this inference we investigated the capacity of 6-OHDA rats to acquire a one-way active avoidance response.

Active Avoidance Deficit

Methods

Ten AL 6-OHDA rats, 8 AL vehicle rats, and 9 AM 6-OHDA rats were trained to acquire a one-way active avoidance response in a single session that occurred during the first week after microinjection. All training was done in a plexiglas chamber (Grayson-Stadler Model 1111; internal dimensions were 30.5 cm long, 30.5 cm wide and 15.3 cm high). The chamber was divided into two compartments of equal size by a partition that had a sliding door (14.0 cm long) at one end. The safe compartment (right side) had a smooth brown vinyl floor laid over the shock bars. The shock compartment (left side) had a floor of stainless steel bars (0.25 cm in diameter and 1 cm between bars). Current was supplied to the floor bars of the shock compartment by activating a constant current shock generator equipped with a shock scrambler (Grayson-Stadler, Model 700GS). White noise entered both compartments from a speaker fixed to the roof of the test chamber.

Testing began after a rat had explored the test chamber for 90 seconds. Jump threshold current was determined for each rat by the method of Turner et al. [25] Jump threshold was the minimal current at which a rat consistently lifted its rear paws off the shock bars.

Avoidance training for each rat began with the foot shock current equal to its jump threshold. A trial began when the sliding door in one end of the partition was removed. If the rat crossed from the shock compartment to the safe compartment within 5 seconds, this movement (approximately two rat body lengths) was an avoidance response. If the rat did not cross within 5 seconds, foot shocks (1 Hz, 1-second duration) were delivered through shock bars for 10 sec. If the rat crossed during the train of shocks, this movement was an escape response. If the rat did not move out of the shock compartment during the 10-second train of shocks, the rat was coaxed by hand into the safe compartment. The rat was left in the safe compartment until just before the next trial began (intertrial interval was 30 seconds). Then it was picked up by the investigator and placed in the shock compartment. Thus the task was always one-way, from left to right.

Training was continued until the rat performed nine consecutive avoidance responses (criterion). If the rat did not reach the criterion in 70 trials, training was discontinued. Because of the poor performance of many 6-OHDA animals, training was discontinued after 50 trials, if a rat had not made one avoidance response.

To insure that the poor performance was not due to insufficient shock current, the shock current was increased to two or three times the jump threshold current (but the current never exceeded 1 mA) if a rat did not make an escape or avoidance response during 10 consecutive trials or if a rat did not reach the criterion in the first 50 trials.

Some of the anterolateral and all of the anteromedial rats were trained under slightly different conditions: (1) the foot shock current for each of these rats equalled the jump threshold current plus 0.2 mA; (2) training of these rats was discontinued at the end of 50 trials. These procedural differences did not produce different results.

Because rats received an unequal number of trials, all escape and avoidance results are presented as the median percentage of total trials.

TABLE 4

ACQUISITION OF ACTIVE AVOIDANCE AFTER ANTERIOR
HYPOTHALAMIC 6-OHDA OR VEHICLE

Experimental Group	n	No. of rats Achieving Criterion for Acquisition	Median Jump Threshold (mA)
AL 6-OHDA	10	0	0.35
AL Vehicle	8	8	0.25
AM 6-OHDA	9	8	0.40

Results

None of the 10 AL 6-OHDA rats acquired the active avoidance response (CAR); all 8 AL vehicle and 8 of 9 AM 6-OHDA rats did (TABLE 4). [26] The failure to acquire the CAR was not dependent upon a change in reactivity to electric shock because the jump thresholds of 6-OHDA rats did not differ from vehicle rats (TABLE 4). The AL 6-OHDA rats that failed to avoid appeared to escape the electric shock normally. [26] Since the escape response was very similar to the required avoidance response, an effective motor sequence was available in AL 6-OHDA rats; but it was not controlled by the complex, distant stimuli that constituted the CS (opening the door in the barrier separating the shock compartment from the safe compartment).

In an attempt to improve acquisition of CAR, five 6-OHDA rats were injected with L-dopa (1-dihydroxyphenylalanine 50 mg/kg i.p., Roche Laboratories, Nutley, New Jersey) 5-10 minutes before avoidance training. L-dopa increased escape responding, but not avoidance responding. [26] The failure of L-dopa to reverse the loss of CAR in 6-OHDA rats contrasts with its success in reversing the loss of CAR in rats treated with reserpine [27] or α-methyltyrosine. [28] This is consistent with the destruction of CA axons and terminals after 6-OHDA, which decreases sites for conversion of L-dopa to norepinephrine or dopamine. Neither reserpine nor α-methyltyrosine has this destructive effect.

AL 6-OHDA rats (n = 9) also failed to *perform* this same CAR on the sixth postinjection day after being trained for 50 trials on the day prior to microinjection of 6-OHDA. [26] This was an impressive defect, because six of nine AL 6-OHDA rats had achieved the criterion of nine consecutive avoidance responses in the training session and all five AL vehicle rats performed the previously acquired CAR normally (four vehicle rats showed savings).

Since previous acquisition of the CAR did not improve performance of the CAR by 6-OHDA rats, we inferred that the 6-OHDA lesion damaged the instrumental use of forward movement, but spared the learning and memory mechanisms. This inference was supported by demonstrating that AL 6-OHDA rats easily learned a taste aversion for saccharin and a one trial passive avoidance response. [26]

It is clear that 6-OHDA microinjections into the AL hypothalamus consistently produced a deficit in forward movement to distant stimuli under three conditions of increasing adaptive complexity—the visual placing test, the open field, and the one-way active avoidance. What kind of neurological damage underlies such a behavioral deficit?

Histological Analysis

Methods

To evaluate the neuropathological reaction to microinjection of 6-OHDA, we injected the AL site of a group of 12 rats with 1.7, 13, or 26 g 6-OHDA in 4 μl of vehicle (0.4 μg ascorbic acid/μl distilled water) and 4 rats with vehicle alone. These rats were killed 2 or 4 days after microinjection, which is the time of maximal neuropathological response. Their brains were perfused with isotonic saline (0.9%) followed by buffered formalin (10%). After storage in buffered formalin (10%) for at least 2 weeks, brains were blocked, embedded in paraffin, and sections at 8 or 10 μm. Alternate sections were taken at intevals of 72–100 μm through the entire hypothalamus and stained by thionine and Woelcke techniques. Brains of some of the 6-OHDA rats that had served as subjects in the behavioral tests were also processed in this manner.

To evaluate the loss of specific catecholamine histoflourescence, 10 AL 6-OHDA rats, 5 AL vehicle rats, 7 AM 6-OHDA rats and 5 AM vehicle rats were killed at least 3 weeks after 6-OHDA injection. Their brains were sectioned with the Vibratome and processed by the glyoxylic acid method. [29]

Results

Two days after microinjection of 4 μl of vehicle (0.4 μg ascorbic acid/μl distilled water) or 4 μl of vehicle containing 1.7, 13, or 26 μg of 6-OHDA, light microscopy revealed very similar pathology. [26] At the tip of the cannula track, there was an area of cell and myelin loss with glial infiltration. There were normal-appearing neurons at the borders of the lesion. The size of the lesion did not vary with the amount of 6-OHDA injected. It was about 250 μm or less after all the doses of 6-OHDA tested. The greatest diameter of the lesion after vehicle injection was about 300 μm.

Four days after microinjection of the largest dose of 6-OHDA, the lesion was similar and vascular proliferation was evident at the borders of the lesion. The maximum diameter of cell and myelin loss was about 300 μm.

The neuropathology of sites injected more than 3 weeks earlier (obtained from rats that had been subjects for the behavioral studies) usually consisted of a thin, linear glial infiltrate within a small area of cell and myelin loss.[21] Less frequently, the injection site could not be definitely determined because there was so little damage seen. A necrotic area encapsulated within glia and measuring as much as 0.5 to 0.8 mm in diameter was occasionally observed.

The loss of CA histofluorescence after AL or AM vehicle microinjections did not extend beyond the region of nonspecific damage observed with light microscopy.[30] The CA loss after AL or AM 6-OHDA, however, was widespread throughout the anterior hypothalamus, limbic forebrain, and neocortex.[30] Both AL and AM 6-OHDA rats showed severe CA loss in parietal and frontal cortex, the hippocampus, and the molecular layer of the piriform cortex. In addition to these common losses, there were CA losses that were specific for the AL or AM injection. Only AM 6-OHDA rats had severe loss of CA in the AM hypothalamus and medial preoptic area. The most extensive CA damage occurred after AL 6-OHDA. The regions of severe loss of CA included the AL hypothalamus, head of the caudate nucleus, nucleus accumbens, dorsal part of the bed nucleus of the stria terminalis, olfactory tubercle, lateral septal nucleus, and the submolecular layers of the piriform cortex. These data are preliminary; more damaged structures may be observed in subsequent material. We do have clear evidence, however, that the CA innervation is intact in the posterior hypothalamus, the posterior half of the caudate, and the upper midbrain.

These histological results confirm the preferential destruction of CA neurons by 6-OHDA. Although there is some nonspecific damage after 6-OHDA, it is restricted to the injection site and appears to be similar to the nonspecific damage produced by vehicle injections. There is a loss of CA fluorescence after 6-OHDA that extends far beyond the nonspecific damage at the injection site. This does not occur after vehicle injections. Since AL vehicle injections did not produce the behavioral deficits observed after AL 6-OHDA, the behavioral deficits correlate with specific CA damage and not with nonspecific tissue damage.

Loss of CA in the AM hypothalamus and medial preoptic area occurred after AM 6-OHDA, but not after AL 6-OHDA. Conversely, AL 6-OHDA injections damaged CA in AL hypothalamus, but not in AM hypothalamus. Since the lateral distance between the AL and AM injection sites was 1.0 to 1.25 mm, these results demonstrate that microinjection of 4 μl 6-OHDA under our conditions spreads a toxic concentration of 6-OHDA less than 1.0 mm in a lateral direction.

The different patterns of CA damage after AL and AM 6-OHDA injections correlate with the different behavioral effects of AL and AM 6-OHDA injections. Recall that AM 6-OHDA did not abolish visual placing or active avoidance (AM 6-OHDA occasionally decreased open field activity, but usually it had no effect; unpublished data, R. C. Young, S. Fink, and G. P. Smith). This means that the CA loss in the AM hypothalamus and medial preoptic area that was produced by AM 6-OHDA injections only is not necessary for the behavioral deficits. The CA denervation of neocortex, limbic forebrain, and olfactory system after AL 6-OHDA correlates with the behavioral deficits. Since the neocortical and hippocampal CA damage occurred after both AL and AM 6-OHDA, it is possible that the behavioral deficits depend on CA denervation of limbic and olfactory structures produced only by AL 6-OHDA. This would favor localization of behavioral function. It is also possible, however, that the behavioral deficits after AL 6-OHDA are due to the more extensive loss of CA. This would favor a "mass action" effect. The available data do not permit us to decide between these alternatives. We are pursuing this question in current experiments.

DISCUSSION

These three behavioral deficits have in common the failure of distant stimuli to control the initiation of forward movement. An important aspect of each deficit is that the motor sequence can be initiated by more proximal stimuli. Rats that don't place their forelimbs to visual stimuli, place to tactile stimuli. Rats that do not use forward movement to avoid distant cues, use forward movement to escape electric shock. Rats that move little or not at all in an open field, move normally in their home cages. From the results in the open field and avoidance tests, the distant stimuli that do not control the initiation of forward movement can be further specified as unfamiliar and not noxious. This characterization is tentative. Much more work will be required to classify the stimuli precisely.

The retention of movement in response to proximal, noxious, and familiar stimuli, but not to distant, unfamiliar stimuli is consistent with the sequence of dissolution of behavioral function after brain damage that Hughlings Jackson[31] described in human patients over 100 years ago and that Teitelbaum has emphasized in his analysis of the behavioral effects of lateral hypothalamic lesions in rats.[32]

The selective loss of reactivity to distant and unfamiliar stimuli after preferential destruction of forebrain CA axons and terminals bears on the hypothesis that the central CA neurons mediate behavioral arousal.[4] Consider our simplest case—the loss of visual placing and the retention of tactile placing. I assume that those behavioral functions are most vulnerable to brain damage that depend upon the most number of synapses (functionally "longer"). This assumption is supported by recent work of Evarts.[33] Evarts provided neurophysiological evidence that the delay between presentation of a conditioned *visual* cue and the electrophysiological response of a pyramidal tract neuron involved in the conditioned motor response of the hand of a monkey is about three or four times as long as the delay between a conditioned *tactile* stimulus of the hand and the response of the same pyramidal tract neuron. The longer delay after the visual stimulus must represent more synaptic processing. The probability of disruption of long polysynaptic paths by forebrain damage is greater than the probability of disruption of shorter polysynaptic paths. This would account for the usual pattern of behavioral dissolution that Jackson observed.

Such speculation offers an explanation for the appearance of the same pattern of behavioral dissolution after damage of the diffuse forebrain CA system if it mediates behavioral arousal. The functionally long polysynaptic path of the visual placing response increases the probability of the signal of the visual stimulus being lost in the synaptic "noise" of competing systems. An arousal system for sensorimotor integration functions to enhance the signal-to-noise ratio. Since CA transmitters usually inhibit synaptic activity,[1] at the synaptic level they would enhance the signal by suppressing the noise of competing systems. By their diffuse distribution, CA neurons could perform this function throughout most of the brain. Because such an arousal function would be more necessary in functionally long, polysynaptic paths than in shorter ones, damage of a forebrain CA arousal system should affect sensorimotor integration of distant stimuli more than integration of proximal stimuli. It is the architectural diffuseness that characterizes both the forebrain CA system and the sensorimotor system for distant stimuli which underlies the common pattern of behavioral dissolution after destruction of sensorimotor tissue or removal of forebrain CA. In my view, arousal is a "permissive" synaptic action of central CA transmitters.[34] Forebrain CA terminals permit optimum sensorimotor integration to occur, but they do not "command" it.

We have recently obtained pharmacological evidence that also favors an arousal defect in these 6-OHDA rats.[35] When AL 6-OHDA rats were tested 15 or 19 days after microinjection of 6-OHDA, they were unresponsive to *d*-amphetamine (2 mg/kg). This dose of *d*-amphetamine produces marked behavioral arousal in normal rats. Since amphetamine exerts its arousal function by releasing central CA, these results add strong support for the hypothesis that forebrain CA mediate behavioral arousal.

The deficits in the initiation of forward movement by 6-OHDA rats have been demonstrated in isolated test situations only. It would be interesting to see how well such rats cope in social or field situations. If they lacked the instrumental use of forward movement to distant or unfamiliar stimuli, they would have to adapt to social and environmental stimuli by passive behaviors. It is easy to imagine behavioral contexts in which passive behaviors alone would not serve them well, but only the acid test of experiment can decide how vulnerable these 6-OHDA rats are to social and environmental stress.

ACKNOWLEDGMENT

I thank Stephen Fink for criticizing this manuscript.

REFERENCES

1. COOPER, J. R., F. E. BLOOM & R. H. ROTH, Eds. 1974. The Biochemical Basis of Neuropharmacology. 2nd edit. Oxford University Press. New York, N.Y.
2. ANDEN, N. E., K. FUXE, B. HAMBERGER & T. HÖKFELT. 1966. Acta Physiol. Scand. **67**: 306–312.
3. DESCARRIES, L. & Y. LAPIERRE. 1973. Brain Res. **5**: 141–160.
4. KETY, S. S. 1967. The central physiological and pharmacological effects of the biogenic amines and their correlations with behavior. *In* The Neurosciences. G. C. Quarton, T. Melnechuk & F. O. Schmitt, Eds.: 444–451. Rockefeller University Press. New York, N.Y.
5. THOENEN H. & J. P TRANZER. 1968. Naunyn-Schmiedebergs Archiv für Pharmakol. und Experiment. Pathol. **261**: 271–288.
6. MALMFORS, T. & H. THOENEN, Eds. 1971. 6-Hydroxydopamine and Catecholamine Neurons. American Elsevier Publishing Co., Inc. New York, N.Y.
7. URETSKY, N. J. & L. L. IVERSEN. 1970. J. Neurochem. **17**: 269–278.
8. LAVERTY, R. & K. M. TAYLOR. 1970. Br. J. Pharmacol. **40**: 836–846.
9. STRICKER, E. M. & M. J. ZIGMOND. 1974. J. Comp. Physiol. Psychol. **86**: 973–994.
10. COOPER, B. R., G. R. BREESE, L. D. GRANT & J. L. HOWARD. 1973. J. Pharmacol. Exp. Therap. **185**: 358–370.
11. NAKAMURA, K. & H. THOENEN. 1972. Psychopharmacolgia (Berlin) **24**: 359–372.
12. JALFRE, M. & W. HAEFELY. 1971. Effects of some centrally acting agents in rats after intraventricular injections of 6-hydroxydopamine. *In* 6-Hydroxydopamine and Catecholamine Neurons. T. Malmfors & H. Thoenen, Eds.: 333–346. American Elsevier Publishing Co., Inc. New York, N.Y.
13. UNGERSTEDT, U. 1968. Eur. J. Pharmacol. **5**: 107–110.
14. HOKFELT, T. & U. UNGERSTEDT. 1973. Brain Res. **60**: 269–298.
15. AGID, Y., F. JAVOY, J. GLOWINSKI, D. BOUVET & C. SOTELO. 1973. Brain Res. **58**: 291–301.
16. POIRIER, L. J., P. LANGELIER, A. ROBERGE, R. BOUCHER & A. KITSIKIS. 1972. J. Neurol. Sci. **16**: 401–416.
17. UNGERSTEDT, U. 1974. Brain dopamine neurons and behavior. *In* The Neurosciences, Third Study Program. F. O. Schmitt & F. G. Worden, Eds.: 695–703. The M.I.T. Press. Cambridge, Mass.
18. IVERSEN, S. D. 1974. 6-Hydroxydopamine: A chemical lesion technique for studying the role of amine neurotransmitters in behavior. *In* the Neurosciences, Third Study Program. F. O. Schmitt & F. G. Worden, Eds.: 705–711. The M.I.T. Press. Cambridge, Mass.

19. SMITH, G. P., A. J. STROHMAYER & D. J. REIS. 1972. Nature New Biol. **235**: 27–29.
20. DE GROOT, J. 1959. Trans. Roy. Netherlands Acad. Sci. **52**: 1–38.
21. SECHZER, J. A. G. N. ERVIN & G. P. SMITH. 1973. Exp. Neurol. **41**: 723–737.
22. GLICKMAN, S. E. 1958. Can. J. Psychol. **12**: 45–51.
23. SMITH G. P. & R. C. YOUNG. 1974. A new experimental model of hypokinesia. *In* Advances in Neurology. F. H. McDowell & A. Barbeau, Eds. Vol. **5**: 427–432. Raven Press. New York, N.Y.
24. YOUNG, R. C. & G. P. SMITH. 1973. Progr. Soc. Neuroscience. p. 189.
25. TURNER, S. G., J. A. SECHZER & R. A. LIEBELT. 1967. Exp. Neurol. **19**: 236–244.
26. SMITH, G. P., B. E. LEVIN & G. N. ERVIN. 1975. Brain Res. **88**: 483–498.
27. SEIDEN, L. S. & D. D. PETERSON. 1968. J. Pharmacol. Exp. Therap. **159**: 422–428.
28. MOORE, K. E. & R. H. RECH. J. Pharm. Pharmacol. **19**:405–407.
29. LINDVALL, O. & A. BJORKLUND. 1974. Histochemistry **39**: 97–127.
30. FINK, J. S. & G. P. SMITH. 1975. Neurosc. Abstr. **1**: 406.
31. JACKSON, J. H. 1958. Evolution and dissolution of the nervous system. *In* Selected Writings of John Hughlings Jackson. Basic Books, New York, N.Y.
32. TIETELBAUM, P. 1971. The encephalization of hunger. *In* Progress in Physiological Psychology. E. Stellar & J. M. Sprague, Eds. Vol. **4**: 319–350. Academic Press, New York, N.Y.
33. EVARTS, E. V. 1974. Sensorimotor cortex activity associated with movements triggered by visual as compared to somesthetic inputs. *In* The Neurosciences, Third Study Program. F. O. Schmitt & F. G. Worden, Eds.: 327–337. The M.I.T. Press. Cambridge, Mass.
34. SMITH, G. P. 1973. The neuropharmacology of thirst. *In* The Neuropsychology of Thirst. A. N. Epstein, H. Kissileff & E. Stellar, Eds.: 231–241. H. V. Winston and Sons. Washington, D.C.
35. ERVIN, G. N. R.C. YOUNG & G. P. SMITH. 1974. Progr. Soc. Neuroscience. p. 202.

THE FUNCTION OF COVERT ORAL BEHAVIOR IN LINGUISTIC CODING AND INTERNAL INFORMATION PROCESSING

F. J. McGuigan

Department of Psychology
Hollins College
Roanoke, Virginia 24020

Empirical and theoretical studies have established that a variety of covert processes occur during the performance of linguistic tasks designated by such terms as "thought" or "cognition."[1-3] These covert events are widespread throughout the body, are extremely complex, and many occur with great rapidity. Contemporary problems of considerable interest concern the specification of functions for such covert processes as the contingent negative variation, evoked potentials, galvanic skin response (GSR) and covert speech muscle activity. Our model has been one in which these brain, muscle, and glandular events perform critical functions in a highly complex internal information-processing system. More particularly, we have hypothesized that these covert processes form: 1) intracerebral circuits (loops) within various brain regions, and 2) circuits between the brain and peripheral mechanisms in the speech musculature, the eyes, the skeletal muscles in the neck, arms, and so on. When activated, these loops serve in the formation and transmission of verbal codes that facilitate internal information processing (cf. References 2-4).

There are numerous historical references that implicate central and peripheral mechanisms in "thought" processes. The report by Delafresnaye[5] is an excellent excursion into brain functioning during thought. Langfeld[6] develops a rich account, dating from the ancient Greeks, of muscular response involvement in thought. Jacobson[7] emphasizes the concept of neuromuscular circuits in the higher mental processes and cites Lilly's interpretation of his studies of 1930–1934 as proving ". . . that the brain had no closed circuits when it came to mental activity" (p. 8). The early behavioristic theories of thinking may also be considered approximations to a "circuit" conception, in that thinking was a composite of covert oral and nonoral language responses in conjunction with brain activity. Watson[8] and his colleagues concentrated mainly on the "surface" (muscular) components of the neuromuscular circuits but still considered the central nervous system to perform critical functions.

Now, with sufficient data to allow us to conclude that: 1) brain events, 2) covert oral responses, and 3) covert nonoral responses occur during the silent performance of language tasks,[1-3] we need to determine how these three classes of covert processes function when complex neuromuscular circuits are activated. Our long-range purpose is to specify neural and muscular interactions during the performance of internal information-processing tasks that have been referred to with terms like "imagination," "cognition," and "thought."

Our procedure in this paper will be to explore possible routes and mechanisms by which impinging linguistic stimuli are transduced and transmitted through various bodily systems during the process of "language perception." Language perception occurs mainly in the auditory modality (for speech perception) and in the visual modality (for reading). In the following, we shall be concerned with speech, although the principles should be generally applicable to other modalities, especially processes involved in reading.

EXTERNAL AND INTERNAL LINGUISTIC CODING

The stream of speech emitted by a speaker is an acoustic analog signal. The problem of characterizing acoustic speech sounds reliably into linguistic units is far from being adequately solved; we will not here consider this problem in any detail, but merely note that the topic has received considerable attention (e.g. References 9, 10).

For some purposes, analog analysis of speech has been productive, but for other purposes quantification of the analog speech signal by means of binary arithmetic has been fruitful. It is especially interesting in this context to note that some *bodily processes,* including those intimately involved in speech, appear to be more effectively represented in binary rather than in analog form. Contractions of a muscle fiber or firing of a nerve impulse, for instance, are relatively discrete (on-off) events that obey the all-or-none law. They thus are not well suited to an analog model in which electrical signals convey information primarily by amplitude or rate of change. Hence we shall attempt to represent selected neuromuscular speech events in binary form and to relate these events to binary representations of analog speech signals. Our concern, however, will be only with the processing of small linguistic units (allophones, words) and not with sentences. It may be useful for the following discussion to emphasize the distinction between allophones and and phonemes: an allophone (e.g. [k] is a concrete instance of an abstract phoneme class (e.g. /k/). Hence, the phoneme /k/ has many different physical (allophonic) realizations ("key," "can," "cool").

Speech Signals Phonemically Represented by Distinctive Features

One prominent characteristic of natural languages is that the many bipolar word pairs can be represented by "yes-no" binary symbols (high-low, inside-outside, etc.). Phonemes also have bipolar characteristics, and it is not surprising that the early descriptions of phonemes (dating from the Hindus about 300 B.C.) carried a notion of binary opposition.[11] Roman Jakobson and his colleagues have successfully exploited these binary characteristics of language and offered a complete binary description of phonemes (Ref. 12). Jakobson regarded phonemes as bundles of *attributes,* a notion similar to that of Twadell's[13] "microphonemes." As a listener monitors the stream of speech, he "detects" instances of these attributes. For example, he detects such instances of attributes as "the buzzing vibrations of the cords of the larynx, called *voicing,* heard during all English vowels (hard, moon, see, etc.) and in certain consonants (z, v, etc.); the hissing breath sounds (as in *h*ard . . . the explosive sounds (like *b*oy) . . . the nasal quality . . . (new) . . ." (Ref. 11, p. 92).

In their 1952 work Jakobson *et al.*[12] proposed 12 possible attributes (distinctive features) of phonemes that may be represented as 12 binary oppositions; for example, a phoneme may have the distinctive feature of being either nasal or oral (it cannot be both); the binary opposition "nasal/oral" may thus be used to specify one distinctive feature of a phoneme. Any phoneme may be uniquely described as a subset of the complete set of 12 distinctive features.

Distinctive features may be represented by means of a set of orthogonal axes that form a phonemic feature space so that each phoneme of spoken speech may be uniquely described by a binary chain of plus and minus feature oppositions. (The reader might look ahead to FIGURE 8, in which a minimal set of nine distinctive features is used to specify in binary form one phoneme (/p/).) Cherry[11] has shown how speech can be plotted as a continuous trajectory of system points from cell to cell of a binary matrix (i.e., from phoneme to phoneme). Using only three dimensions, an acoustic speech trajectory is illustrated to the left of FIGURE 1.

The system of distinctive features has been applied in principle to five levels of speech analysis; Twaddell,[13] Cherry,[11] and Jakobson and Halle.[14] These five speech levels may be summarized as follows: 1) a physiological level in which speech is produced; 2) an articulatory level in which the position, shapings, and dimensions of the speech organs, are specified; 3) an acoustic level for the physical analysis of sounds; 4) that of physiological reception, in the ear and subsequent afferent neural activity; and 5) in perception at the "psychological level" where semantic processing occurs.

While distinctive features may be specified for all five linguistic levels, a relatively refined matrix has been worked out only for level 3, the acoustic level at which auditory stimuli are transmitted as air vibrations. There has been some considerable description of distinctive features at the articulatory level (level 2), but these have been presented only in prose and not specified in detail.[14] Certainly a priority effort for linguists is to define phonemes by specifying distinctive feature matrices for other levels. Our purpose here will be to use the descriptions of speech as acoustic stimuli for the listener (level 3) as a basis for considering response aspects of speech within the listener (levels 4 and 5).

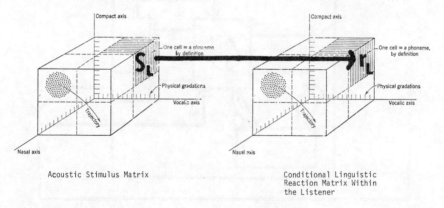

Acoustic Stimulus Matrix

Conditional Linguistic
Reaction Matrix Within
the Listener

FIGURE 1. Representation of a phoneme as a conditional acoustic linguistic stimulus (S_L). The stimulus evokes a corresponding perceived phoneme within the listener, represented as a conditional linguistic response (r_L) (adapted from Cherry.[11]).

Speech Perception and Distinctive Features

When speech stimuli impinge on the listener, they produce internal events wherein there is perception of the linguistic input. Our general notion will be that the perception occurs when the stimulus elements, represented by a matrix of distinctive features, evoke events within the listener that may be represented by a corresponding reaction matrix. An acoustically represented instance of a phoneme as a stimulus might thus evoke a corresponding phoneme instance in a reactional matrix system within the listener. Such a stimulus-response relationship is characterized in FIGURE 1, using only three dimensions. When a language stimulus (S_L) that is emitted by the speaker impinges on the listener, it evokes a covert language reaction pattern, a portion of which is represented to the right (r_L).

There is, incidentally, good evidence that discrete binary contrasts in language (as in FIGURE 1) *can* be differentially conditioned; for example, words that have been naturally or experimentally conditioned as "good" vs. "bad" differentially evoke psychophysiologically measured covert conditional responses.[15,16] Furthermore, conditional language responses generalize to other words along complex dimensions (e.g. Ref. 17) between stimulus objects and corresponding words,[18] and so on.

NEUROMUSCULAR EVENTS IN INTERNAL INFORMATION PROCESSING

To this point we have developed the general notion that linguistic stimuli (continuous signals) can be represented in binary code, and that these stimuli evoke perceptual processes within the listener that may also be represented by a systematically related binary system. We shall now sketch out some neuromuscular processes by which linguistic codes might be generated and transmitted within the language recipient.

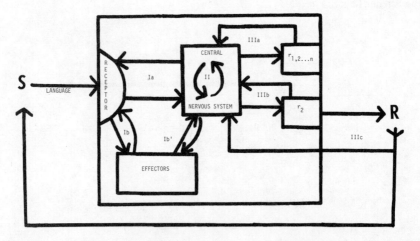

FIGURE 2. Schematic representation of potential circuits during internal information processing. Covert processes in the receptors, brain, muscles, and glands (measured by EEG, EMG, GSR, etc.) serve as the basis for inferences about these hypothesized loops within a person.

There is abundant anatomical and physiological evidence about specific circuits (loops) between the brain and a wide variety of peripheral mechanisms (e.g. Ref. 19). A paradigm for specifying classes of circuits that might serve linguistic functions during information processing is presented in FIGURE 2.

The first kind of circuit (designated Ia) occurs when stimuli excite receptors, whereupon afferent neural impulses evoke brain events that result in efferent impulses back to the receptor. Such loops must reverberate for some time following stimulus reception. There is also the probability of extra-CNS loops between receptors and other peripheral mechanisms, like receptor-speech muscle-brain circuits (circuit class Ib and Ib') (cf. Ref. 20).

The second general class of circuit (for sensory integration) would consist of strictly intracerebral loops (II). These may include circuits between the cortex and subcortical regions (cf. Penfield,[21]) as well as complex transcortical loops such as Hebb's[22] cell assemblies.

Finally, there are three possible loops between the brain and effectors: circuit class IIIa, in which one covert response class ($r_{1,2}$. . . n) leads to a series of additional covert responses; IIIb, in which one covert response (r_2) is an antecedent ("determiner") of an overt response (R); and IIIc, where the consequences of an overt response (R) include both internal signals (to the central nervous system) and external signals that interact with stimulus input (S_L), as in overt speech. Circuits IIIa and IIIb involve only internal signals from the response, whereas in circuit IIIc the response produces both internal *and* external signals.

We shall now consider circuits of the classes I, II, and III in greater detail. As mentioned earlier, man's two major modes of information processing are auditory and visual. In evolution, the auditory modality was probably the more basic (for language), which is a major reason for giving speech priority over reading.

It is important in the following discussion to emphasize that when we refer to circuits and loops, we mean *classes* of these circuits. That is, we do not imply that there is a single neuron conducting a single impulse along a circuit. Rather, circuits must carry complex volleys of numerous neural impulses simultaneously along parallel channels all throughout the body. Hassler[23] has detailed some circuits that neurologically function in parallel. Tomatis[20] points out that auditory stimuli influence the vagus nerve, which widely distributes signals, including those that are transmitted to the viscera.

FIGURE 3 is a somewhat expanded representation of the internal information processing circuits that are hypothesized in FIGURE 2. To begin to appreciate the complexity of the neuromuscular systems with which we shall deal, and to gain an indication of their ability to meet the processing requirements of our model, we may note, as an example, that there are 130 million rods and cones in the eye. These cells make junction with one million nerve fibers; this ratio of 130:1 indicates that there must be exceeding complex events in the transfer of information from the receptor to the optic nerve. On the motor side, the oculomotor nerve contains 25,000 fibers, and the muscles that produce eye movements have approximately three muscle fibers for each nerve fiber. This ratio of one neural fiber to three muscle fibers invites thought about the transfer of information back from the brain to the eye musculature. For comparison with the optic and oculomotor nerves, cranial nerves contain about 70,000 fibers, whereas motor roots of spinal nerves contain about 100,000 fibers. Estimates are of some 10 billion cerebral neurons, and although uncounted, there must be even more muscle fibers in human bodies in which more than half of the weight is muscle.

But to proceed, we may note that all internal linguistic events following stimulus input necessarily are "abstract," since phonemic and semantic entities are obviously not present in the acoustic signal. Consequently, the assertion of such linguistic entities as phonemes and meaning reactions requires processing of the stimulus input. After considering the initial processing of the signal in the periphery, we shall turn to systems involving central events.

Peripheral Processing

How might the peripheral events represented in FIGURES 2 and 3 function linguistically? First, there are receptor mechanisms *per se* that transduce input signals during initial stimulus processing. Stevens and House[24] emphasize the importance of this peripheral receptor analysis in speech perception by citing a number of neurophysiological studies that indicate that "fairly complex processing takes place peripherally. Therefore, the peripheral auditory mechanism must impose on the input signal a much more radical transformation than a simple frequency analysis. The processing probably provides considerable information concerning attributes of the signal that are relevant to the discrimination of various linguistic categories or features." (p. 48)

More important than the linguistic processing in which auditory stimuli are transduced to neural impulses, however, are those receptor processes that might function as components of circuits of the classes Ia and Ib.

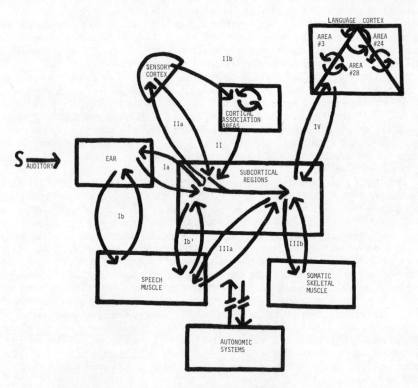

FIGURE 3. Possible neuromuscular circuit classes in internal information processing.

Receptor-Subcortical Circuits (Class Ia)

Once the auditory signal enters the ear, nerve cells in the cochlea of the inner ear are activated as a function of the vibration frequencies that have impinged on the external auditory meatus and on the eardrum. The resulting afferent neural impulses are conducted along the auditory nerve (consisting of some 30,000 afferent neurons) to the cerebrum, following which efferent impulses return to the receptor; the continuous operation of this loop forms the class of circuit designated Ia. This well-described type of receptor-brain circuit may function during short-term memory by temporarily holding linguistic units so that the perceiver can form the units into a grammatical context (as discussed later in this paper).

Receptor-Speech Muscle-Brain Circuits (Class Ib)

The second possible loop might serve a peripheral speech function by involving the ear directly with the speech musculature. Wyczoikowska[25] implicitly hypothesized such a loop in explaining why her subjects reported that they felt strong impulses in the tongue when listening to auditory stimuli. Her subjects reported, for instance, that they heard words with "vibrating motions" in the tongue during thought. The physiological basis was her specification of the lingual and the glossopharyngeal nerves between the ear and the tongue, so that stimulation of the ear might directly innervate the tongue, facilitating the perception of external speech. Stevens and House[24] cite an even earlier reference to a speech perception model that is based on the active internal replication of the external stimulus, namely, von Humboldt in 1836 held that the human being repeats immediately that which he has just heard. They then propose an elaborate, active model of speech perception in which the listener participates equally with the talker—the listener internally generates the speaker's message just as if he were to operate as the talker (rather than as the listener). As Stevens and House[24] point out, this is the concept of "analysis by synthesis" put forward by Halle and Stevens.[26] A similar view is also suggested by Cherry,[11] as discussed later in this paper. A variety of other kinds of research also indicate that the speech muscle may be intimately involved in the processing of external linguistic stimuli within the listener. Such data, consistent with the interpretation of a class of circuits like Ib, are summarized in a forthcoming publication.[27]

In this section, we have noted that during peripheral linguistic processing, signals are continuously transmitted from the ears to subcortical levels and return, by way of the circuit class Ia of FIGURE 3. Signals also possibly arrive at subcortical levels from an ear to speech muscle circuit (pathways Ib and Ib' that are in parallel with loop Ia). We shall now consider the next "step" in internal linguistic processing, namely, how signals from external stimuli that enter two ears become integrated into one perceptual phenomenon.

Sensory Integration Circuits (Class II)

The acoustic signals that arrive at the thalamic-brainstem-midbrain regions by the class of circuit designated Ia may interact with impulses that ascend from the speech muscle by path Ib'. Regardless of whether one or both of these classes of loops function linguistically, afferent flow into the subcortical region sets off additional ascending and descending loops simultaneously. The ascending circuit is to the sensory (in this case auditory) cortex by way of loop class IIa of FIGURE 3. (A number of specifications of auditory pathways through the brain stem and midbrain are available, e.g. Goldstein.[28]) The descending loops from subcortical levels to the skeletal musculature (loop classes IIIa and IIIb) will be considered in the next section.

Some evidence for the existence of a pathway Ib' from the speech muscle to the cortex (II) is summarized in McGuigan.[27] One example is the work of Bowman and Combs,[29] who stimulated the distal portion of the hypoglossal nerve, which arises in the tongue, and recorded evoked potentials in the contralateral sensory motor cortex with a latency of only 4–5 msec.

Penfield and Jasper[30] have presented evidence for a circuit that consists of nerve fibers running from the lower brain stem through the thalamus to the sensory cortex and back down to the thalamus (p. 474). With regard to impulses descending from the cortex to subcortical levels, Goldstein[28] suggests that a peripheral stimulus delivered to any portion of the auditory, visual, or somesthetic receptive fields activates one and the same central "association" system (specified in Ref. 28, p. 1517) in an undifferentiated way; this cortical region, he holds, constitutes part of a generalized thalamocortical system, but its function[29] is unclear: "Little is known about what sort of associations between diverse sensory inputs might be accomplished by a system conveying no information other than that *some* stimulus has been presented *somewhere* . . ." (p. 1519). Such an undifferentiated central association system could be extremely important in the present context. One reason is that a system like this might function to transfer signals from one modality to another. For instance, if the cortical association system is activated by a visual stimulus, it might direct impulses into somesthetic channels to activate the body musculature. Hence, when one silently reads prose, this central neurophysiological system might direct the internal visual stimuli into muscle channels to covertly activate the oral skeletal muscle, as detailed in McGuigan.[2] Edmund Jacobson (personal communication) has held that an external stimulus becomes meaningful when it is transferred into another modality; perhaps the central association system performs such an intermodal transfer function. We thus indicate that impulses from the sensory (auditory) cortex descend in parallel back to the subcortical regions, first directly (IIa) and secondly through the cortical association areas (IIb). As these subcortical-sensory cortex-association cortex loops continue to reverberate in *both* hemispheres, the incoming auditory signals from the two ears may be integrated into one perceptual phenomenon; additional integration may occur in the central association areas with internal signals arriving from various other bodily sources (speech muscle, viscera, etc.).

Linguistic Processing Loops: Cortical-Covert Behavior Interactions (Classes IIIa, IIIb, IV)

In FIGURE 3, loops of the classes IIIa and IIIb reverberate simultaneously with loop class II. That is, while sensory integration is occurring (II), subcortical-skeletal muscle loops run simultaneously (and in parallel) between 1) the subcortex and the speech musculature (IIIa), and 2) from the subcortex to and from the other skeletal muscles of the body (IIIb). By hypothesis,[2] a function of loops IIIa and IIIb in FIGURE 3 is to produce conditional (muscle) response patterns that participate in the formation of verbal codes that are afferently carried back to the brain by loop class IV. When circuit IV is activated, there is lexical and semantic processing wherein the listener understands (perceives) the incoming linguistic stimuli.

Several kinds of evidence for circuits from the speech muscle to the brain are summarized in McGuigan.[27] For example, Sauerland and Mizuno[31] found evidence for a specific reflex between the tongue and laryngeal musculature such that afferent impulses are carried by hypoglossal fibers from extrinsic and intrinsic portions of the tongue to the brainstem, following which the intrinsic laryngeal musculature is activated. Presumably, impulses from the brainstem then ascend to the cortex. Relevant to this circuit is the work of Ojemann,[32] who showed that the lateral thalamus is an integrating center for various activities concerned with speech. We have also already noted that Bowman and Combs[29] specified an afferent pathway from the tongue to the sensory-motor cortex by way of the hypoglossal nerve.

Sussman[33] offered the general conclusion that there is a centripetal pathway that conveys sensory information from the muscle-spindle end organs in the tongue to the brainstem by a hypoglossal-to-cervical nerve route and a hypoglossal-to-lingual nerve route, and then from the medulla on to the higher cortical regions.

Penfield specified three major cortical speech areas that are relevant to circuit IV: Wernicke's area (#28), Broca's area (#3), and that in the supplementary motor-area (#24). Penfield electrically stimulated these three speech areas and concluded that all three have effective axonal connections into the thalamic nuclei. These three areas may thus form the cortical components of loop IV, and interactions among these language regions and other cortical areas may constitute transcortical loops (II) of FIGURE 2, such as Hebb's[22] cell assemblies. Semantic processing may then proceed through circuit IV somewhat in the manner proposed by Osgood[34] in his theorizing about representational (meaning) reactions (r_M's), as well as his $\overline{s\text{-}s}$ and $\overline{r\text{-}r}$ events, which he also places at the cortical level.

As far as the peripheral components of circuits IIIa and IIIb are concerned, we have abundant evidence that numerous covert skeletal muscle responses occur throughout the body during the silent performance of linguistic tasks (for example, see Ref. 3). We may expect the speech musculature to be the most prominent in linguistic coding processes; the generalization is that covert oral language responses occur in *all* linguistically competent individuals, even though the amplitude may be extremely low in highly proficient people (e.g. References 3,35). Nonoral skeletal muscle responses during linguistic processing also must be emphasized; examples are heightened covert behavior in the preferred arm during reading, memorizing, and listening,[36,37] and covert dactylic responses in the deaf while thinking.[38,39]

We now must consider the critical question of whether or not the speech musculature actually can function in the generation and transmission of a verbal code, as we have hypothesized in the interaction of circuits IIIa and IV. The following evidence, added to that previously cited, suggests an affirmative answer.

Sussman[33] considered the nature of the information carried by the afferent pathways from the tongue, and, relying on the work of Bowman and Combs,[40] concluded that "Not only can the higher brain centers be kept informed as to the *initiation* of a high-speed consonantal gesture of the tongue but also as to the *attainment* and subsequent *release* of that gesture. . . . The neuromuscular system of the tongue has been shown to be a built-in feedback system that can signal the length and rate of movement of a muscle" (p. 266). Consequently, ". . . it is logical to assume that the *afferent discharge pattern emanating from the tongue should contain high-level distinctive information.* Such discriminative information can be provided by the differential frequency discharge patterning of the muscle spindles due to the orientation of the extrafusal fibers relative to the direction of movement" (p. 267).

Another line of research that supports the hypothesis that the speech-muscle functions in the generation of a verbal code has resulted in evidence of a discriminative relation between speech-muscle behavior and the phonemic system during various cognitive processes. For example, Blumenthal[41] showed that tongue electromyograms were of significantly greater magnitude when subjects thought of saying lingual-alveolar verbal materials (that would require major tongue movements during *overt* speech), compared to when they thought of saying bilabials. In a series of experiments, Locke and Fehr[42] reported more covert lip activity during the subvocal rehearsal of labial words, relative to nonlabials. More recently, McGuigan and Winstead[37] reported that covert responses in the tongue are relatively pronounced when the subject is reading, memorizing, and rehearsing prose that is heavily loaded with lingual-alveolar material, whereas covert lip behavior is especially pronounced while reading, memorizing, and rehearsing prose that is dominated by bilabial material. Of more direct significance to speech perception, one extremely well-relaxed subject listened to sentences and words loaded with either labial or nonlabial verbal material. While listening to labial material, this subject significantly increased lip electromyograms but did not do so while listening to comparable nonlabial material.[4] In short, it seems that the particular class of verbal material (bilabial, lingual-alveolar, etc.) silently processed evokes relatively heightened covert activity in the speech muscle that would be used for the overt production of that class of verbal material. One possible interpretation is that the speech muscle covertly generates a verbal code that is related to the phonemic system.

Other relevant data are that there are heightened tongue electromyograms (EMG) during perceptual clarification ("The Gilbert & Sullivan effect") as reported by Osgood and McGuigan.[43] In that Gilbert and Sullivan study, auditorially unclear words being sung in operetta choruses were perceptually clarified by simultaneously presenting the words in visual prose. It was McGuigan's (but not Osgood's) hypothesis that the "feedback" from the speech musculature when the subjects silently read the matching prose produced the auditory clarification by interacting with central meaning processes. This did *not* happen when unrelated prose was read or when no auditory clarification was reported subjectively by the subjects. A second in a series of four studies planned by Osgood and McGuigan employed the same paradigm, with the exception that instead of meaningful words sung in the operettas, meaningless auditory prose (spoken to the subjects in the Finnish language) was used. Even with the meaning reactions removed, there was still auditory perceptual clarification accompanied by heightened tongue EMG.[27] These data are consonant with the conclusion that the speech musculature does carry distinctive information to the brain.

The next question is whether a system of feature oppositions can be fruitfully employed to describe the information generated during the complex interaction of muscle-fiber contraction and muscle receptor stimulation, and consequent discharge of afferent neural impulses.* An empirical specification of precise patterns of muscle fibers responding as a function of patterns of distinctive feature oppositions (like those to be presented later in FIGURE 8) would be fantastically complex. No electromyographic work to date has even approached the refined laboratory analysis that would be required for measuring speech-muscle activity for coding distinctive features during language reception. Even the much simpler problem of specifying relationships between muscle activity and distinctive features during speech *production* (vs. perception) has not led to extremely impressive results. Harris[44] reported one line of research, for example, that followed from the proposal of Jakobson *et al.*[45] that the "tense" member of the opposition pair (see FIGURE 8, tense/lax, #7) leads to more forceful articulation than does the "lax" member. As Harris points out, the "tense-lax" distinction is meant to be the primary one between "voiced" and "voiceless" consonants, so that instances of the phoneme class /p/ should demand greater muscular tension when produced than for /b/. Harris cited four studies in which this expectation was examined by measuring force of orbicularis oris contraction in the lips. In three studies, she states that the differences between /p/ and /b/ were not significant, but a small difference was found in the fourth. There is, however, more encouraging evidence later. For example, Hirose and Gay[46] found that the posterior cricoarytenoid muscle participates in laryngeal articulatory adjustments, particularly for the voiced/voiceless distinction. They state that "there is a consistent increase in PCA (posterior cricoarytenoid) activity for voiceless

---

*We emphasize the muscular aspects of this peripheral complex because muscle activity has been relatively more susceptible to study in the normal human through electromyography, and probably has resulted in more valuable empirical findings during cognitive processing.

consonant production regardless of phoneme environment" (pp. 135–138). They also reported that vocalis and the lateral cricoarytenoid muscles both appear to be activated in the production of vowel segments, but rather suppressed for consonantal segments.

Raphael[47] also tested the view that tongue muscles are physiologically more tense for tense symbols of the tense-lax opposition in production than for the lax instances of this opposition. Raphael found that there is consistently greater activity, as hypothesized, on the part of the genioglossus muscle (a flat, triangular muscle, the strongest of the extrinsic tongue muscles that forms most of the substance of the tongue) for the items linguistically classified as tense, than for their counterparts that were hypothesized to correspond to the "lax" members of the oppositions.

Researchers have apparently concentrated more on electromyographic recording of speech-muscle patterns during speech production because of the relatively greater difficulty of studying such patterns during speech perception. It is likely that the muscle pattern-distinctive feature relationships are the same or very similar during both processes, so that inferences can be made from data during speech production to speech perception. We would expect only greatly reduced amplitude during perception. Because they are learned together, Cherry[11] even suggests that speech perception and speech production are one and the same phenomenon: ". . . that when we listen to someone speaking, we are also preparing to move our own vocal organs in sympathy—not necessarily motor responses, but subthreshold—and that our imitative instincts of childhood never leave us. Paget, for instance, comments upon our instinctive recognition of mouth position when hearing speech" (p. 293). On this point Cherry also says that "the representations we carry in our heads, of speech sounds, are likely to be formed of data concerning vocal organ configurations, the cavity resonances (formants), the larnyx frequencies, et cetera" (p. 294). (These statements closely resemble those of Wyczoikowska[25] and others presented earlier in this paper.) MacNeilage[48,49] presents the related suggestion that the phoneme may be a basic unit stored in the nervous system as a fixed articulatory position, a positional target, uniquely related to fixed positions of the articulators for a given phoneme.

Electromyographical research of speech muscles is in its infancy, and there has been but limited success. Yet we should eventually be able to specify unique speech muscle response patterns as a function of distinctive features, not only during production but also during perception. To achieve this highly refined level of analysis, we require much more sensitive and precise techniques than those previously used. One promising approach is that of Isley and Basmajian;[50] by implanting fine wire electrodes, these researchers were able quite precisely to specify various speech muscle patterns during the performance of a variety of oral tasks (but unfortunately for us they did not include speech activities).

It *would* be fortunate if the relationships between muscle states and distinctive features are the same for all the five speech levels previously mentioned, including those for speech production and speech perception. In developing our model for perception, we shall make this assumption and consider that speech-muscle response patterns produce distinctive feature codes.

The implication from this section is that such codes, carried by circuit classes III and interacting with circuit class IV, could thereby produce "semantic interpretation," "ideas," and the like.

NEUROMUSCULAR EVENTS AND LOOP TIMES

We have identified a number of reactions that occur at various locations throughout the body and have hypothesized that they are components of circuits like those of FIGURE 3. We have, furthermore, suggested a temporal order for these various neuromuscular events, sequentially labeled by the symbols I, II, III, and IV. The circuits I, II, III, and IV, however, have been merely hypothesized to serve the linguistic functions that we have specified. Furthermore, the empirical findings employed to sketch out such circuits were almost exclusively lacking in temporal information—although the previously cited data indicate that such circuits quite possibly do exist, they do not show that they actually perform such linguistic processing functions as we have hypothesized. We are, in fact, far from the highly inventive physiological experimentation that would allow us to precisely specify such internal information processing circuits with confidence. One step toward that goal is to bring to bear relevant temporal data that already do exist; such a step still will not answer the question as to whether or not those circuits function linguistically, but such temporal data could at least indicate which circuits are and are not possible. Lashley's[59] classical arguments (followed by Hebb[22] and others) against a "chain model" for high-speed serial behavior, for instance, were in large part based on temporal data which, incidentally, were either irrelevant to his argument or erroneous (cf. McGuigan[2]).

The approach that we propose here will be based on a rather limited sample of data relevant to duration and temporal relationships among the events specified in FIGURE 3. If this limited effort seems to help us establish some empirical guide lines and constraints for our information-processing model, a more extensive effort could be considered. It is hoped that this approach will eventually increase the probability of making successful indirect inferences (but not more than that) about actual linguistic neuromuscular circuits. However, even the relatively small sample of data that follow are complex, and difficult for the reader (as well as for the author) to relate precisely to the model of FIGURE 3. The results of our efforts in this section might therefore be diligently studied by the especially interested reader. The reader less interested in such psychophysiological detail might review FIGURE 4 more generally, considering primarily the principle of relating such temporal information to the circuits of FIGURE 3, and that such extremely rapidly firing circuits as we have hypothesized apparently are physical possibilities.

To establish some perspective, let us first consider the amount of time required for running off a total S-R unit; as a simplification, we shall use values for simple (as opposed to choice) reaction time. Unfortunately, a sizeable portion of a subject's "reaction time" as classically measured is artifactual, due to the mechanical lag of the switch-closing apparatus. For instance, McGuigan and Boness[51] electromyographically measured a latency for an overt finger response of about 185 msec following stimulus onset, whereas the value obtained from the actual closing of the microswitch was about 225 msec. Furthermore, perhaps 75 msec of the classically measured reaction time is due to the duration of the motor period (the time from the electromyographically measured onset of the muscle response to the overt response of switch closing). Other variables that may have little to do with information-processing time might also need to be removed from classical reaction time measures, such as muscle-membrane depolarization time of perhaps 13 msec.[52]

Our initial guidelines thus suggest an approximate temporal interval of some 100 msec between the external stimulus and the overt response for the simplest input-output situations; it is during some such interval that at least some of the internal information processing circuits of FIGURE 3 might function, eventuating in one or more of the three classes of response circuits specified in FIGURE 2. Of course, many circuits are still "looping" *after* this simple response is made.

In attempting to specify events temporally between the external stimulus and the overt response, we can rely on several kinds of studies. For one, there are studies of internal events immediately following onset of the external stimulus (prior to the overt response), such as evoked brain potentials. We can also use various "internal reaction time measures" in which a stimulus was applied at a point of some internal system and consequent reactions in other regions within the body were measured prior to an overt response. Similarly, there are studies in which covert events immediately prior to the overt response have been studied. By integrating the results of such classes of studies we may be able, in a sense, to put together some of the pieces of the "internal information processing jig saw puzzle" so that we can make sensible inferences about these very rapid, complex, interacting events that occur between external stimuli and overt responses. Continued accumulation and integration of such temporal information thus might allow us to eventually specify with some precision complex classes of circuits like those of FIGURE 3.

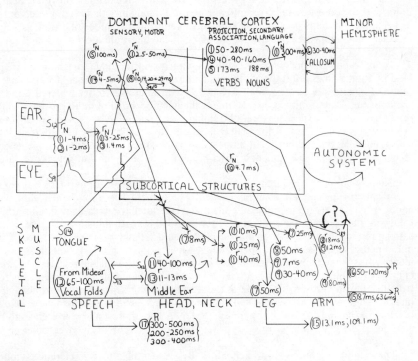

FIGURE 4. A sample of temporal values of events within hypothesized internal information-processing circuits.

FIGURE 4 includes a sample of temporal values for potential circuit components. We note that input from both the ear and the eye enter subcortical regions that include the thalamus, brainstem, midbrain, *et cetera*. These afferent neural impulses are then transmitted to the skeletal musculature (represented at the bottom of FIGURE 4) and simultaneously to the higher regions of the brain (represented at the top); in particular, we represent impulses "descending" to the oral and nonoral musculature, and "ascending" to the sensory and motor cortex of the dominant cerebral hemisphere. Later, various other cortical regions are involved in the processing (the projection areas, secondary cortex, association areas, and especially the language regions). At the upper right of FIGURE 4, intercerebral transmission is indicated through the corpus callosum; ascending neural impulses from the thalamic level are also transmitted directly to the minor hemisphere. Additionally, we represent complex but slow circuits between the central nervous system and the autonomic nervous systems (to the right of FIGURE 4); these circuits are of great behavioral importance, of course, but are excluded from detailed consideration here. Finally, when the skeletal musculature is sufficiently contracted, overt responses result, as indicated by the Rs to the right of the skeletal muscle representation at the bottom of FIGURE 4.

With this overall sketching out of neuromuscular circuits, let us now turn to a sample of time values for the various events hypothesized as circuit components.

The initial event in FIGURE 4 is receptor processing. We cannot, however, offer a unitary, constant estimate of receptor-processing time, since this event is a complex of a number of subprocesses and also is a function of a number of variables. (For instance, one subprocess in the ear is the cochlear microphonic wave which takes about 3 msec to traverse the length of the human cochlea.[28]

Total receptor-processing time for the ear is shorter than for the eye. While holding light flashes constant at 500 mμ and a duration of 100 msec, Chapman[53,54] reported latencies of the first spike, recorded with microelectrodes inserted into the retina of the intact bullfrog, as varying in the neighborhood of 60 to more than 800 msec. He concluded that measures of frequency and number of spikes recorded at the eye may be good indices of the neural messages that reach higher centers.[53]

Because of the difficulty (or impossibility) of specifying a standard value for receptor-processing time, this first processing event is not quantitatively represented in FIGURE 4.

Davis'[55] summary of latencies for various auditory evoked potentials has some overall organizational value for us. Evidently recognizing the above-stated difficulty about specifying receptor-processing time, Davis reports events measured temporally following the cochlear microphonic. After the external stimulus is processed in the ear, he reports that the first neural reaction has a latency of some 1-4 msec. This initial neural event is depicted in FIGURE 4 beneath the term "nerve impulse" and is identified as being from our first reference (Davis) by means of the reference symbol ①; the event that initiates this neural reaction in the ear is identified by S$_1$ (S is for stimulus and the subscript "1" relates the stimulus to the neural reaction time ① by means of reference ① , viz., Davis). The recorded event is specified as a *neural* reaction in the auditory nerve by the symbol r$_N$. A listing of all of the references to be considered here is offered in TABLE 1, with the references given completely in REFERENCES.

The second reference below "nerve impulse" is identified by the reference symbol ② ; this is the work of Amadeo and Shagass,[56] who measured an evoked potential over the sensory cortex at approximately 1-2 msec following stimulus impingement. They reasoned that this was too fast to actually be a cortical event and that it was possibly from the auditory nerve. Hence, we also represent this event in FIGURE 4 as an extremely rapid potential following stimulus impingement (the stimulus is specified as the subscript 2 in S$_{1,2}$ within the ear). The reference symbol② in FIGURE 4 is also cited as reference 2 in TABLE 1.

Next in time following the auditory nerve event, Davis[55] reports evoked potentials from the brainstem and midbrain. Davis states that reactions from the cochlear nucleus to the medial geniculate body can be grouped together, and occupy a time zone of about 3-25 msec (after the cochlear microphonic); since the Davis reference for this event is the same as before, we also refer to this subcortical event by ① .

Below that for Davis is reference ③, in which Jewett *et al.*[57] reported widely distributed potentials from the scalp with an initial peak latency as short as 1.4 msec. They interpret these potentials as being generated in brainstem auditory structures. Perhaps they occur because external auditory stimuli may be transduced and transmitted through the body prior to the tympanic membrane (cf. Ref. 20.). We shall also note later that Bickford *et al.*[58] report a muscle response to an auditory stimulus with a latency as short as 8 msec. Such data make it clear that these neuromuscular circuits function with great rapidity, far more rapidly than the relatively slow time values of about 60 msec on which Lashley[59] and Hebb[22] based some of their reasoning about high-speed serial order behavior. They also indicate some apparent contradictions.

TABLE 1

CITATIONS FOR TIME VALUES IN FIGURE 4*

---

1. Davis (1973)[55]
2. Amadeo & Shagass (1973)[56]
3. Jewett, Romano & Williston (1970)[57]
4. Morrell & Salamy (1971)[60]
5. Teyler, Roemer, Harrison & Thompson (1973)[61]
6. Filbery & Gazzaniga (1969)[62]
7. Bickford, Jacobson & Cody (1964)[58]
8. Hammond (1955)[63]
9. Evarts, 1966[64], 1973[65])
10. Bernhard, Bohm & Petersén (1953)[66]
11. Goldstein (1968)[28]
12. Shearer & Simmons (1965)[67]
13. McCall & Rabuzzi (1973)[68]
14. Bowman & Combs (1969)[29]
15. Gatev & Ivanov (1972)[52]
16. Bartlett (1963)[69]
    Botwinick & Thompson (1966)[70]
    Hathaway (1935)[71]
    Hilden (1937)[72]
17. Ertl & Schafer (1967)[73]
    Faaborg-Anderson & Edfeldt (1958)[74]
    Hirano & Ohala (1969)[75]

---

*r_N in FIGURE 4 refers to a neural reaction; r is a skeletal muscle response.

Each neural and muscular event in FIGURE 4 obviously does not cease at the point indicated; rather, each is but one component of a complex neuromuscular circuit with additional consequences. This continuous nature of each event is, in each case, represented by an ongoing arrow.

Most interestingly for us, Davis discussed "sonomotor" muscle responses that occur with a latency between 10 and 50 msec. Sonomotor muscle responses, he indicates, are reactions to acoustic stimuli that are especially prominent when recorded at the inion, over the temporalis, or the postauricular muscle. Davis adds that "the response may be a reproducible sequence of waves with peaks separated by about 15 msec" (pp. 466–467). These findings suggest central-peripheral loops such as we have indicated in the head-neck muscle region of FIGURE 4 by the reference symbol for Davis viz., ①, at 15 msec intervals, viz., at 10 msec, 25 msec and 40 msec. Davis adds: "The presence of myogenic responses, if consistent, is the valid sign of activity in the acoustic centers and reflex pathways of the brainstem. . . ." (p. 467).

Following the brainstem and midbrain potentials of 3–25 msec, we represent in the sensory-motor cortex by the (Davis) symbol ①, fast vertex potentials with latencies of 25–50 msec; for simplicity, this event class is indicated only in the dominant hemisphere of FIGURE 4.

The next temporal event reported by Davis is the class of slow vertex potentials (N_{100}-P_{200}-N_{280}) that constitute a complex generated by the primary projection areas and in the surrounding secondary association areas. This complex is indicated as issuing from the 25–50 msec class of events in the sensory and motor cortex running to the projection (etc.) areas; it is specified by the time region 50–280 msec in the upper-middle representation of the cortex. Still later than the 50–280 msec events are reactions (P_{300}), diffuse in origin, that occur at 300 msec or more latency.

Morrell and Salamy[60] reported events with latencies similar to those of Davis' 50–280 msec cortical events, and these are represented below ① in the projection (etc.) areas by ④; in particular, they measured the onset of a negative wave that was especially prominent in the left temporoparietal region with a latency of about 40–50 msec. This wave reached a maximum at about 90 msec after signal onset, following which there was a positive ongoing event that peaked at about 160 msec.

Also within the general time interval of Davis' 50–280 msec were some interesting values reported by Teyler et al.,[61] as indicated by their reference symbol ⑤. They found that auditory linguistic stimuli elicited larger evoked potential reactions in the dominant (vs. the minor) hemisphere. Pooling values from the two hemispheres, latency for verbs in the evoked wave form was reliably shorter than for nouns (verb latency = 181 msec, noun latency = 186 msec). More importantly, the latency to verb forms was significantly shorter than to noun forms in the left hemisphere, verb latency = 173 msec vs. 188 msec; evoked-response latencies showed not only hemispheric asymmetries but also significant linguistic form-class differences, with verbs having a shorter latency than nouns. The latency of an evoked wave form to clicks did not vary significantly as a function of hemisphere.

Finally, to the upper, far right of FIGURE 4, interhemispheric transmission time was estimated as 30–40 msec by Filbey and Gazzaniga;[62] cf. (⑥).

Let us now concentrate more extensively on circuits involving the skeletal musculature, represented at the bottom of FIGURE 4. We have already noted the rapid responses at 10 msec, 25 msec, and 40 msec in the head and neck that issue from the subcortical region identified by the ①, 3–25 msec temporal interval.[55] Perhaps related to that 10-msec response is the 8-msec neck response reported by Bickford et al.,[58] as represented by ⑦. This response results from the neural pathways at the thalamic region from the ear (the events indicated at the 3–25-msec portion of the subcortex). Bickford also reported, with a latency from stimulus impingement, responses at 25 msec in the arm and 50 msec in the leg, as indicated in each of those three muscle regions by ⑦.

Hammond[63] applied the stimulus of a sudden pull that stretched the biceps, and recorded human biceps EMG responses with a latency of 18 msec, represented as ⑧ in the arm-muscle region. There was a second biceps response to the same stimulus with a latency of about 50 msec in humans. The stimulus S_8 in the upper right-arm region is represented as setting off a circuit of unknown nature (indicated by the question mark) returning to the arm to produce the 18-msec response. We also represent a stimulus, S_9, below the Hammond reference for the work of Evarts[64,65], on the monkey. Evarts stimulated the hand and recorded arm EMG responses with latencies of 12 msec, of 30–40 msec, and with a third phase at about 80 msec. We represent by ⑨ the fastest (12 msec) response as being similar to that recorded by

Hammond at 18 msec, with unspecified mediators, because Evarts suggests that these reactions were too rapid to involve the sensory-motor cortex. We also represent the afferent neural impulse from the stimulus in the hand ($S_{8,9}$) as continuing to the sensory cortex (⑨), where Evarts measured neural reactions (r_N) with latencies of 10 msec, 14 msec, 20 msec, and 24 msec in various regions. Descending impulses from the cortex (⑨) are shown to produce a potential in the ventral root with a latency of 4.7 msec; this event (represented as ⑩ in the subcortical region) was recorded by Bernhard *et al.*[66] as resulting from a stimulus (S_{10}) in the primate motor cortex. We illustrate this neural circuit continuing on from the cortex discharge (⑨ to S_{10}) to the forearm to produce an EMG event in the forearm (⑨) with a latency of 7 msec from cortical stimulation.[65]

To summarize this particular circuit, the stimuli ($S_{8,9}$) in the arm produced reactions (⑨) in the sensory-motor cortex with latencies between 10 and 24 msec; resulting cortical stimulation S_{10} produced a ventral root reaction at 4.7 msec (⑩), continuing on to an arm EMG reaction, at 7 msec (⑨); there is also Evarts' EMG response at 30–40 msec ⑨, similar to Hammond's response (⑧) with a latency of 50 msec to S_8. Evarts' conclusion is that the sensory motor cortex can play a role in mediating this hand-arm circuit and possibly account for the 30–40-msec EMG response recorded by him, and also account for the 50-msec response recorded in man by Hammond. Resulting from the cortical event represented by ⑨, we also indicate a circuit descending to the arm with unknown mediation that results in the reaction (⑧) to $S_{8,9}$ with a latency of 80 msec.

To continue the reaction to an auditory stimulus, we represent an impulse from the subcortical region (①) to the middle-ear muscle producing a response (⑪) with latencies ranging between 40 and 100 msec.[28] A stimulus resulting from middle-ear contraction may set off a response in the vocal folds from 65 to 100 msec later; this is represented as starting with S_{12} in the middle-ear region resulting in the response represented by ⑫.[67]

The speech and eye musculature is the most refined of all the skeletal muscle, capable of producing very precise and localized responses. Many motor units in these regions consist of only two or three muscle fibers, suggesting the relatively great capability of these systems to function in the transmission of highly refined units of information. Some representative speech muscle events are as follows.

McCall and Rabuzzi[68] stimulated the internal laryngeal nerve of the cat (S_{13}) and noted middle-ear muscle responses indicated by ⑬ (in the tensor tympani with a latency of 13 msec, in stapedius with a latency of 13 msec, and in cricothyroid with a latency of 11 msec).

They concluded that these reflex responses are mediated by a central reflex arc between the internal laryngeal nerve and the motor supply to the tympanic muscles. One interpretation is that the tympanic muscle reflex may have a function in vocalization, such as that it is responsible for the contraction of the middle-ear muscle in association with speaking. McCall and Rabuzzi summarize a number of references that support the conclusion that contraction of middle-ear muscles precedes the production of sound. It is interesting to note in this connection that middle-ear muscles also contract prior to rapid eye movements in the dream state.

To illustrate further the great rapidity with which neuromuscular circuits may function, particularly those involving the speech muscles, we may note that Bowman and Combs[29] stimulated the distal portion of the hypoglossal nerve in the tongue (S_{14}) and recorded a reaction in the contralateral sensory-motor cortex with a latency of 4–5 msec (⑭).

In psychology (and elsewhere too) we use the term "response," *both overt and covert,* as if a response is a simple, instantaneous, on-off event. Such abstraction and categorization is often necessary, but we must not obscure the fact that what we abstract as a response, be it overt or covert, is a part of an extremely complex ongoing stream of events. We have earlier discussed the relationship between the covert buildup of muscle activity, measured by EMG, that "bursts" into an overt response. But even that covert antecedent of an overt response, or even a covert response that is not an immediate antecedent of an overt response, is extremely complex and can be studied in great detail at molecular levels. The measurement of excitation-contraction latency in human muscles by Gatev and Ivanov[52] is illustrative. The excitation-contraction latency is the interval between the onset of the action potential and the onset of the muscle contraction; it is the time during which the electrical activity of the muscle changes into mechanical activity, which is an essential stage in the transmission of neural impulses to the contractile elements of the muscle. For the two muscles that they studied, the excitation contraction latency of *flexor carpi ulnaris* was 8.7 msec and of *gastrocnemius lateralis* 13.1 msec. The contraction time was also shorter in *ulnaris,* i.e., 63.6 msec vs. 109.1 msec. We represent at the right bottom of FIGURE 4 by ⑮ the 8.7-msec excitation-contraction latency for *ulnaris.* The contraction time of 63.6 msec is also shown. The similar values for the leg region are also specified following ⑮ for the Gatev and Ivanov reference.

Values for the motor period, the time between onset of skeletal muscle contraction and the overt response, are indicated to the right of the skeletal muscle region of FIGURE 4 as ⑯. For arm and hand muscles, the onset of the covert response occured some 50–120 msec prior to the onset of the overt response; these values for the motor period are not individually repeated, but are summarized under reference 16, 69–72, in TABLE 1. The time by which covert EMG onset in speech muscles occurs prior to audible speech sound has been measured as 200–500 msec by several investigators. These references are collectively summarized under reference 17, 73–75, in TABLE 1.

We have, in this section, attempted to specify some of the temporal values for components of our hypothetical neuromuscular circuits. We first calculated a minimal value for the processing of an external stimulus to overt response unit as approximately 100 msec. Apparently, circuits of the nature discussed under references ⑧, ⑨, and ⑩, (in which some 30 msec is consumed between the arm to sensory-motor cortex to ventral root to arm) could function within this time period, perhaps for sensory integration as in our circuits Ib′–II. Presumably circuits like our III–IV that serve lexical-semantic functions would reverberate for some additional time; perhaps such ongoing circuit processes are represented in the "Projection, Secondary Association, Language Cortex" region of FIGURE 4 with values for events following stimulus impingement of several hundred milliseconds. It is, however, as we well recognized at the beginning of this section, difficult to do more than establish approximate constraints for a linguistic processing model with this approach. Nevertheless, even these very approximate estimates suggest that the extremely rapid brain-muscle-brain-muscle circuits that we have hypothesized *are* physical possibilities; one must be very impressed with the finding, for instance, that stimulation on the tongue produces a contralateral cortical event with only a 4- or 5-msec latency ⑭. In short, while we have been able only to illustrate this approach here, it does appear promising, and, with considerably more information that is suitably organized, we might be able to specify rather precisely these neuromuscular circuits and their temporal order of activation in internal information processing.

CONDITIONAL LINGUISTIC RESPONSE PATTERNS AND CODING

We have assumed that in the learning of a language, some auditory linguistic unit (perhaps an allophone) acquires the stimulus function of evoking a complex bodily reaction. We have characterized the acquisition of this stimulus-response relationship as one that, it is hoped, obeys the laws of conditioning, so that we refer to the stimulus as a conditional (discriminative) stimulus, and to the response pattern as a conditional linguistic response pattern. In this section we shall consider the question of what it means to ascribe a linguistic function to the conditional covert behavior that occurs during the performance of cognitive tasks.

Earlier, we emphasized the potential importance of being able to represent the analog speech stream in binary phonemic coding, and we noted the related fact that many neuromuscular processes are discrete, on-off events, so that, at a molecular level, they too can be well represented in binary form. Hence the discriminative stimulus-conditional response relationship depicted in binary form in FIGURE 1. The principal neuro-muscular events that are on-off, of course, are single nerve impulses and single muscle-fiber contractions, both of which obey the all-or-none law. The major issue to which we shall now turn concerns the way in which the skeletal musculature, particularly that in the speech region, might function in the generation of internal linguistic codes.

We have cited considerable evidence that the peripheral components of Loops IIIa and IIIb in FIGURE 3 become especially active during the performance of linguistic tasks. The general conclusion throughout the literature has been that "amplitude of covert oral behavior increases during 'thought' tasks." However, since muscle fibers obey the all-or-none law, it cannot be that muscle fiber responses *per se* increase in amplitude. Rather, it must be that as electromyographical measures of muscle activity increase in amplitude, the muscle fibers contract more rapidly, and/or the number activated per unit time increases. Therefore, the conclusion that increased amplitude of covert oral (and nonoral) behavior facilitates the performance of language tasks, more precisely stated, is that there is an increase in the *rate* with which oral muscle fibers contract, and/or there is an increase in the total *number* contracting per unit time. In either case, the increased muscle fiber activity increases the excitation rate of the receptors embedded in the muscles, causing an increase in the afferent neural activity fed back from the musculature. This increased neuro-muscular activity, we assume, is evoked by external conditional language stimuli and constitutes a conditional response pattern, as represented by the matrices of FIGURE 1. It is this conditional muscle responding that, in theory, facilitates internal information processing by generating a linguistic code that is carried to the brain (by circuit IIIa of FIGURE 3). Furthermore, the amount of muscle fiber-afferent neural impulse activity should be indicative of the amount of information generated and transmitted. Consider, for instance, a person who experiences difficulty in performing some linguistic task, e.g. one who does not adequately comprehend the prose that he is reading. Under such circumstances there is an ("automatic") increase in the amount of speech muscle activity (commonly called "subvocalization"), with the consequent increases of afferent neural impulses. Hence the individual, experiencing a need for a larger amount of internal information, generates that increase primarily in his speech muscle and transmits it to the brain, especially to the cortical linguistic regions. The amount of covert speech muscle activity generated should therefore be related to linguistic proficiency, the difficulty of the task, and so on. For example, an accomplished reader or writer would need to generate but a minimal amount of verbal information in his oral region (the minimal amount of information still being sufficient to allow him to perform the task adequately). But a poor reader, or a good reader under distracting conditions, needs to send a greater amount of verbal information, presumably with some redundancy, to his brain (redundancy is often necessary in various avenues of life to achieve understanding; e.g., the effective teacher makes the same point in different ways, and more than once).

The relevant data support the above reasoning.[76] More particularly, previous research has indicated that amplitude of covert oral behavior is inversely related to reading proficiency when proficient vs. unproficient subjects are *selected* for comparison; but amplitude increases when proficiency is *experimentally* increased. Experimentaly produced decreases of covert oral behavior possibly reduce reading proficiency. Amplitude of covert oral behavior also increases as textual and environmental demands increase. The general empirical conclusion, then, is that increased covert speech-muscle activity is benesiia in the performance of language tasks, and our interpretation has been that such responses are beneficial because they perform a linguistic function, thus justifying the term "covert oral *linguistic* behavior."[2] We now need to consider the kind of linguistic code that might be generated by the skeletal musculature during linguistic behavior. We also must consider how such an afferently carried code might interact in the brain; that is, how circuit class IIIa functions with circuit IV.

We have seen that linguistic stimuli evoke, by hypothesis, complex patterns of conditional covert oral and nonoral responses, and we have placed emphasis on the oral responses produced by the speech musculature. These conditional response patterns must consist of an enormous number of spatially distributed muscle fibers which, at any given instant, may be specified as those that are in a state of contraction and those that are relaxed (lengthened). To represent the state of the skeletal muscle-fiber system, we can employ a response matrix like that to the right of FIGURE 1. In such a complex, three-dimensional matrix, each cubic cell in the matrix could represent one speech-muscle fiber. A conditional response pattern can then be represented in a large matrix whose cells, at any instant, are in the state of on or off. Following the principle of FIGURE 1, a discrete conditional stimulus input would evoke a complex discrete pattern of covert oral and covert nonoral conditional linguistic responses. This binary pattern would be the muscular events at the periphery of loops IIIa and IIIb of FIGURE 3.

An attempt to represent the speech-muscle system by means of three dimensional matrices appears in FIGURE 5. Various speech muscles are identified to the right. Each speech muscle is then represented in the three dimensional space such that the a dimension is height, b is depth (into the body), and c is breadth or width (across the body). For instance, the muscles of the lips are systematically represented in terms of motor units, and each motor unit is subdivided into the appropriate number of muscle fibers. For example, the first cube (a_1, b_1, c_1) is the cell in a three-dimensional space for one particular muscle fiber; the cube a_1, b_1, c_2 represents a spatially adjacent muscle fiber. The state of each muscle fiber at any given time t_1 is represented with + if the fiber is in contraction, or by – if it is relaxed; 0 indicates the absence of a muscle fiber at that particular spatial location. Coded afferent volleys are set off from each set of speech muscles (the lips, tongue, chin, etc.). The precise nature of these afferent neural impulses is determined by the complex state of the muscle fibers in the set of three dimensional matrices, e.g., by the entire set of the three values +, 0, and –.

Let me offer a brief summary and preview of the notions being developed. External linguistic stimuli become discriminative stimuli that evoke spatially distributed responses in the oral musculature. These responses may be described in binary form as consisting of muscle fibers throughout the entire speech musculature; each fiber may be in an on or off state. Once evoked, a given muscle-fiber pattern activates the system of receptors embedded in the muscle spindles and tendons to generate a unique afferent neural impulse volley that is coded for a given allophone, such as $[p_1]$ (recall that an allophone is a concrete instance of an abstract phoneme class). Another, similar, afferent neural volley would be coded for another allophone of the same phoneme class that differed in some specifics (e.g., $[p_2]$). Whereas the two volleys would be produced by two different patterns of muscle fiber contraction, there would be a considerable number of muscle fibers in common on-off states. That is, two such neural volleys would be coded for the same phoneme class because of the commonality of antecedent muscle-fiber contractions. But there would be slight differences in their coding because the muscle fiber patterns for the slightly different allophones of the same phoneme class would also differ somewhat. In short, differences between neural codings for different allophones are due to small, instantaneous differences in muscle-fiber states.

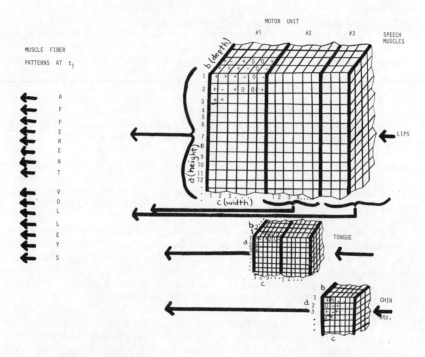

FIGURE 5. Muscle-fiber patterns and resultant afferent neural volleys at time t_1.

The neural volleys that result from muscular contraction transmit a phonetic code that contains distinctive features and nondistinctive features; the nondistinctive features, in effect, constitute "noise," being events unique for each allophone. The common characteristics of the muscle-fiber patterns and the resulting neural impulses produce the coding for distinctive features. That is, the muscle fibers which can only have an on-off function still can generate a unique event (a distinctive feature) within a phonetic code. The unique event (coding) depends on the precise fiber combination that contracts at any instant; similarly for the resulting on-off neural events of the afferent neural volley.

Once the ascending phonetic code interacts with the linguistic regions of the brain, in some (unknown) sense the appropriate phomeme is perceived ("produced," "restructured," "retrieved"). For instance, if the afferent neural volley is coded for the allophone [p], the distinctive features carried in a neural code may match those distinctive features for the phoneme / p /, producing ("retrieving," or whatever) that phoneme; the nondistinctive features of the afferent volley might in some sense be ignored by such a central processor (though they might not be ignored in another volley, since what may be nondistinctive for one phoneme pair, may be distinctive for another; the central processor would apparently have to have a property that allows it to identify distinctive vs. nondistinctive features as a function of class of phonetic input, probably making such decisions within a grammatical context).

We have previously concluded that covert oral behavior ("silent speech") occurs in everybody, but is more pronounced in some people, and under certain environmental conditions. When covert oral behavior becomes especially pronounced, there is an "eruption" into "subvocalization"; consequently, external speech stimuli are emitted in the form of slight "whispering" that can be amplified and to some extent understood by a listening experimenter.[77-79] Such exaggerated covert oral behavior produces additional coding beyond what is normally required, so semantic processing is facilitated. The additional coding is probably redundant to that which is normally generated. A precise analysis of increased neuromuscular activity might yield a large number of parameters that could function in the generation and transmission of this additional redundant coding. One could be a spatial system, so that different combinations of cells of FIGURE 5, with considerable overlap, could generate simultaneously two allophones of the same phoneme class, like $[p_1]$, and $[p_2]$. These two generated afferent volleys could then be transmitted simultaneously, in parallel, to the brain. Or, the heightened covert oral muscle responding when reading prose could be, instead of spatially redundant, temporally redundant. In temporal redundancy, the same muscle-fiber patterns for a given allophone contract more than once, in succession, transmitting identical but successive volleys to the brain.

If the amount of redundancy produced by subvocalization is *still* insufficient to produce comprehension, the information processor may "break into" overt speech, pronouncing aloud the word or words that are difficult for him to comprehend; hence, as often happens in everyday life, an individual will overtly repeat what is said or read, adding a further redundant, externally generated auditory signal that impinges on his eardrum (this would be Loop IIIC of FIGURE 2).

We should also not forget that any given oral pattern is also associated with a complex covert nonoral response pattern. Hence, a conditional linguistic stimulus evokes *both* oral and nonoral components. Especially prominent components of nonoral patterns occur in the preferred arm and hand, possibly due to conditioning while learning cursive writing of prose. Other localized conditional muscle patterns may also be evoked, such as heightened behavior in the left wrist during processing of a word like "wristwatch."

The body thus also has information-processing redundancy in the sense that an external linguistic stimulus may have several symbolic representations in different parts of the body, so that several oral and nonoral regions may generate coded afferent neural patterns. When the neural volleys reach the language regions of the brain they may activate some kind of representation of the external stimulus (by way of Loops IIIa and IIIb to Loop IV of FIGURE 3). In exploring the coding principle further, for simplicity, we shall continue to consider only the speech musculature.

Complex conditional patterns in the autonomic system must also occur; though we are not considering such responses here, they *have* received considerable attention (e.g. Ref. 80). Circuits involving the autonomic doubtlessly add much richness to internal behavior, adding "emotional tone" to linguistic units (certain words evoke feelings in the pit of the stomach).

To continue with FIGURE 5, the on-off status of speech muscle fibers constitutes a pattern during speech perception at a given instant, time t_1. By adding a temporal dimension to the matrix, we can represent continuously changing covert response patterns as a function of the changing linguistic input. Such a matrix appears in FIGURE 6; in the column to the right the various speech muscles are specified according to their motor units and the fibers of each motor unit. Hence, the first cell in FIGURE 5, which we labeled as a_1, b_1, c_1, at time t_1 was in an "on" state, as indicated by the + in the first cell of the first row of FIGURE 6. In the first Time column (under t_1), the status of the other muscle fibers of FIGURE 5 are represented for all of the speech musculature. Columns t_2, t_3, ... t_n indicate the status of the speech musculature at times following t_1. For instance, the first fiber a_1, b_1, c_1 is contracted at time t_1; it is also contracted at time t_2, but is relaxed at time t_3.

To the left of these spatial-temporal matrices, we summarize (under "Coded Muscle Pattern At Times:") the coded status for each muscle fiber in binary arithmetic. Hence, for fiber a_1, b_1, c_1, the spatial-temporal status is specified by "110," and so on. In short, we now have a spatial-temporal matrix that determines the coded afferent impulses, the latter being represented to the far left of FIGURE 6. Once in this binary form, we are now in a position to treat the code in a powerful fashion, using formal models that have far-reaching consequences, such as those employed by Rouvray[81] and Fienberg.[82]

In short, as the covert linguistic response pattern changes in the ongoing generation of a verbal code, Loops IIIa, and IIIb of FIGURE 3 reverberate; the muscle pattern activity is transduced from a spatially represented binary code (that changes as a function of time) into an afferent neural code that ascends to the language regions of the brain.

To emphasize some points briefly: The patterns of neural impulses generated by the continuous firing of muscle fibers ascend from the speech muscle (circuit IIIa) and from the nonspeech muscle (circuit IIIb); these volleys are integrated at the thalamic level above the thalamic relay stations,[23] and also at the thalamic level with impulses descending from the sensory cortex (II). The consequence of this processing and integration is the activation of loop class IV of FIGURE 3 that runs to the language regions of the brain.

This general hypothesis, incidentally would appear to accord with the work of others who have taken totally different points of view from ours. For one, Studdert-Kennedy[83] proposed that there are processes that convert the neuroacoustic input into neurophonetic representations, and that additional processes transform entities at the neurophonetic level into neurophonemic representations. When there is transfer from the neurophonetic level to the neurophonemic level, external speech is perceived. By our model, the neuroacoustic input (in Studdert-Kennedy's terms) is converted, at least in part, by covert activation of the speech musculature; when the resulting afferent neural volleys, phonetically coded, reach the linguistic and motor regions of the brain, the phonetic code is processed to reproduce the appropriate phonemes "stored" there. Our coding function of oral behavior is also consonant with the findings of Estes,[84] that phonemic encoding of visually presented letters was obtained when vocalization was permitted at input, but phonemic encoding was not present when vocalization was suppressed. Similarly, Rubenstein et al.[85] concluded that visual word recognition entails phonemic recoding through auditory/articulatory processes. Hintzman[86] holds the very relevant view that subvocal rehearsal has a recoding function in short term memory.

Liberman et al.[87] suggest that during perception the listener generates speech to transform auditory stimuli into instructions to the vocal mechanism that give rise to those patterns. The production of sounds is made with different articulatory

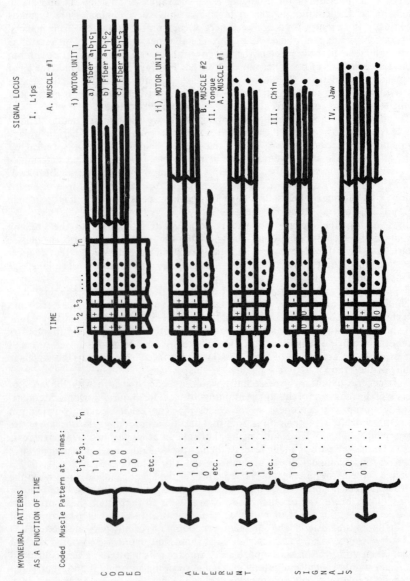

FIGURE 6. Myoneural patterns as a function of time.

maneuvers so that the listener makes a natural division of acoustic stimuli into articulatory categories. In perceiving sounds, the listener transforms the auditory stimuli to his articulatory patterns so that the listener makes sharp discriminations phonemically. For example, if an allophone of the phoneme class / p / enters the ear, the listener transforms the auditory stimulus to an articulatory category for that phoneme. Such reasoning involves covert oral behavior along the lines of our model.

Jakobson and Halle[14] speculate about relationships between linguistic and physiological functioning, particularly regarding motor events during speech perception. In particular, they suggest that sonority features might be related to the amount, density, and spread of nervous excitation, while tonality features relate to the location of this excitation; they expect that neural reactions to sound stimuli will eventually supply a differential picture of distinctive features at this level, which would certainly be an impressive accomplishment. At the "psychological" level, which they consider to be the study of speech sounds that illuminate the perceptual correlates of the diverse distinctive features, the perception of each feature is independent of the other, as if separate channels were involved. This conclusion, based on the work of Miller and Nicely,[88] is consonant with our assumption that internal linguistic processing proceeds in "parallel" channels. During perception, the listener correlates the incoming message with a code that is common to himself and to the speaker, leading Jakobson and Halle to study relationships between motor acoustic and perceptual coding rules. The listener, in decoding a message, thus extracts distinctive features from the perceptual data. During perception, Jakobson and Halle hold that kinaesthetic feedback (our circuit IIIa) of the listener plays a role in this decoding process.

A summary of, and expansion on, the events in FIGURE 6 is presented in FIGURE 7, with illustrative phonetic coding for the afferent volley of neural impulses. The changing status of the speech muscle is represented in binary form to the right of FIGURE 7 as a function of time. For instance, the first set of coded muscle-fiber patterns, represented at the top of FIGURE 7 as occurring at time t_1 through t_n (designated Series 1), are from the first column of FIGURE 6 labeled "Coded Muscle Pattern At Times: t_1." Hence, pattern number t_1 is represented in FIGURE 6 as a column of 1 1 1 0, etc., and that pattern is also depicted behind the t_1 of FIGURE 7. Similarly, the pattern under the second column of FIGURE 6, labeled t_2, is 1 1 0 0, and so on; this pattern is represented behind t_2 of FIGURE 7, and likewise for t_3. This first series of muscle-fiber patterns occurring at the times t_1 through t_n includes the *entire* speech musculature. That muscle pattern then generates the afferent neural volley that is represented in FIGURE 7 as being coded (through a transformation represented by the broken line) for the distinctive features 1 through 9 that describe a particular phoneme, as listed in FIGURE 8. This transformed code (that must be the result of an *exceedingly* complex transformation) carried by the neural volley is coded – for feature 1 (the nonvocalic feature), + for feature 2 (the consonantal feature), – for feature 3 (the diffuse feature), etc. This particular neural coding for features 1 through 9 is for the allophone [p] that matches the coding for the phoneme / p /.[14] In short, in series 1 of FIGURE 7 the afferent neural impulses transmit the distinctive and nondistinctive features for the allophone [p], and this allophone instance of the phoneme class / p /, is indicated by the nine –, +, and 0 (for nondistinctive features) symbols. This phonetic coding for the allophone [p] is then transmitted to the brain for central processing, whereupon the phoneme / p / is produced (retrieved, perceived).

The second in the series (Series 2) of muscular states (labeled t_1' through t_n' in FIGURE 7) generates the afferent neural patterns represented for the features +, –, –, –, 0, 0, 0, 0, etcetera; this pattern represents the neural coding for the allophone [i].

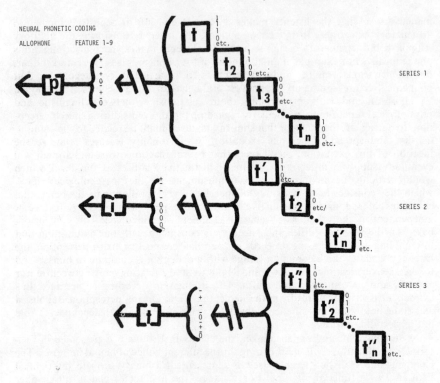

FIGURE 7. Phonemic coding as a function of temporal-spatial afferent neural patterns.

The still later neural volley (Series 3) represented by t_1'' through t_n'' represents the neural coding for the allophone [t]. In short, the status of Jakobson and Halle's nine feature oppositions listed in FIGURE 8 are for the allophones [p], [i] and [t], as specified in the three series of FIGURE 7. When this coded phonetic volley reaches the language regions of the brain, the phonemes / p /, / i / and / t / are successively processed. Following the perception and integration of these three phonemes, the word "pit" is "perceived." Let us see how, by the hypothesis of this paper, this entire process might work.

Nine distinctive features are listed in the left colum of FIGURE 8. As we have noted, at any given instant an acoustic language stimulus may be characterized, as in column I, by the members of the oppositions specified by the binary chain of pluses and minuses (as well as by the blanks). To distinguish / p / from, say, / b /, number 7 is the critical feature. We emphasize this distinction by placing feature 7 toward the bottom of FIGURE 8. That is, by including the "tense" feature (+), the stimulus is coded as a member of the class / p /; however, should opposition #7 be the "lax" feature (−), the stimulus would be coded as an instance of the phoneme / b /.

The acoustic stimulus that impinges on a person then evokes a speech-muscle pattern (through circuits Ib and/or IIIa of FIGURE 3), as indicated in column II of FIGURE 8. In the example of perceiving the phoneme / p /, the acoustic stimulus evokes the topmost pattern of muscle-fiber contraction indicated as Series 1 in FIGURE 7 at the times "t_1, t_2 . . . t_n" for the allophone [p]. Although there is a complex transformation between the binary chain for the acoustic stimulus (column I) and the binary chain that represents the speech-muscle response pattern (column II), for simplicity we assume constant, nontransformed, feature relationships between these and the remaining columns of FIGURE 8.

Once the acoustic stimuli (column I) evoke a pattern of speech muscle-fiber contraction (column II), there results a unique afferent neural volley characterized in column III of FIGURE 8. This volley represents the coding in FIGURE 3 carried by the loop class IIIa that activates loop class IV. The coded afferent volley in this example then produces perception of ("retrieves") a phoneme (like $/p/$) in the central processing represented by column IV; perhaps the phoneme is a central motor program, as suggested by Osgood (personal communication).

The issue of the unit of linguistic perception is a complex one, but the principles developed here probably do not depend on the outcome of the issue. It is possible that the perceptual unit is the phoneme, following which words are perceived. This possibility is represented in column IV as the process by which the internal phonetic stimuli from the speech musculature evoke the phoneme $/p/$. The remainder of some specifiable acoustic language unit, like a word, may then be similarly processed with additional afferent volleys arriving in the brain almost simultaneously with that for [p]—in this example, the phonetic neural stimuli that evoke the phoneme $/p/$ are followed by the neural volleys that evoke the phonemes $/i/$ and $/t/$. As represented at the bottom of FIGURE 8, when the Series 2 and Series 3 neural volleys coded for [i] and [t] follow [p], the word "pit" is evoked, perhaps from a lexical store; lexical and semantic processing is represented in column V of FIGURE 8. Had, however, the "lax" member of opposition 7 been a component of the external language stimulus (in place of the "tense" member) the phoneme $/b/$ instead of $/p/$ would have been perceived, as indicated in the lower part of opposition 7 in column IV of FIGURE 8. "Perception" of $/b/$ when followed by $/i/$ and $/t/$ would produce the word "bit" instead of "pit" from a lexical store.

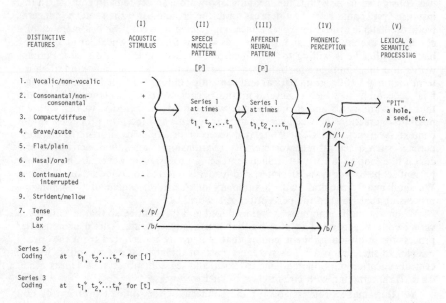

FIGURE 8. Coding processes within the listener that lead to word perception.

As far as the central nervous system aspects of the model is concerned, we do not have sufficient neurophysiological knowledge to say much about lexical and semantic storage systems; it is in fact difficult today to go much farther than Lashley's[59] trace system. But it *is* reasonable to assume that speech perception occurs when coded afferent neural impulses enter the brain and in some sense match the appropriate lexical and semantic representations of their corresponding externally impinging linguistic units. This is the process represented by loop IV of FIGURE 3.

We have hypothesized that perception occurs when the afferent neural volleys represented by a binary chain, such as the −, +, −, +, −, −, + for [p] in FIGURE 8, matches some comparably represented engram within a memory matrix (perhaps like Osgood & Hoosain's[89] semantic feature matrix). Lashley's search for the engram suggests to us that the lexical and semantic systems extend throughout the entire cerebrum, although there apparently are differential contributions of the dominant vs. minor cerebral hemispheres (cf. References 90 and 91).

Pribram[92] has suggested, in effect, that Lashley's trace system operates through a holographic kind of process. If so, when the afferent impulses for a linguistic unit make a holographic match, there would be retrieval of the impinging verbal unit. Other possible retrieval processes could involve electrochemical matching of a central representation, resonance matching, or some system that is as yet almost completely unexplored, such as matching magnetic signals within the brain.

How a word (like "pit") is processed is, of course, an enormously complex matter (and a subject of lively controversy). In some way during processing the units of a word must be integrated, following which a representation of the word is evoked so that the word is recognized and meanings are associated with it (e.g., for "pit," the listener thinks of a depression in the ground, or whatever). This is the process that Penfield[21] calls "translation," in which "ideas" occur. In column 5 of FIGURE 8 we merely note this semantic and lexical processing. It is certain, though, that the meaning of a perceived word within a sentence is not specified unambiguously when it is considered in isolation; the meaning of a word also depends on context. In this instance "pit" could refer to a depression in the ground; or if the sentence concerns fruit, the listener would interpret a meaning related to seed; if he is a member of a commodity exchange he may interpret it as a locus for selling wheat, or he may be a bettor, so that he is willing to "pit" his horse against another, and so on. Perhaps words and their units are partially processed, and then held in some kind of short-term memory until a grammatical and semantic context is formed, thus allowing a final decision as to which of several meanings each word in a sentence will take. By thus involving words and their meanings with short-term memory, we can consider possible interactions between central storage systems and receptor processes. In this context Averback and Coriell[93] related receptor processes to short-term memory; perhaps such a central-receptor memory relationship is a result of activation of a circuit like loop Ia in FIGURE 3. Such sentencing processes, however, are beyond our present scope of study, and the interested reader is referred to Osgood[34] on this topic. We shall merely conclude with a summary of our development of the phonemic processing that leads to the perception of a word.

When a stimulus impinges, it is transduced and transmitted so that, eventually, a verbal code is generated in part by the skeletal musculature. This neuromuscular processing results in phonetic coding that is neurally transmitted from the speech muscles to the central nervous system; arrival of the afferent neural volleys lead to central evocation of phonemes, and to lexical and semantic processing. This is circuit class IIIa interacting with circuit class IV of FIGURE 3.

We thus make progress toward the solution of the difficult problem of how centrally stored phonemes are evoked, with the hypothesis that the covert muscle activity generated during silent linguistic processing produces a phonetic neuromuscular code that is centrally processed to evoke phonemes from central storage—a word (in this example, "pit") is thus perceived and interpreted.† There is then efferent flow back to the musculature that involves a meaning reaction (r_m). According to Osgood (cf. References 43 and 89), r_m is represented as a complex code of *semantic features* (componential mediator components, $\pm r_{m_1} \cdots - r_{m_n}$) which initiates complex, continuing muscle-brain-muscle-brain circuit reverberation. However, in Osgood's view, although mediator components (r_m) and complexes (r_m) have their origins in overt behavior in the history of the organism, in contemporary mature performances they are purely central mediation processes, not requiring motor activation and feedback.

It is important to observe that the phonetic code generated by the speech muscles, while not itself meaningful, is responsible for making differences in meaning. For instance, if one perceives the letter D, followed by the letters AD, the tongue is primarily responsible for generating an afferent neural volley phonetically coded for [D], and "DAD" is perceived. Had, however, "M" been sensed, the lips would be the primary agent for generating a phonetic coding for [M] which, when followed by AD, leads to the perception of "MAD." In this way the speech muscle can be responsible for semantic differences.

We have considered events during linguistic perception in which the impinging linguistic stimulus unit is recognized (by evocation from a lexical store) and interpreted (through semantic processes). Once a meaning reaction is evoked, it may then produce mediating stimulation that leads to additional verbal units in complexly concatenated linguistic chains. These concatenated response sequences include associations, perhaps like the implicit associative responses discussed by Bousfield *et al.*[94] and by Underwood.[95] The interactions among such implicit associative reactions must be *exceedingly* complex,‡ and we again emphasize that internal information processing must proceed simultaneously in a number of "channels," and not according to a single-unit, single-channel linear processing model.

We must conclude by emphasizing that our attempt to represent these extremely complex, reverberating neuromuscular events in discrete form, and in diagrams, as we have throughout this paper, is highly artificial and greatly oversimplified. The most complex neuromuscular diagrams of the human mind that we could offer would still fall far short of an adequate account of internal language processing, probably the most complex phenomenon in nature.

ACKNOWLEDGMENTS

My great appreciation is expressed to Charles E. Osgood for his help with this work.

---

† Hebb's[22] cell assemblies would thus be evoked by the phonetic code ascending by circuit IIIa (together with other central and peripheral antecedents), leading to word perception. The phonetic coding from IIIa would, in Osgood's[34] system, evoke phonemes represented within the motor and nervous system that function at Osgood's program ($\overline{r}$-r) level.

‡ Although nothing like the complexities of understanding and creating *novel* sentences, which we do most of the time.

REFERENCES

1. McGUIGAN, F. J. 1966. Thinking: Studies of Covert Language Processes. Appleton-Century-Crofts. New York, N.Y.
2. McGUIGAN, F. J. 1970. Covert oral behavior during the silent performance of language tasks. Psychological Bull. **74:** 309–326.
3. McGUIGAN, F. J. 1973. Electrical measurement of covert processes as an explication of "higher mental events." *In* The Psychophysiology of Thinking. F. J. McGuigan and R. A. Schoonover, Eds.: 343–385. Academic Press. New York, N.Y.
4. McGUIGAN, F. J. 1973b. Conditioning of covert behavior—some problems and some hopes. *In* Contemporary Perspectives in Conditioning and Learning. F. J. McGuigan and D. B. Lumsden, Eds. V. H. Winston & Sons. Washington, D.C.
5. DELAFRESNAYE, J. F., Ed. 1954. Brain Mechanisms and Consciousness. Charles C Thomas. Springfield, Ill.
6. LANGFELD, H. S. 1933. The historical development of response psychology. Science **77:** 243–250.
7. JACOBSON, E. 1973. Electrophysiology of mental activities and introduction to the psychological process of thinking. *In* The Psychophysiology of Thinking. F. J. McGuigan and R. A. Schoonover, Eds.: 3–31. Academic Press. New York, N.Y.
8. WATSON, J. B. 1930. Behaviorism. Revised edit. Norton. New York, N.Y.
9. FOSS, D. J. & D. A. SWINNEY. 1973. On the psychological reality of the phoneme: Perception, identification, and consciousness. J. Verb. Learning Verb. Behav. **12:** 246–257.
10. FUJIMURA, O. 1972. Acoustics of speech. *In* Speech and Cortical Functioning. J. H. Gilbert, Ed.: 107–165. Academic Press. New York, N.Y.
11. CHERRY, C. 1957. On Human Communication. M.I.T. Press. Cambridge, Mass.
12. JAKOBSON, R., G. FANT & M. HALLE. 1952. Preliminaries to speech analysis. Acoustical Lab Report (13). M.I.T. Press. Cambridge, Mass.
13. TWADDELL, W. F. 1935. On defining the phoneme. Language Monographs **16:** 1–62.
14. JAKOBSON, R. & M. HALLE. 1971. Fundamentals of Language. 2nd revised edit. Mouton. The Hague, The Netherlands.
15. VOLKOVA, V. D. 1953. On certain characteristics of the formation of conditioned reflexes to speech stimuli in children. Fiziol. Zh. SSSR **39:** 540–548.
16. ACKER, L. E. & A. E. EDWARDS. 1964. Transfer of vasoconstriction over a bipolar meaning dimension. J. Exper. Psychol. **67:** 1–6.
17. RAZRAN, G. 1939. A quantitative study of meaning by conditioned salivary technique (semantic conditioning). Science **90:** 89–91.
18. COFER, C. N. & J. P. FOLEY. 1942. Mediated generalization and the interpretation of verbal behavior: I. Prolegomena. Psychol. Rev. **49:** 513–540.v
19. McGUIGAN, F. J. & R. A. SCHOONOVER, Eds. 1973. The Psychophysiology of Thinking. Academic Press. New York, N.Y.
20. TOMATIS, A. 1970. *In* Language. The Ideas of Dr. Alfred Tomatis. A. E. Sidlauskas. Unpublished manuscript. University of Ottawa. Ottawa, Canada.
21. PENFIELD, W. 1969. Consciousness, memory, and man's conditioned reflexes. *In* On the Biology of Learning. K. Pribram, Ed.: 129–168. Harcourt, Brace & World. New York, N.Y.
22. HEBB, D. O. 1959. The Organization of Behavior. John Wiley & Sons. New York, N.Y.
23. HASSLER, R. 1966. Thalamic regulation of muscle tone and the speed of movements. *In* The Thalamus. D. P. Purpura & M.D. Yahy, Eds.: 419–438. Columbia University Press. New York, N.Y.
24. STEVENS, K. N. & A. S. HOUSE. 1972. Speech perception. *In* Foundations of Modern Auditory Theory. Vol. 2. J. V. Tobias, Ed. Academic Press. New York, N.Y.
25. WYCZOIKOWSKI, A. 1913. Theoretical and experimental studies in the mechanism of speech. Psychol. Rev. **20:** 448–458.
26. HALLE, M. & K. N. STEVENS. 1959. Analysis by synthesis. *In* Proceedings of the Seminar on Speech Compression & Processing. Vol 2. Air Force Cambridge Research Center. Cambridge, Mass.

27. McGuigan, F. J. Principles of Covert Behavior—A Study in the Psychophysiology of Thinking. Prentice-Hall. Englewood Cliffs, N.J. In press.
28. Goldstein, M. H., Jr. 1968. The auditory periphery. In V. B. Mountcastle, Ed. Medical Physiology. Vol. II. The C. V. Mosby Co. St. Louis, Mo.
29. Bowman, J. P. & C. M. Combs. 1969. The cerebrocortical projection of hypoglossal afferents. Exp. Neurol. 23: 291–301.
30. Penfield, W. & H. Jasper. 1954. Epilepsy and the Functional Anatomy of the Human Brain. Little, Brown, and Co. Boston, Mass.
31. Sauerland, E. K. & N. Mizuno. 1968. Hypoglossal nerve afferents: elicitation of a polysnaptic hypoglossal-laryngeal reflex. Brain Res. 10: 256–258.
32. Ojemann, G. A. 1975. Language and the thalamus: Object naming and recall during and after thalamic stimulation. Brain & Language 2. In press.
33. Sussman, H. M. 1972. What the tongue tells the brain. Psychol. Bull. 77: 262–272.
34. Osgood, C. E. 1957. Motivational dynamics of language behavior. In Nebraska Symposium on Motivation. M. R. Jones, Ed.: 348–424. University of Nebraska Press. Lincoln, Neb.
35. Edfeldt, A. W. 1960. Silent Speech and Silent Reading. University of Chicago Press. Chicago, Ill.
36. McGuigan, F. J. & S. C. Bailey. 1969. Covert response patterns during the processing of language stimuli. Interam. J. Psychol. 3: 289–299.
37. McGuigan, F. J. & C. L. Winstead, Jr. 1974 Discriminative relationship between covert oral behavior and the phonemic system in internal information processing. J. Exp. Psychol. 103: 885–890.
38. Max, L. W. 1937. Experimental study of the motor theory of consciousness: IV. Action-current responses in the deaf during awakening, kinesthetic imagery and abstract thinking. J. Comp. Psychol. 24: 301–344.
39. McGuigan F. J. 1971. Covert linguistic behavior in deaf subjects during thinking. J. Comp. Physiol. Psychol. 75: 417–420.
40. Bowman, J. P. & C. M. Combs. 1968. Discharge patterns of lingual spindle afferent fibers in the hypoglossal nerve of the rhesus monkey. Exper. Neurol. 21: 105–119.
41. Blumenthal, M. 1959. Lingual Myographic Responses During Directed Thinking. Abstract of a dissertation presented to the Graduate College, University of Denver. Denver, Colo.
42. Locke, J. L. & F. S. Fehr. 1970. Subvocal rehearsal as a form of speech. J. Verb. Learning Verb. Behav. 9: 495–498.
43. Osgood, C. E. & F. J. McGuigan. 1973. Psychophysiological correlates of meaning: essences or tracers? In The Psychophysiology of Thinking F. J. McGuigan & R. A. Schoonover, Eds.: 449–483. Academic Press. New York, N.Y.
44. Harris, K. S. 1971. Vowel stress and articulatory reorganization. In Status Report on Speech Research (Oct.–Dec.): 167–178. Haskins Laboratories. New Haven, Conn.
45. Jakobson, R., C. G. M. Fant & M. Halle. 1963. Preliminaries to Speech Analysis. M.I.T. Press. Cambridge, Mass.
46. Hirose, H. & T. Gay. 1971. The activity of the intrinsic laryngeal muscles in voicing control: an electromyographic study. Status Report on Speech Research (Oct.–Dec.): 115–142. Haskins Laboratories. New Haven, Conn.
47. Raphael, L. J. 1971. An electromyographic investigation of the feature of tension in some American English vowels. In Status Report on Speech Research: 179–191. Haskins Laboratories. New Haven, Conn.
48. MacNeilage, P. F. 1970. Motor control of serial ordering of speech. Psychol. Rev. 77: 182–195.
49. MacNeilage, P. F. & L. A. MacNeilage. 1973. Central processes controlling speech production during sleep and waking. In The Psychophysiology of Thinking. F. J. McGuigan & R. A. Schoonover, Eds.: 417–448. Academic Press. New York, N.Y.
50. Isley, C. L. & J. V. Basmajian. 1973. Electromyography of the human cheeks and lips. Anat. Rec. 176: 143–147.
51. McGuigan, F. J. & D. J. Boness. 1975. What happens between an external stimulus and an overt response?—A study of covert responses. Pavlovian J. In press.

52. GATEV, V. & I. IVANOV. 1972. Excitation-contraction latency in human muscles. Agressologie **13:** 7-12.
53. CHAPMAN, R. M. 1961. Spectral sensitivity of single neural units in the bullfrog retina. J. Opt. Soc. Am. **51:** 1102-1112.
54. CHAPMAN, R. M. 1962. Spectral sensitivities of neural impulses and slow waves in the bullfrog retina. Vision Res. **2:** 89-102.
55. DAVIS, H. 1973. Classes of auditory evoked responses. Audiology **12:** 464-469.
56. AMADEO, M. & C. SHAGASS. 1973. Brief latency click-evoked potentials during waking and sleep in man. Psychophysiology **10:** 244-250.
57. JEWETT, D. L., M. N. ROMANO & J. S. WILLISTON. 1970. Human auditory evoked potentials: possible brain stem components detected on the scalp. Science **167:** 1517-1518.
58. BICKFORD, R. G., J. L. JACOBSON & T. R. CODY. 1964. Nature of average evoked potentials to sound and other stimuli in man. Ann. N.Y. Acad. Sci. **112:** 204-218.
59. LASHLEY, K. S. 1951. The problem of serial order in behavior. *In* Cerebral Mechanisms in Behavior, L. A. Jeffress, Ed. John Wiley & Sons, Inc. New York, N.Y.
60. MORRELL, L. K. & J. G. SALAMY. 1971. Hemispheric asymmetry of electrocortical responses to speech stimuli. Science **174:** 164-166.
61. TEYLER, T. J., R. A. ROEMER, T. F. HARRISON & R. F. THOMPSON. 1973. Human scalp-recorded evoked-potential correlates of linguistic stimuli. Bull. Psychonomic Soc. **1:** 333-334.
62. FILBEY, R. A. & M. S. GAZZANIGA. 1969. Splitting the normal brain with reaction time. Psychonomic Sci. **17:** 335-336.
63. HAMMOND, P. H. 1955. Involuntary activity in biceps following the sudden application of velocity to the abducted forearm. J. Physiol. **127:** 23P-25P.
64. EVARTS, E. N. 1966. Pyramidal tract activity associated with a conditioned hand movement in the monkey. J. Neurophysiol. **21:** 1011.
65. EVARTS, E. N. 1973. Motor cortex reflexes associated with learned movement. Science **179:** 501-503.
66. BERNHARD, C. G., E. BOHM & I. PETERSÉN. 1953. Investigations on organization of cortocospinal systems in monkeys (*Macaca mulatta*). Acta Physiol. Scand. **29:** 79.
67. SHEARER, W. M. & F. B. SIMMONS. 1965. Middle ear activity during speech in normal speakers and stutterers. J. Speech Hear. Res. **8:** 203-207.
68. McCALL, G. N. & D. RABUZZI. 1973. Reflex contraction of middle-ear muscles secondary to stimulation of laryngeal nerves. J. Speech Hear. Res. **16:** 56-61.
69. BARTLETT, N. R. 1963. A comparison of manual reaction times as measured by three sensitive indices. Psychol. Rec. **13:** 51-56.
70. BOTWINICK, J. & L. W. THOMPSON. 1966. Premotor and motor components of reaction time. J. Exper. Psychol. **71:** 9-15.
71. HATHAWAY, S. R. 1935. An action potential study of neuromuscular relations. J. Exper. Psychol. **18:** 285-298.
72. HILDEN, A. H. 1937. An action current study of the conditioned hand withdrawal. Psychol. Monogr. **49:** 173-204.
73. ERTL, J. & E. W. P. SCHAFER. 1969. Eratum-cortical activity preceding speech. Life Sci. [1] **8:** 559.
74. FAABORG-ANDERSON, K. & A. W. EDFELDT. 1958. Electromyography of intrinsic and extrinsic laryngeal muscles during silent speech correlation with reading activity. Acta Otolaryngol. (Stockh.) **49:** 478-482.
75. HIRANO, M. & J. OHALA. 1969. Use of hooked-wire electrodes for electromyography of the intrinsic laryngeal muscles. J. Speech Hear. Res. **12:** 362-373.
76. McGUIGAN, F. J. 1973. The function of covert oral behavior ("silent speech") during silent reading. Int. J. Psycholinguistics **2:** 39-47.
77. GOULD, L. N. 1950. Verbal hallucinations as automatic speech. Am. J. Psychiatry **107:** 110-119.
78. McGUIGAN, F. J., B. KELLER & E. STANTON. 1964. Covert language responses during silent reading. J. Educ. Psychol. **55:** 339-343.
79. McGUIGAN, F. J. 1966. Covert oral behavior and auditory hallucinations. Psychophysiology **3:** 73-80.

80. GRINGS, W. W. 1973. Cognitive factors in electrodermal conditioning. Psychol. Bull. **79:** 200–210.
81. ROUVRAY, D. H. 1973. The search for useful topological indices in chemistry. Am. Sci. **61:** 729–735.
82. FIENBERG, S. E. 1974. Stochastic models for single neuron firing trains: a survey. Biometrics **30:** 399–427.
83. STUDDERT-KENNEDY, M. The perception of speech. *In* Current Trends in Linguistics. Vol. 12: Linguistics and adjacent arts and sciences. T. A. Sebeok, Ed. In preparation. Mouton. The Hague, The Netherlands.
84. ESTES, W. K. 1973. Phonemic coding and rehearsal in short-term memory for letter strings. J. Verb. Learn. Verb. Behav. **12:** 360–372.
85. RUBENSTEIN, H., S. S. LEWIS & M. A. RUBENSTEIN. 1971. Evidence for phonemic recoding in visual word recognition. Center for the Information Sciences. Lehigh Univ. Bethlehem, Pa.
86. HINTZMAN, D. L. 1967. Articulatory coding in short-term memory. J. Verb. Learn. Verb. Behav. **6:** 312–316.
87. LIBERMAN, A. M., F. S. COOPER, K. S. HARRIS, P. F. MACNEILAGE & M. STUDDERT-KENNEDY. 1967. Some observations on a model for speech perception. *In* Models for the Perception of Speech and Visual Form. W. Wathen-Dunn, Ed.: 68-87. M.I.T. Press. Cambridge, Mass.
88. MILLER, G. A. & P. E. NICELY. 1955. An analysis of perceptual confusions among some Englsh consonants. J. Acoust. Soc. Am. **27:** 338–352.
89. OSGOOD, C. E. & R. HOOSAIN. 1974. Salience of the word as a unit in the perception of language. Percept. Psychophys. **15:** 168–192.
90. NEBES, R. D. 1974. Hemispheric specialization in commissurotomized man. Psychol. Bull. **81:** 1–14.
91. SPERRY, R. W. 1973. Lateral specialization of cerebral function in the surgically separated hemispheres. *In* The Psychophysiology of Thinking. F. J. McGuigan & R. A. Schoonover, Eds.: 209–229. Academic Press. New York, N.Y.
92. PRIBRAM, K. H. 1971. Languages of the Brain. Experimental Paradoxes and Principles in Neuropsychology. Prentice-Hall. Englewood Cliffs, N.J.
93. AVERBACK, E. & A. S. CORIELL. 1961. Short-term memory in vision. Bell Syst. Tech. J. **40:** 309–328.
94. BOUSFIELD, W. A., G. A. WHITMARSH & J. J. DANICK. 1958. Partial response identities in verbal generalization. Psychol. Rep. **4:** 703–713.
95. UNDERWOOD, B. J. 1965. False recognition produced by implicit verbal responses. J. Exp. Psychol. **70:** 122–129.

LANGUAGE AND THE ACQUISITION OF LANGUAGE-TYPE SKILLS BY A CHIMPANZEE (*PAN*)*

Duane M. Rumbaugh and Timothy V. Gill

*Georgia State University, and
Yerkes Regional Primate Research Center
Emory University
Atlanta, Georgia 30303*

INTRODUCTION

Recent studies[1-4] have served to raise the distinct probability that language is not a uniquely human attribute. To assess that probability accurately is not without serious risks and difficulties. The answer to the question, "Is the ape capable of human-type language skills?" clearly pivots on the definition of language. The definition of language, in turn, will have profound implications for the resolution of a number of other interrelated issues. For example, is language a skill/process apart from those acquired through classical and instrumental conditioning?[5] To what degree does language rely upon intelligence and related cognitive processes? What are the dimensions of similarity and difference that separate human-type language from the diverse forms of communication employed by animals?

Other important questions bear upon the evolutionary origins and the ontogenetic acquisition of language skills. Is human-type language contingent upon unique genetic endowment? What were the etiological factors that in the early hominoids selected for whatever genetic endowments were necessary for the emergence of language? What kinds of stimulation and learning experiences are requisites to the emergence of initial language skills in the human child and which ones are requisites to the refinement of the highest, most abstract linguistic competencies? Are there sensitive age periods during which certain learning experiences must take place for optimal language development to occur?

Consideration of most of these questions is beyond the scope of this paper. The one that clearly is not, however, is the one addressed to the definition of language.

If language is defined in terms of communication by means of vocal sounds and specifically *human* speech (Webster's unabridged dictionary), then it is clear that the answer to the question, "Is the ape capable of human-type language skills?" is unequivocally *No*. Efforts to teach apes literally to speak have met with such limited success that there is no longer reasonable justification to anticipate that apes with their normal larynges will ever master human-type speech. The apes' vocal tracts possibly do not provide for the production of most of the phonemes used in human speech.[6]

It is our view that although speech might be the most natural and efficient linguistic medium, it is not essential to language. Were it the case that man did not possess his highly evolved larynx, nonetheless he probably would still have language and language-type communication. Relevant to this point is the convincing case that has been carefully formulated by Hewes[7] in support of the conclusion that initially man's language was *not* vocal, but gestural. We must look beyond human speech to determine the essentials of language processes and language-type communications.

Furthermore, it is our position that the definition of language should not rest

*This research was supported by NIH grants HD-06016 and RR-00165.

90

upon the universals (e.g. design characteristics[8]) of natural, human, spoken languages. Without question, the specification of design characteristics have been of great value in the analysis of man's languages; however, a distinction should be drawn between universal *design* characteristics and the *essential* operations of language. In other words, not all attributes/functions of man's spoken languages are necessarily germane to language-type communication. Prior to an attempt to define the essential characteristics of language, the term communication should be considered.

Communication

Altmann, in his analysis of social communication and its structure, defined social communication as "a process by which the behavior of an individual affects the behavior of others." (Ref. 9, p. 326.) His position is consonant with Cherry's,[10] which holds communication as "the relationship set up by the transmission of stimuli and the evocation of responses."

It is of significance that Gardner and Gardner,[1] in a major report of their work with the chimpanzee subject, Washoe, couched their study in terms of two-way communication, not language. Their selection of the American Sign Language,[11] a form of gestural communication widely used by deaf persons, was predicated by their belief that that "medium of communication would be compatible with the species-specific capacities of the chimpanzee and would permit [Washoe] to achieve a significant level of two-way communication."[1] This position was both conservative and defensible. Their work demonstrated that two-way communication between man and chimpanzee was possible, a finding which proved to have such an impact that to have cast its interpretation in terms of language might have proved quite counterproductive to the future prospects of continued research of that type.

We agree with those who view language as a subset of the broader phenomenon, communication.[8,9,5,12] The point should not be overlooked, however, that at some point interorganismic exchange becomes so plastic, so rich, and of such high information value that it can and should be said that a linguistic-type of communication exists. But what, then are the distinctive/essential/fundamental attributes that communication must have for it to be so termed? We propose that a basic differentiation should be made between language and language-*type* communication.

Language

We define language as the use of symbols interactionally so as 1) to define covertly information that subsequently might be publicly transmitted, 2) to encode into signals/words selected information, covertly symbolized, for transmission/broadcasting thereof, providing thereby the possibility that the information might be received and covertly interpreted by others, and 3) to interpret the linguistic-type transmissions of others. This definition focuses attention upon the generation of new information through the use of symbols interactionally and upon the perception/interpretation of information transmitted by others. Since the transmission *per se* of the words/signals falls short of "communication," it seems imperative that the above processes be included in a definition of language.

A clear implication of our definition is that what is commonly termed "language" is essentially a totally private type of phenomenon. It allows for a Daniel Defoe's Robinson Crusoe even in isolation to be very linguistic in attempts to adapt, problem-solve, and create. We use our linguistic skills even while alone. The prime requisite for this type of linguistic competence is level of cognitive function. It is assumed that the covert interactional use of symbols is inherently provided for when cognitive functioning (e.g. abstractive powers, intelligence), with its attendant properties for concept formation, the recognition of dimensions of similarities and differences amongst diverse aspects of the environment, and the ability to hypothesize and infer, reaches some critical level. The operations of the higher levels of intelligence, for which the majority of mature humans is noted, are presumed to have the inherent capacity to generate symbols that initially serve idiosyncratically to index and to organize at least selected relationships among aspects of the perceived environment.

Language-Type Communication

Communication of a linguistic-*type* between two beings becomes possible when they are able to achieve agreement *by whatever means* as to the symbolic meanings of signals (e.g. words, lexical units) that can be efficiently produced for purposes of transmission. Since the symbolic meanings of signals (i.e., lexical units, words) to be used in the public transactions can be subject to rather capricious definition, it follows that the signals' elements (e.g. phonemes, gestures, lines, characters, etc.) and the processes for producing them must be plastic and open, as opposed to being fixed and closed, as is the case with the vast majority of signals used in species-specific animal communications.

Symbols and Signals

Symbols, then, are presumed to be both the medium and product of private (covert), higher-order intellectual function. *Signals,* by contrast, are public in quality, and their meaning is contingent upon two or more social beings agreeing, by whatever means, upon their symbolic referents. Collectively the signals, as lexical units, serve in the language-*type* transmissions of speech, the printed page, the American Sign Language for the Deaf, and other media.

The meanings of words are never universally fixed and unequivocal. Whereas a general public agreement can be reached as to the meaning of a word, each individual retains a certain degree of idiosyncraticity in his definition, because words as signals are only referents for symbols that are covert and private: only in the covert, private language processes of the individual might words ever be the equivalent of symbols.

Signals/words used in language-type transmission are never totally free of ambiguity, either individually or in their interactional usage. Consequently, in the final analysis it is the individual, private language system and its intellectually contingent processes (including generous usage of inference) that allows for the linguistically-coded information received from others to be processed and interpreted with any accuracy whatsoever.

The power of language-type communication rests in the interactional use of signals or words, each of which has been defined at least minimally to allow for use in combination with other words in a manner that allows for the very efficient linguistic-type encoding of information to be exchanged between beings, e.g. to be communicated. Clearly, if an individual's working vocabulary is limited to 500 words/signals, his thoughts are not limited to 500 symbols. Rather, the symbolic referents of words can be changed as a result of their interactional use. For example, the four words—the, box, violet, and paint—in their permutations allow for 24 different four-word strings, each of which potentially might serve as a sentence. (A sentence is here defined as the use of words interactionally for public transmission of a privately generated unit of information.) Two of the permutations of the four aforementioned words are *paint, the, violet, box* and *paint, the, box, violet*. The first of these makes a perfectly good sentence, "Paint the violet box." The meaning of that sentence is relatively clear; the box that is violet-colored should have its color altered via painting. The second permutation also forms a perfectly good but different sentence, "Paint the box violet." The instruction is given to paint the box a specific color, i.e. violet. The information of the second sentence can be transmitted, though awkwardly, with probable success through either of two other permutations, "Violet paint the box," and "Paint violet the box." And if it is allowed that the word "violet" may serve as a referent to a person (name of) as well as to a color, the permutations allow for a specific person to be specified for the painting, "Violet, paint the box!" and for three additional ways of asserting that: "Paint, Violet, the box!", "The box, Violet, paint!", and "Paint the box, Violet!" The permutations also allow for "Box the violet paint," and now the message is that the violet-colored paint is to be put into a box. These sentences should suffice to exemplify how, through the interactional use of signals/words, language-type communication affords considerable power both for the encoding of language-based information and for doing so in a variety of ways.

THE LANA LANGUAGE PROJECT

Origin

The Lana Language Project was launched to determine whether a computer-based system could be developed to facilitate and objectify research into the language-type skills evidenced by the chimpanzee in other studies.[1-4] The senior author of this paper is responsible for the germinal idea of bringing to bear the technology of modern electronics so as to automate the majority of procedures in research bearing upon the question, "Is the ape capable of human-type language and communication skills?" The second author was initially assigned the role of lead behavioral research technician; however, over the course of the past four years his role has evolved to that of co-investigator. It was Professor Harold Warner, Chief Biomedical Engineer of the Yerkes Primate Center, who in a number of initial discussions with the senior author of this paper contributed the electronics engineering expertise and opinions thereto relating to justify pursuit of the research program.[13]

Once satisfied that electronics engineering might be incorporated into the methods and operations of a unique approach to the study of chimpanzee language-type skills, the senior author, through the good graces of the late distinguished primatologist Clarence Ray Carpenter, made contact with and invited to the project-planning Professor Ernst von Glasersfeld and Mr. Pier Pisani of the University of Georgia's Department of Psychology and Computer Center, respectively. Professor von Glasersfeld, a psycholinguist, in cooperation with his computer-specialist colleague, Pier Pisani, was primarily responsible for the development of a language that might be accomodated by a relatively small computer. That language has been termed *Yerkish*, in honor of Robert M. Yerkes, the distinguished founder of the laboratories which now bear his name. The colleagueship and insightfulness of Professor Josephine V. Brown of the Department of Psychology, Georgia State University, and Mr. Charles Bell, an electronics technician of the Yerkes Primate

Center, proved invaluable at many important junctures in the design and implemen-tation of the Lana Language Project.

It was the success of the husband-and-wife team, Beatrice T. Gardner and R. Allen Gardner, of the Psychology Department of the University of Nevada, that gave the initial stimulus to the senior author to consider pursuing research of the type which gave rise to the Lana Language Project. The Gardners[1] demonstrated through their work with Washoe, who was about one year old at the beginning of the project, that at least one chimpanzee had considerable facility both to produce and to apparently understand the meaning of a number of words (hand-produced signs of the American Sign Language for the Deaf).

Washoe eventually developed a lexicon of better than 130 words, but more important than the number of words mastered was what she did with them. Even in the initial stages when Washoe had mastered only 10 words, she began to chain them in ways that suggested rudimentary syntax. Although analyses[14] reveal several commonalities between Washoe's stringing of signs and the child's stringing of words, it is our opinion that it should not be concluded that Washoe was observing or adhering to any set of rules for the structuring of the rudimentary sentences. Since no particular set of rules had to be observed in the stringing of signs, it might well be that Washoe's preferred sequences, which suggest syntactical use, were the result of simple habits, acquired/formed primarily by the models thereof afforded by her attendants.

Notwithstanding that point, it was clear that Washoe was doing impressive things with her signs. Reflecting upon the first phase of their project, the Gardners concluded: "Washoe's intellectual immaturity, the continuing acceleration of her progress, the fact that her signs [did] not remain specific to their original referents but were transferred spontaneously to new referents, and the emergence of rudimentary combinations all suggest [ed] that significantly more [could] be accomplished by Washoe [in] the subsequent phases."[15] (Tense altered by authors).

Washoe's transfer of signs from their original to new referents is exemplified by her use of the sign for "open." She initially used the sign when she wanted to get through a closed door, one of three particular doors used daily. "Washoe transferred this sign to all doors; then to containers such as the refrigerator, cupboards, drawers, briefcases, boxes, and jars; and eventually—an invention of Washoe's—she used it to ask us to turn on water faucets." (Ref. 15, p. 670.) Other impressive examples of transfer of sign usage occurred with the words "hat," "more," "dog," "cat," and "key."

Premack's[2] study with Sarah chimpanzee provided perhaps the most tantilizing evidence at the time for anticipating that eventually an ape might be able to employ syntax creatively, as in conversation. His methods entailed the use of plastic segments as the functional equivalents of words. Their sequential arrangement on a board allowed for variations in instructions/messages, even though the words employed were held constant. Sarah evidenced competence in discerning the meaning of a number of different sentences, the meaning of the negative ("Sarah take banana" versus "No Sarah take banana"), the differentiation between "sameness" and "difference," the names of various things, the use of words of various dimensional classes (color, shape, and size), the meanings of selected prepositions, the meaning of "if-then" contingency statements, and, apparently, the interpretation of compound sentences.

Perhaps the most important observation was that Sarah came to describe objects that were not present but that were represented by their respective plastic segments. With a small piece of blue plastic serving as the word for apple, Sarah described "apple" as red, round, and "with a stem," as opposed to being green, square, and "without a stem." It was the referent (apple) that was described, and not the salient attributes of its signal (a blue piece of plastic).

Fouts,[16] who studied with the Gardners, has pursued language studies with chimpanzees at the Institute for Primate Studies in his association with the University of Oklahoma. One of his chimpanzee subjects, Lucy, is noted for having "named" a number of things: four citrus fruits were labeled *smell fruits;* a radish was called *food* for three days and then called *cry hurt food* after one was tasted; and the labels *drink fruit* and *candy drink* were applied quite aptly to watermelon. Brazil nuts were termed *rock berries* and ducks dubbed *water birds.* To these authors, Lucy's assignment of such descriptive names serves to suggest that she recognizes/abstracts the salient attributes of things and generically clusters diverse items of her environment in accordance with their dimensions of similarity. These research findings also stimulated us to advance the research into the language-like skills which chimpanzees can acquire in certain contexts, hopefully, with the advantages of modern technology and computerized operation.

A Computer-Based System

Details of the computer-controlled training system that was designed and built for the study have been provided elsewhere.[17] In brief, a PDP8E computer and a parser [18] mediate and monitor all linguistic-type events, be they between the chimpanzee and the computer or between the chimpanzee and the human experimenter (FIGURE 1).

FIGURE 1. Lana (at age 4½) at the keyboard. The overhead bar must be depressed for the keyboard to be activated. Each key has on its surface a geometric pattern (lexigram) that designates its function or meaning. Depression of a key results in a facsimile of the key's lexigram produced on a projector above the keyboard. The locations of the keys are changed frequently to ensure that keys are selected on the basis of their lexigrams, not positions.

Through computerized operations, we intended to achieve round-the-clock operations, seven days a week, enhanced objectivity of records of linguistic events/episodes, greater efficiency and reliability in training, and, eventually, a method that might be applied broadly for the possible benefit of children who for various reasons find language acquisition extremely onerous.

The design of a unit that would allow for linguistic input by the ape subject into the computer-based system was conceptually problematic. We decided that the actual production of a word would be a function of events that took place in the system following rather simple motor responses by the ape subject. The performance of the correct motoric response (key pressing), however, would require accurate perceptions, discriminations, and choices.

We decided that keys on a console would be used as words in the Lana Language Project (probably influenced by Premack's use of plastic segments as words). The keys would not be used to spell words; they would be the words. Each word was to be represented by a unique geometric configuration embossed on the surface on one of the keys. The keys and the console were designed to allow for ready relocation of the keys' positions, so that their locations could not serve as reliable indices of function. Somewhat arbitrarily, it was decided that the system would provide for a six-word-long sentence at a maximum, not including specific markers for statements of request and question, and yet another key, the "period" key, which when depressed would serve to signal the computer that an expression had been terminated and was to be evaluated for correctness.

Yerkish [19]

The Yerkish language is strictly visual; no vocalizations are involved. Its grammar is correlational; the language is, nonetheless, open and does provide for different ways of expressing a given message or a statement. Words that are conceptually related are put into a single category. Thus, there are not nouns, verbs, adjectives, and so on, as in English.

The Channel of Communication

The ape can express itself linguistically by the selection and depression of the appropriate word keys in accordance with the grammar of Yerkish. As a given key is depressed, a facsimile of the geometric configuration (e.g. a lexigram) on the key's surface is produced by one of the projectors above the keyboard console. There are two rows of projectors—one for producing the statements generated through use of the subject's keyboard, and one for producing that generated through use of the experimenter's keyboard—which are referred to as the "send" and "receive" projector rows, respectively. In a given row, there is a left-to-right production of the facsimiles of the lexigrams on the keys depressed.

The first projector can produce the symbols for only PLEASE, NO, YES, and "?". PLEASE and "?" serve to activate subroutines in the computer's program appropriate for communications of request or question, respectively. This first projector is bypassed for any sentence/expression that does not begin with one of the four foregoing words. The next six projectors can produce any of more than 1,000 Yerkish lexigrams (words). This is accomplished through the selective activation of one or more of the twelve lamps in each projector. Each of these six projectors holds identical film materials, consisting of nine design elements (such as a rectangle, circle, and wavy line, all of which can be superimposed to form unique configurations) and three primary-colored film segments. Since the twelve lenses for these lamps all focus upon the rear-view projection screen which forms the front of a given projector, the selective activation of the lamps produces a facsimile of the lexigram that is on the surface of the key that has been depressed. It is through these two rows of projectors that linguistic-type exchanges occur between the subject and the human experimenter.

The experimenter's keyboard, while the functional equivalent of the ape's keyboard, is comprised of simple push-buttons labeled with English abbreviations that code the keys' functions. The location of this keyboard relative to the ape's keyboard is given in FIGURE 2.

All linguistic events are recorded through the computer's activation of a teleprinter and a paper-tape punch. Expressions of the experimenter are flagged with a specific marker to allow for clear separation between that said by the ape and that said by the experimenter.

Under the ape's keyboard console, and under the control of the computer, is an array of dispensers for vending requested foods and drinks, and a variety of objects (blanket, ball, and miscellaneous toys and objects). To the side of the keyboard console is a screen for the projection of photographic slides and another for the projection of motion pictures; there are also systems that produce stereophonic music and that open a window for a view out-of-doors, all contingent upon the correct request being formulated.

Tactics

Very early in the Lana Language Project it was decided that the subject (Lana, two years old, initially) would spend most of the 24 hours of each day in the language-training situation. Lana's quality of life would be a direct function of her linguistic expertise; even opportunity for daily exercise and play outdoors would be made contingent upon appropriate request. This proved to be a wise decision, for we have had essentially no problem in getting her to use the keyboard and to use it accurately. (Turning off the keyboard for a brief period of time came to be a very effective form of punishment to discourage counterproductive behaviors.)

Initially, an orangutan (*Pongo*) subject lived in the language-training situation with Lana to the end of providing her social stimulation. Because the orangutan and Lana had lived together for many months prior to the commencement of study, they were well adapted to each other. We had originally hoped that both might simultaneously benefit from the language training. Within the first few weeks of the study, however, the slower subject was removed because her presence seemed to be both interfering with Lana's working at the keyboard and restricting her linguistic expressions to the barest necessities of life: food and drink. Lana evidenced essentially no interest in the movies, music, slides, or the opportunity to view the outdoors by asking that the window be "opened" until shortly after the orangutan was removed from her quarters. It is believed that the incentive value of these events increased as social companionship, particularly during the evening hours when no humans were in attendance, decreased. Social stimulation was from that point on to be provided by behavioral technicians who, upon specific and appropriate request, would enter her room and then tickle, swing, or groom her, again upon the appropriate request being formulated—PLEASE TIM/SHELLEY SWING/ TICKLE/GROOM LANA. They also would allow Lana to groom them if her formulation was PLEASE LANA GROOM TIM/SHELLEY, and if they elected to answer, YES.

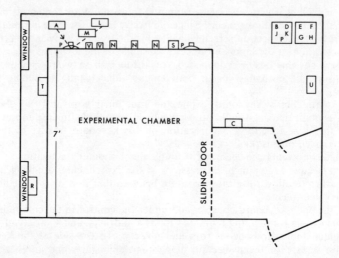

FIGURE 2. Diagram of the language training room. A = Lana's keyboard; C = Experimenter's keyboard; B, D, E, F, G, H, J, & K = computer and interfacing complex; M, L, V, N, S, & P = projectors and vending devices for foods, liquids, objects, etc.; T = projection screen; R = window; and U = teleprinter.

Despite the restrictions upon Lana's opportunity for social stimulation and interaction, she is, comparatively speaking, a well-adjusted chimpanzee, particularly for those which are captive-born and reared. She is not given to excessive behavioral aberrancies/stereotopies and is emotionally quite stable. Reports of her linguistic progress will substantiate the point that her social milieu has been compatible with both rapid acquisition and facile use of various skills of the linguistic type.

Initial Operations, Training, and Testing Methods

The system became operational in December, 1972, but it was not until February 1, 1973 that its operation was highly reliable. The entirety of 1972 had been spent in finalizing the design and fabricating the system. (FIGURE 3)

Lana's initial training was with a 5 × 5 matrix of keys on one board. She was taught the use of specific keys in combinations with others through a variety of training techniques. Initially, manual guidance was used, which entailed taking Lana's finger to the key to be depressed and thereby pressing the key. The technicians also modeled the correct responses. As Lana developed affinities for the technicians, she appeared to benefit and promptly came to imitate what they had done.

Subsequently, pointing to the correct key was sufficient to inform Lana what should be done next. Eventually, verbal guidance (admonitions by the technicians including "Push it!", "Yes," "No," and "Finish it!") proved to be effective for use at a distance, as in the case when Lana was at her keyboard and the human experimenter was at the one adjoining her room.

Since we were procedurally feeling our way during the initial acquisition periods, training of new skills often proceeded in other than a totally preplanned manner. We were attempting to discern methods that would and would not work. But the *testing* of Lana's proficiency level always employed tight controls. Once it was believed that she had reached a plateau in the aquisition of a skill, testing took place under controlled conditions to ensure that there would be no cueing on the part of the technicians regarding the correct choice. Controls incorporated included (1) the

FIGURE 3. Lana (at age 2½) working with the original keyboard.

shielding of the experimenter from Lana's view by positioning the experimenter behind opaque shields; (2) use of experimenters not involved in the training of specific skills; (3) the counterbalancing of experimenters across test sessions; and (4) the use of trial one performance measures in response to randomly sequenced trials of more than one type.

Lana's initial training consisted of pressing a single key to request and to obtain M & M candies. She was next required to precede each such request with PLEASE and to follow it with depression of the PERIOD key (the PERIOD key served to signal the computer that an expression had been terminated). The next stage entailed the introduction of what might be termed a modified holophrastic-type training, suggested by Ernst von Glasersfeld. The keys for a correct request—for instance, MACHINE GIVE M & M—were placed in the correct order in a row and were coupled together electrically so that the depression of any one of the three keys resulted in the activation of all. Depression of the PLEASE key before and depression of the PERIOD key after depression of any one of the holophrase keys were still required.

Upon mastery of this phase, the object requested was separated from the "holophrase." Specifically, Lana then had to make one key depression for PLEASE, a second key depression for MACHINE GIVE, a third key depression for M & M, and a fourth key depression for PERIOD. The last phase was to then require that she press each word key separately, the keys still being in the correct order within a row. Mastery of this phase resulted in the order of the keys being scrambled first within a row and then being scrambled randomly within the 25-key matrix of the first console.

We installed a "go-bar" to force certain consistencies upon the ape as it worked at the keyboard. The bar was so-called because it had to be pulled down to activate the keyboard, thereby avoiding the possibility that the subject might respond rapidly with alternate hands. It was inevitable that Lana would climb up onto the bar, as apes are prone to do with any structure; however, it was not anticipated that as she climbed her foot would from time to time accidentally hit and depress keys. (Initially the surfaces of the keys protruded approximately one-eighth of an inch beyond the aluminum plate that formed the console, in the interest of making the keys readily accessible for responding.) Such a context was fortuitous because it provided the initial evidence that Lana had come to attend to and indeed equate the projected facsimilies of the lexigrams with those on the surfaces of the keys. We noticed that if the PLEASE key had been one accidentally depressed, Lana apparently took note of it when she came to the keyboard to formulate a statement, for she would look alternately between the depressed key and the projected image of the likeness of the key. (It should be noted at this point that when a key is depressed it gains an additional level of brilliance, a characteristic which was incorporated into the keyboard so as to give the subject assistance in referring back to keys that had been depressed.) Noting that the PLEASE key was bright and that a facsimile of it was produced on the first projector overhead, she simply added to it to compose a sentence, as for food or drink, rather than do the unnecessary act of pressing the PLEASE key as the first word of a statement of request.

It was also noted during the first four months of training that Lana came to be sensitive to errors that she made during the course of formulating a sentence. Specifically, if she made a mistake in word order, she became prone to depress the PERIOD key promptly rather than continue the sentence to no avail. Depression of the PERIOD key always results in the erasure of the images on the projectors and the resetting of the keyboard regardless of the correctness of that word string which precedes the depression of the PERIOD key. This was indication, then, that Lana had begun to discern not only the lexigrams that differentiated the keys, regardless of their locations, but the sequencing of the lexigrams in terms of what would and what would not constitute a sentence acceptable to the system—acceptable in the sounding of a tone and in the delivery of an incentive for which she had asked.

Reading and "Writing"

These observations led to four experiments [4] that demonstrated that Lana had at least rudimentary reading and sentence-completion skills. In the first two of these studies, three-word valid and invalid sentence beginnings were given to Lana through use of the experimenter's keyboard. One of the valid sentence beginnings was PLEASE MACHINE GIVE, to which Lana could add M & M, WATER, MILK, PIECE OF BANANA, PIECE OF APPLE, and so on, any incentive which might be transferred to Lana. A second valid sentence beginning was PLEASE MACHINE MAKE, to which she could add either WINDOW OPEN, MUSIC, or MOVIE— any state or event that the computer was capable of producing through activation of appropriate component parts of the system.

Along with these valid sentence beginnings, *in*valid sentence beginnings were presented on a random basis. Invalid sentence beginnings were ones that could not constitute, by virtue of their order, the beginnings of sentences that might be completed in accordance with the Yerkish grammar. Along with simple inversions in otherwise correct beginnings, such as PLEASE GIVE MACHINE and PLEASE MAKE MACHINE, were random combinations of words, such as PLEASE WINDOW TIM and PLEASE DOOR M & M.

Lana reliably differentiated the valid from the invalid sentence beginnings, as indicated by the fact that with about 90% accuracy she would attempt to complete and did complete accurately sentences that had valid beginnings. By contrast, and again with about 90% accuracy, she promptly depressed the PERIOD key in response to the presentations of invalid sentence beginnings. This was tantamount to rejection of the invalid sentence beginnings; in general, she did not expend energy in attempts to finish such sentence beginnings.

In the last two of the four experiments in reference, we presented the beginnings of a number of sentences familiar to Lana, familiar in the sense that she had been taught them through the training procedures initially employed. In these two experiments the sentences were started and stopped at every possible point on a random basis up to the very last word. The observations indicated that with about 90% accuracy Lana would pick up and complete the sentence from wherever we had left off.

In summary, the results of these four studies indicated that Lana discerned the various lexigrams and attended to their serial order. She could read and she could write, if the production of words through the depression of keys on her keyboard was taken as a form of writing.

Use of Yes and No

Lana had been trained to respond "yes" or "no" in response to questions regarding the state of the window and door, specifically whether they were open or shut. In response to such questions, Lana had to look at either the door or the window and then respond either "yes" or "no" in accordance with the nature of the question. Subsequently, on her own, she extended the use of "no" to serve as a protest. It first occurred when Shelley Pogue drank a coke in the anteroom. Lana came up to the door with her hair erect and did a "foot stomp." She then went to the keyboard and pressed the key for "no." The same event occurred later the same day when Lana saw Shelley eating an apple and she had none.

Naming–Training

Throughout the course of Lana's training she came to use lexigrams that corresponded to certain items and events of her environment. As she asked PLEASE MACHINE GIVE PIECE OF CHOW PERIOD, and she did so thousands of times, she received a piece of monkey chow. Whenever she asked PLEASE MACHINE GIVE WATER PERIOD, a sip of it was made available to her through use of a stainless steel straw. The question was posed, "Could Lana 'name' the object so obtained?" More specifically, would she learn to respond correctly by naming an object when the object was coupled with the question posed through the computer "?WHAT NAME OF THIS PERIOD"?

Lancaster[20] observed that the ability to name objects allows one to refer to the surrounding environment and to use language in a manner that is not simply oriented to extant motivational states. The mastery of naming skills, then, might be quite fundamental to the acquisition of other language skills, for it allows for reference to things and events of the environment. (Interestingly, a search of the literature reveals a dearth of research on the acquisition of naming-skills by children.)

Lana was 2.75 years old when naming-training commenced in the summer of 1973. At the time, she had been in language training for seven months. She had become totally dependent on her keyboard capabilities for essentially all of her nourishment and for special stimulation, such as movies, music, and her seemingly insatiable desire to be tickled.

The specific procedures and detailed results of this study are to be found in a report by Gill and Rumbaugh.[21] Briefly, in the pretraining phase a specific response of key depression was established as in "ITEM-NAME" NAME-OF THIS, to the query, ? WHAT NAME-OF THIS, where "ITEM-NAME" refers to the lexigram previously established for the exemplar presented. (The "of" portion of "name-of" was included as a single lexigram, rather than using a separate lexigram, due to the previous establishment of the use of that word in connection with "piece," to form the phrase "piece of." The word "name-of," then, served as a function, whereas "piece of" served as a referent to a portion of a larger unit.)

In the main name-training phase, the word keys for M & M, BANANA, WHAT, NAME-OF, THIS, AND "?" were turned on, as well as other keys normally on during the day—PLEASE, MACHINE, GIVE, MAKE, MOVIE, MUSIC, WINDOW, OPEN, WATER, PIECE, OF, and PERIOD. M & M chocolate candies and slices of banana were used as the items to be named. The question, ? WHAT NAME-OF THIS, was stated through use of the experimenter's keyboard; with the depression of the key for the last word of that sentence, either M & M candies or banana slices were shown to Lana through use of a small plastic tray held in the experimenter's hand.

Over the course of two weeks and approximately 1600 trials, Lana learned to respond differentially to these two exemplars by responding appropriately M & M NAME-OF THIS PERIOD or BANANA NAME-OF THIS PERIOD. At the end of this phase of training, Lana was presented with these two types of naming-trials where the sequence of the objects was strictly random. During 100 trials she achieved the predetermined criterion of 90% correct.

The test of Lana's ability to transfer naming-skills from the two objects in the training phase to other objects was tested first by use of an array of five exemplars: pieces of apple, pieces of monkey chow, pieces of bread, juice, and a soccer ball. These five items had been requested hundreds of times during previous months. These five items, together with M & M and banana slices, were presented for ten trials that involved the presentation and request for names of either M & M or banana. Of considerable interest is the fact that she was correct on the first presentation of ball, responding BALL NAME-OF THIS PERIOD. On the last five trials of each of the five items she was 80% correct. On the seventh and tenth times through the naming trials she was without error.

A second transfer test was conducted with two additional items, milk and blanket. These were the last two items that at the time had been worked for by Lana in her language-training situation. She was correct on the first naming-trials for both of these items, reasonable evidence in support of the contention that in the initial training Lana had learned more than just to respond differentially to the two exemplars, M & M and banana slices. She had learned that things have names.

Subsequently, she has acquired names of new things quite readily and has at times even apparently inferred the name of something. Specifically, she was being taught the name of the projected image as from a 35-mm slide projector. The second author, through use of his keyboard, typed the request PLEASE MACHINE MAKE SLIDE, whereupon three slides were automatically projected on the screen adjacent to Lana's keyboard. Without being requested to do anything, Lana went to her keyboard and used the key for "slide" for the first time as she typed out SLIDE NAME-OF THIS PERIOD. Too, interspersed with requests that her movie be shown (per request it plays for 30 seconds) there have been statements MOVIE NAME-OF THIS, with the successive requests PLEASE MACHINE MAKE MOVIE PERIOD. Also, she has named spontaneously all of her food items during evening hours, while eating each, in turn.

During the naming-training sessions, Lana also came to use the word THIS as a referent to things for which she had no names. That word was used in a number of sentences during the evening hours when it might be said that she was either "trying out new combinations" or was "babbling." Examples were: PLEASE MACHINE GIVE PIECE OF THIS PERIOD and PLEASE MACHINE NAME THIS PE-RIOD.

Through the course of the naming-training study, she learned to make declarative sentences and to respond properly to the interrogative. She also developed on her own the use of the interrogative marker, in apparent imitation of the experimenter's use of it. For example, she daily asked, ? TIM MOVE INTO ROOM PERIOD, to which is responded either YES or NO. In point of fact, there was no need for her to substitute ? for PLEASE in the above sentence, for previously she had always used PLEASE and gained the entrance of Tim—but she did so.

Use of "Stock" Sentences for Other Than the
Originally Intended Purpose

On February 21, 1974, Lana first used one of her "stock" sentences (e.g. one taught her for a specific function) for other than its initial and intended purpose in an apparent and appropriate manner. It was late morning; Lana had had her milk, and Beverly Wilkerson, a technician, was about to leave, since it was that time. Beverly got some bread and put pieces into the dispenser so that Lana might ask the system for them. What Beverly forgot to notice was that she failed to turn on the correct dispenser. Beverly was about to leave the area as Lana typed:

Lana:	*Please machine give piece of bread.* (No bread was forthcoming.)	5:25 p.m.
	Please machine move into room.	5:26 p.m.
	Please Shelley.	5:27 p.m.
	Please Tim.	5:27 p.m.
	? Beverly move behind room.	5:27 p.m.
Beverly:	*Yes.* (And she moved behind the room to check why it was that the bread had not been delivered upon completion of Lana's initial request.)	5:27 p.m.

Beverly found the difficulty, corrected it, and Lana got her bread. From that point on, Lana was very prone to use the request to have someone move behind the room when equipment failures were sensed, or perhaps more precisely, when incentives otherwise vended were not.

Another instance of Lana's so doing is exemplified by events of Saturday, December 14, 1974, when Michael Haberman had loaded two of the dispensers with pieces of monkey chow and apple. As he left the area of the vending devices, Lana asked twice for pieces of chow, which she got, and then twice for pieces of apple, which she did not get. As Mike was about to leave the room, Lana came to the glass door and hooted and whimpered. Mike turned around and looked at her; with a "pout face," she moved to the keyboard and asked, ? YOU MOVE BEHIND ROOM PERIOD. As Mike moved to "behind the room," Lana typed out PLEASE MACHINE GIVE PIECE OF APPLE PERIOD, whereupon Mike saw that the apple dispenser was jammed and not working. It was as though her typed request was to direct his attention to the one of the two devices that had failed to work. Correction of the problem resulted in Lana's repeatedly asking for slices of apple, and successfully so.

In brief, although Lana had learned through specific training to ask persons to move behind the room to position them behind the window for viewing when the blind was lowered via appropriate request, she came to use the sentence to problem solve when instances of equipment malfunction resulted in her not getting the incentives requested from the system. It is possible that Lana's initial use of a stock sentence (February 21, 1974) in a novel way/context was critical to the emergence of the conversation, as discussed in the next section.

Conversations

Coke

The word THIS was a key word in the first conversation that might be adjudged as having been substantive, novel, and appropriate to the context. On March 6, 1974, in the late afternoon, the second author was drinking a Coca Cola, as he was prone to do. He was standing in full view of Lana; she had an unobstructed view of him through the glass sliding door of her chamber. It is important to note that Lana had learned the lexigram for "coke" and had requested it hundreds of times through her system through use of the sentence PLEASE MACHINE GIVE COKE PERIOD. Despite that fact, Lana made apparent reference to Tim's coke through use of the word THIS, as the following conversation reveals:

Lana:	*? Lana drink this out-of room.*	4:05 p.m.
Tim:	*Yes.* (And he opened the door to allow Lana to come out and have a drink of his coke. This exchange and the drink of coke were repeated two times in succession.)	

Reflecting upon this event and acknowledging that Lana knew the name for Coca Cola, Tim reentered the anteroom about 4:40 p.m. with another coke in hand and intentions that become apparent in the following transactions which ensued:

Lana:	*Please machine give coke.* (But there was no coke in the vending device controlled by the system.)	4:41 p.m.
	Please Lana drink coke this room. (Perhaps she intended to say "out-of" instead of "this," as she had said in the first instance, recorded above. That possibility notwithstanding, Tim responded—).	4:42 p.m.
Tim:	*No.*	
Lana:	*? Lana drink this out-of room.* (And in response to this question, Tim countered with one focused upon the meaning of the word "this.")	4:42 p.m.
Tim:	*? Drink what.*	
Lana:	*? Lana drink coke out-of room.*	4:43 p.m.
Tim:	*Yes.* (And Lana was allowed to join Tim in the anteroom for a sip of coke. She was then returned to her room.)	
Lana:	*? Lana eat coke out-of room.*	4:44 p.m.
Tim:	*No eat coke.* (The sentence is in error for coke is not to be "eaten.")	
Lana:	*Please.*	4:44 p.m.
	Please Lana drink coke out-of room. (Although the sentence is correct, Tim elected not to honor it.)	4:44 p.m.
Tim:	*No.*	
Lana:	*? Lana drink coke out-of room.*	4:45 p.m.
Tim:	*Yes.* (And she was allowed to do so.)	4:45 p.m.

This exchange meets our fundamental definition of a conversation: 1) there must be a linguistic-type of exchange/communication between two beings; 2) there must be novelty in at least one of the communications transmitted by each of the two beings; and 3) the topic/subject of the exchange must remain relatively organized and constant across time.

The first conversation is significant in many ways. First, Lana had had no specific training that was intended to cultivate conversational exchanges. She initiated and then sustained the exchange through appropriate response. Second, her first sentence, ? LANA DRINK THIS OUT-OF ROOM, was both novel and appropriate to the incentive toward which she was apparently motivated, i.e., Tim's coke. This sentence was a combination of one that grew out of the naming-training sessions as noted earlier, that is, the use of the word "this" as a referent for various items of her environment. The phrase "? Lana drink" had been taught her through modeling and reinforcement provided by the technicians in training sessions. But it was Lana who came to use the sentence, "? Lana drink this." In this conversation, she added to that sentence the phrase "out-of room." That phrase had been used in two sentences that she had been specifically taught as requests to be taken outdoors. They were, LANA MOVE OUT-OF ROOM PERIOD and ? TIM/SHELLEY/BEV CARRY LANA OUT-OF ROOM PERIOD.

That the addition of that phrase was other than a chance event is supported by the fact that the initial exchange at 4:05 p.m. was repeated twice; e.g., she used the sentence three times successively in order to obtain the coke. Additional points of significance are that even though she was flexible in her linguistic formulations in the exchange which commenced at 4:41 p.m., all of her formulations were "coke"-oriented. When one sentence did not yield the incentive, another of a similar type was employed. Most significant, we believe, is the fact that when asked by Tim, ? DRINK WHAT PERIOD, in response to her question, ? LANA DRINK THIS OUT-OF ROOM PERIOD, she responded in a precisely correct manner: she deleted the word "this" and substituted for it the specific word "coke" to formulate the sentence, ? LANA DRINK COKE OUT-OF ROOM PERIOD.

On March 18, 1974, Lana asked ? SHELLEY TICKLE LANA OUT-OF ROOM PERIOD (1:41 p.m.), and then later asked ? SHELLEY GROOM LANA OUT-OF ROOM PERIOD (4:01 p.m.), additional instances as to Lana's transfer of a linguistic innovation from one situation to another. Again, on March 20, she asked ?TIM TICKLE LANA OUT-OF ROOM PERIOD (4:22 p.m.). The reader should take note that the foregoing exchange and those given in other sections of this paper are unabridged.

Question-Answer

On March 9, 1974, Lana seemingly posed the question to herself, ? LANA MAKE WINDOW OPEN PERIOD. At any rate, forthwith there followed two requests, PLEASE MACHINE MAKE WINDOW OPEN PERIOD, and she viewed the outdoors.

Stylistics and the Pronominal?

On April 12, 1974, Lana modified a request in a manner that basically qualifies as "stylistic variation." Tim had coffee which he was drinking:

Lana: *Please Tim give drink.*
Tim: *No.*
Lana: *Please Tim give this.*
Tim: *Yes.* (And did so.)

Stylistic variation is suggested both in the fact that she referred (presumably) to the coffee as a "drink," when in Yerkish the word is an activity, not an object. Stylistic variation is also suggested in the fact that the nonspecific referent "this" was substituted for "drink." The example also serves as one of pronominal reference, where the pronoun of the "this" was used in lieu of the specific name, "coffee," which she knew as the name of the liquid being drunk by Tim.

Use of "Lana" as the Indirect Object. On April 22, 1974, Lana first used her name as an indirect object. This was strictly on her own initiative; no specific training had been given to encourage her to do so. Her first use of it in this way was ? TIM GIVE LANA BALL PERIOD.

Use of "This" to Denote a Specific Thing. On April 25, 1974, Tim entered the anteroom with his cup of coffee. Lana's question was ? TIM GIVE LANA THIS COFFEE PERIOD, to which Tim said YES, and shared it with her.

Move it Through Space. On April 30, 1974, another very important conversation took place, again one that was initiated by Lana. On April 29, Lana had been very disinclined to work in her training and testing session; consequently, her evening ration of food was restricted to make her hungrier for the following morning work-session. On the morning of April 30, Tim Gill entered the anteroom and, holding a large pitcher of cold milk in one hand and his morning cup of coffee in the other, stood in full view of Lana. The following exchange transpired:

Lana:	*Milk name-of this.*	8:54 a.m.
Tim:	*Yes.*	
Lana:	*Milk name-of this.*	8:55 a.m.
Tim:	*Yes.*	
Lana:	*Milk this.*	8:56 a.m.
	? Tim give Lana coffee. (She relishes black coffee!)	8:57 a.m.
Tim:	*No.* (Although at times he has honored that request, he elected not to,	

for it was the milk, not the coffee, that was the incentive appropriate to
her state of heightened food-motivation.)

Lana:	*? Tim move milk coffee.* (This was the first suggestion that she was going to ask Tim to move something from one point to another in space. She had not received specific training to ask that this be done.)	8:58 a.m.
Tim:	*(No response.)*	
Lana:	*? Tim move behind room.*	8:58 a.m.
Tim:	*Yes.* (Whereupon Tim set down the pitcher of milk and moved behind the room to the general area of the vending devices, where the milk would ordinarily be loaded into the machine. Lana's response was to hoot with apparent disturbance; piloerection and a furrowed brow were also noted. In a few seconds, Tim returned to the anteroom, picked up the milk, and stood once again in Lana's full view.)	
Lana:	*Milk of this coffee.*	8:59 a.m.
	? Tim give milk name-of.	9:00 a.m.
	? Tim move milk behind—(The sentence was not completed; however, Tim interpreted it to mean that Lana did not know how to finish what promised to be a novel question that was quite appropriate to the context.)	
Tim:	*? Behind what.*	
Lana:	*? Tim move milk behind room.* (And with this statement Lana had, for the first time, asked that an animate move something other than their own bodies from one point to another in space.)	9:01 a.m.
Tim:	*Yes.* (And he loaded the vending device with milk and Lana commenced to work for it by repeatedly asking—)	
Lana:	*Please machine give milk.*	9:02 a.m.

The significance of this conversation is that first, Lana spontaneously named the desired incentive. Probably because of her heightened hunger state, the pitcher of milk was one of the more salient things of her environment. Second, Tim was asked to "move behind the room," possibly as a way of asking that he move the milk back there and load it into the device for vending. (As noted above, Lana had on previous occasion asked technicians to "move behind the room," not just to position themselves behind the window for viewing, but in response to not being able to get the foods or liquids which they had just loaded into the vending devices.)

Third, and most significant of all, Tim was, in the final analysis, asked to move the desired incentive behind the room. Lana had never been trained to ask that something be moved from one point to another in space, and the technicians had never announced to her that they were going to move "something" from one point to another in space *except* their own bodies. To clarify this point, when Lana asks, TIM/SHELLEY/BEV MOVE INTO ROOM PERIOD, they usually respond, YES TIM/SHELLEY/BEV MOVE INTO ROOM PERIOD. And as stated earlier, Lana can ask that she be allowed to "move out-of room" or to be carried "out-of room" in order to be taken outdoors for play and exercise. Lana extrapolated, it would seem, that she could request that persons move materials from one point to another in space from having learned that she could ask that either they (e.g. their bodies) or she could be moved or transported through the formulation of specific requests. This conversation was repeated in essence on May 1, 2, and 7, as well as on several subsequent occasions. She remains very prone to use again and again novel linguistic expressions that result in the solving of problems.

Give Name-of This. On Monday, May 6, 1974, Tim began testing Lana on her skills in naming a bowl and a metal can in response to the question, *? WHAT NAME-OF THIS.* It was through the course of the three previous days and on Friday, May 3, in particular, that she had learned to assign their respective names. She had been enticed to learn their names in the following way: The receptacle was baited with M & M candies; when she named the receptacle correctly it was handed to her and she was allowed to extract them.

At 11:30 a.m. on Monday, May 6, Tim started to teach her the name of *box* (a small cardboard box) baited with M & M candies. The key for *box* was on her keyboard, but she had not been taught its meaning. The following conversation commenced at 11:36 a.m., with Tim holding the cardboard box in his hand and sitting in the anteroom facing his keyboard:

Lana:	*? Tim give Lana this can.* (Seemingly she was calling the "box" a "can.")	11:36 a.m.
Tim:	*Yes.* (And he gave her the empty can used in the initial sessions, though it seemed clear that she wanted the box with the M & M's.)	
Lana:	*? Tim give Lana this can.*	11:42 a.m.
Tim:	*No can.* (Which meant that Tim did not have the can to give to her as it had just been given to her.)	
Lana:	*? Tim give Lana this bowl.* (In this instance, it seemed that she was calling the "box" by a name appropriate to the second of the two previously used objects in naming-training.)	11:43 a.m.
Tim:	*Yes.* (And he gave her the empty bowl used in the previous sessions, which she promptly discarded.)	
Lana:	*? Shelley* (The sentence was not finished.)	11:43 a.m.
Tim:	*No Shelley.* (A way of saying Shelley was not present.)	
Lana:	*? Tim give Lana this bowl.* (Before Tim could answer, she continued . . .)	11:44 a.m.
	? Tim give Lana name-of this.	11:45 a.m.
Tim:	*Box name-of this.* (Thereby giving her the name of the vessel which she apparently wanted.)	
Lana:	*Yes.* (Quite interestingly, this is the response which technicians give when Lana does something correct.)	11:46 a.m.
Lana:	*? Tim give Lana this box.*	11:47 a.m.
Tim:	*Yes.* (Whereupon he gave it to her. She immediately ripped it open and extracted the M & M candies.)	

At 1:01 p.m. the same day, Tim presented Lana with another vessel, a cup, for which Lana at the time had no name. It, too, was baited with M & M candies. She first asked Tim for its name and then asked Tim for it by name—cup. Once again, it was observed that Lana was ready to transfer a newly acquired linguistic skill to a similar problem situation.

The primary significance of the foregoing conversation was that Lana came to ask that the name of something be identified and that she then used that information forthwith to ask that it be given to her. Though we had asked *her* many times to name things through the course of naming-training sessions, at no point had we trained her with this specific intent that she ask us to name something for her. She apparently abstracted from the many instances in which we had asked her to name things that she reciprocally might ask us for the names of things.

It should be noted that after Tim gave Lana the name of *box*, Lana commented, YES. As noted above, the technicians typically respond in that way whenever Lana is correct in her answers. (Though an interpretation of Lana's "intentions" in responding with YES immediately after being given the name, box, is problematic, it is suggested that this was the best way she had of saying, "That's what I wanted to know!")

Use of "to." On May 9, 1974, training commenced to introduce the use of the word "to," as a preposition to be placed before her name, which she had come to use as an indirect object. The word "to" was introduced in the following manner:

Tim:	*? Tim give can to Lana.*
Lana:	*Yes.* (And Tim gave the can to her.)

       ? Tim give bowl to Lana.
Tim: *Yes.* (And he gave it to her.)

Lana had been shown at this point the correct use of the word.

On the next day Lana was shown the use of "to" again. Tim initiated conversations with Lana involving its use. Lana was prone to ask correctly ? TIM GIVE BALL TO LANA; however, at times she did err and said, ? TIM GIVE LANA TO BALL PERIOD. On May 11 and 12 there were other short training sessions.

The first *spontaneous* and correct usage of "to" by Lana occurred on May 13. Lana was busy eating her monkey chow. Tim held up a ball where he stood in the anteroom, whereupon she asked:

Lana: *? Tim give ball to Lana.*
Tim: *Yes.* (And he gave the ball to her.)

All in all, not more than 30 minutes were necessary for Lana finally to use the preposition "to" on her own. From that point on it was the general rule that "to" was used prior to her name when it was used as an indirect object.

A Request for the Typical. Perhaps the first occasion in which Lana gave evidence that she had "missed" a common occurrence for the time of day was on May 20, 1974. The episode occurred just a few minutes before 9 o'clock. Tim had just finished cleaning Lana's room and she had not yet been fed. Tim had just left Lana's room and was sitting on the stool in the anteroom drinking his morning coffee. There was no milk present in the area when the following episode commenced:

Lana:	*? Tim move into room.*	8:58 a.m.
Tim:	*No.*	
Lana:	*? Tim give.*	8:59 a.m.
	? Tim give milk behind room.	8:59 a.m.
Tim:	*No give.* (Incorrect use of "give.")	
Lana:	*? Tim move milk behind room.*	9:00 a.m.
Tim:	*Yes.*	

Tim did go to the kitchen then and got milk for Lana, which she repeatedly worked for by asking PLEASE MACHINE GIVE MILK PERIOD. It is important to note that it was at this time of day that Lana normally obtained her milk.

Orange (Fruit) = the Apple which-is Orange (Color). Later in the same month, (May 28, 1974) Lana generated her first name for something she apparently wanted, but was handicapped in requesting it, because she had no name given to her for referring to it. The object was the fruit, orange, one of Lana's preferred fruits. At approximately 10:00 a.m., the following conversation transpired:

Tim:	*? What color of this.*	10:10 a.m.
Lana:	*Color of this orange.* (Which is certainly correct!)	10:11 a.m.
Tim:	*Yes.*	
Lana:	*? Tim give cup which-is red.* (This probably was an attempt to request the orange; however, in that there was a red cup which is part of her object/color naming materials, Tim responded—)	10:13 a.m.
Tim:	*Yes.* (Whereupon he gave her the cup, which she discarded.)	10:14 a.m.
Lana:	*? Tim give which-is shut.*	10:16 a.m.
	? Shelley give.	10:16 a.m.
Tim:	*No Shelley.*	10:16 a.m.
Lana:	*Eye.* (A frank error, probably.)	10:16 a.m.
	? Tim give which-is orange.	10:21 a.m.
Tim:	· *? What which-is orange.*	10:21 a.m.
Lana:	*? Tim give apple which-is green.* (Lana frequently confused the keys for the colors orange and green at this point in time.)	10:22 a.m.

Tim: *No apple which-is green.* (A way of saying, I have no green apple to give.)

Lana: *? Tim give apple which-is orange.* (Whereupon she bounded with   10:23 a.m. apparent enthusiasm to the door to receive "the orange-colored apple.")

Tim: *Yes.* (And he gave it to her.)   10:23 a.m.

This scenario was repeated three times with intervals of five minutes between them, during which time Tim left the room and Lana ate the orange, which had been given to her. On the three repetitions, however, Lana promptly asked for the orange as "the apple which-is orange" and did not make any of the errors recounted in the first portion of the above conversation. Once again, Lana carried forward for effective use a novel linguistic formulation that had proved effective in a problem-solving situation.

Lana subsequently asked for other things in ways that suggested that she had taken note of their most salient characteristics. For instance, when offered an overly-ripe banana, she asked for it as "the banana which-is black." Too, she had come to ask habitually for a coke when she saw the technicians drinking it; in response to one of them drinking a Fanta orange drink, she asked for "the coke which-is orange," the word "coke" probably referring to the bottle and with the phrase "which-is orange" reflecting the observation that the color was different from normal.

The One in the Bowl. On another occasion (January 23, 1975) Lana coped with the problem of asking for an orange in still other ways, revealed in the following conversation. Tim took an orange and put it into an orange-colored bowl so that Lana would not be able to ask for the orange fruit by color.

Lana: *Lana want eat ball which-is black.* (The use of black as a color was a   4:34 p.m. frank error.)

Tim: *? This ball which-is black.* (And he held up a black ball from the   4:35 p.m. object/color training set.)

Lana: *Lana want ball which-is orange.*   4:36 p.m.

Tim: (Tim then held up an orange ball from the object/color training set.)

Lana: *Lana want eat ball which-is orange.*   4:40 p.m.

Tim: *No eat ball which-is orange.* (A way of saying that ball is not to be eaten.)

Lana: *Lana want eat this* (pause) *in bowl.*   4:43 p.m.

It is suggested that when Lana responded, LANA WANT EAT BALL WHICH-IS ORANGE PERIOD, in response to Tim's holding up literally an orange ball, that Lana was attempting definition/naming of that which she wanted in terms of what she would do with it; i.e., she would *eat* it. It is further suggested that when Tim admonished her, NO EAT BALL WHICH-IS ORANGE PERIOD, in reference to literally an orange tennis ball, that Lana then shifted to defining that which she wanted by its location, *as well as* in terms of what she "intended" to do with it. This definition/naming of that which she wanted in terms of where it was and what she would do with it seems inherent in her last statement, LANA WANT EAT THIS (pause) IN BOWL PERIOD. Lastly, it is suggested that the pause noted in the generation of that sentence was time required for her literally to decide upon how it might be designated still another way.

We will consider more conversational materials and events later; however, in the interests of chronology, attention at this point will be shifted to other topics.

Training in Object and Color Naming

To further cultivate object- and color-naming skills, a set of training materials was devised that would allow for naming-training and -testing regardless of color, and vice versa. The materials selected were ball, box, can, cup, shoe, and bowl. Six of each item type were obtained and were colored blue, purple, red, black, yellow, and orange. In summary, the set of training materials consisted of six items, with each item being represented in six different color states, for a total of 36 items.

Lana was initially trained to name the objects regardless of color and then to give the color of the item regardless of its name in response to the questions, ? WHAT NAME-OF THIS PERIOD, and ? WHAT COLOR-OF THIS PERIOD, respectively. Correct responses would be cast (Items-name) NAME-OF THIS PERIOD, in the instance of object-naming and COLOR-OF THIS (color-name) PERIOD, in the instance of color-naming. Initial training was done with the objects hand-held by the technician and presented to her for inspection upon termination of the question for either object or color-naming.

Training in object-naming continued until Lana was able to perform at least 90% correct within a randomly sequenced list of the items for a total of 96 trials. Since guessing should produce correct choices only one sixth of the time, this was a very strict training criterion. Next, color-naming was instituted to a similar criterion. In the interests of objectification and experimental control, the objects were then photographed and projected on a screen, next to Lana's keyboard, so that a transfer test of her object/color naming skills might be conducted without the experimenter in Lana's room. That she had only minimal difficulty in correctly giving either the name or the color in response to the projected pictures of the items of the training set supports the conclusion that she perceptually equated physical objects with their projected images. Just as she perceptually equated the lexigrams on the projectors, which were at best facsimiles of the lexigrams embossed on the surfaces of the keys of her console, she perceptually equated the projected pictures of items with the physical equivalents thereof. Davenport and Rogers[22] had observed in their cross-modal studies that chimpanzees were able to use either high quality color or black-and-white photographs of objects for high-level haptic perceptual equating. "We can now conclude that apes can perceive a photograph of an object *at first sight*. In addition, the . . . study supports our earlier finding that in some animals a mediative/representational process does exist, even in the absence of verbal language; and this process permits the animal to match-to-sample across sensory modalities."[22]

During the summer of 1974, training was instituted to bring Lana to a point where she could give either the name or the color of an item projected on the screen in response to the appropriate question. Prior to this point, Lana excelled in giving either names or colors within the course of a session; however, she had difficulty in shifting sets from giving names to colors and vice versa. Details of this work are available elsewhere;[23] in brief, Lana succeeded in giving the object's name or its color with 80% proficiency on a randomly sequenced course of 180 trials.

At the suggestion of Susan Essock, training was instituted with more than one object present at a time in order to allow eventually for the asking of Lana to give either the name of an item designated by its color or the color of an object designated by its name. Specifically, with, for example, a blue box, a red can, and a black shoe laid out before her on a given trial, she might be asked to respond to "? What color of this shoe period," the answer to which would be "Color of this shoe black," and to respond to "? What name of this which-is blue," with "? Box name-of this which-is blue." Over the course of 180 test trials with *three* objects present, randomly selected for each trial, and with the question posed for color, Lana was 79% correct (17% = chance). On a subsequent test (36 trials) with *six* objects present, each item with its own distinctive color, Lana's performance accuracy *increased* to 89% correct. This improvement in performance was likely due to the fact that when the number of test items increased from three to six, Lana would first inspect the objects, as she had done when three objects were present on a given trial, then go to her keyboard and type out the first part of her answer, for example, "Color of this shoe—," and then visually check back before committing herself to the identification of the color of that shoe for that particular trial. In short, she introduced a *second* visual check as to the correct answer, something she had not done when only three items were present on a trial.

Lana was next asked to name an object of a specific color when either three or six different objects (each of different colors) were presented. She responded to the question, "?What name-of this which-is (color-name)," with, "(Object-name) name-of this which-is (color-name)." She was correct on 92% of the 36 test trials when three objects were present and 97% correct on the 36 test trials when six objects were present. As a final test, the questions, "? What name of this which-is (color-name)," and "? What color of this (object-name)," were randomly interspersed; Lana was 94% correct. Clearly, she could both differentiate between what was requested as well as correctly answer.

Cross-Modal Tests

The capacity of normal humans to judge sensory inputs from two or more sensory modalities for sameness/difference is remarkably excellent. Within reasonable error limits a human can, for example, judge a stimulus source as "an apple" regardless of whether it is seen, felt, tasted, or smelled. Within reasonable limits, the normal human can look at a stimulus—for example, a triangle—and select from two or more others the one that is most like the triangle seen. The ability to cross-modally perceive dimensions and degrees of sameness and difference are highly integrated in man and probably serves to help organize and to keep track of the events of a highly dynamic environment.

That a public, productive language is not a requisite to the mediation of certain cross-modal perceptions was demonstrated by Davenport and Rogers;[24] their apes were able to match one of two objects haptically sensed (palpated) with a sample that was visually accessible. In the last phase of their study, apes were able to select one of two haptically available novel stimuli so as to match the one visually accessible appreciably better than chance. They concluded that this experiment demonstrates the presence in apes of a meta-modal concept of stimulus equivalence that is based on a mediation process independent of verbal language.

We considered the question, "Might Lana's linguistic-type skills facilitate execution of cross-modal perceptions?" To answer this question, Lana was initially taught to respond "same" or "no same" to pairs of stimuli presented visually, half of which were comprised of identical stimulus members and half of which were comprised of qualitatively different stimulus members. Initially her response was to say "same" or "different," but problems in mastery of these responses resulted in shifting her response to "same" and "no same."

Next, Lana was trained and tested for her ability to identify the six objects that comprised her set of object/color materials: ball, box, can, cup, shoe, and bowl. She was taught to reach through a small hole in a box and to palpate the object present on a given trial and then to give its name in response to the question posed by the experimenter through the computer, ? WHAT NAME-OF THIS PERIOD.

Within 29 trials Lana had eliminated all errors in naming these familiar objects via haptic perception. Interestingly, the ball was correctly identified on its first presentation. Its uniform attribute of "roundness" perhaps made it the simplest of all, but that Lana was correct on naming even one correctly on the first presentation is probably significant.

The first cross-modal test of sameness/no-sameness (difference) was conducted with all possible pairings of the six objects named above presented for a total of 60 trials. On those trials, where a haptically sensed stimulus was compared with another one visually sensed, she was 92% correct. It should be noted that this was Lana's first true cross-modal test; there had been no extensive pretraining in cross-modal problems of the type employed by Davenport and Rogers in the first phase of their experiment referred to above. In phase I, the subjects of Davenport and Rogers had required a minimum of 1,000 trials to achieve a stated criterion of excellence prior to work in pahse II. Lana did initially that which took the apes trained by Davenport and Rogers several months to achieve. Note was taken of the fact, however, that for Lana the objects were both familiar and had names.

To assess the role of familiarity apart from names *qua* names, a set of 60 stimulus pairs was obtained from Dr. Davenport. As these materials were totally new to Lana, they were "nameless." Materials for constituting 30 of the pairs were held in reserve so that they would be totally novel at the time of cross-modal test. The materials for constituting the remaining 30 pairs were made available to Lana for handling and generalized nonspecific investigation morning and afternoon for two weeks prior to the conduct of cross-modal tests and for visual inspection (outside her room) 24 hours each day. In that test, with half the pairs being constituted of the novel items and half comprised of familiar items, and within each of those groups half the pairs being comprised of identical items and half of different items, Lana was significantly better (80% correct) when judging familiar objects than when judging novel objects (57% correct). Familiarity apart from names facilitated cross-modal perception.

In the next study we attempted to assess the degree to which names apart from familiarity *qua* familiarity facilitated cross-modal judgments of sameness/difference. In this study we used five foods for which Lana had names: M & M candies, bread, banana, apple, and monkey chow biscuits. All of these materials were very familiar to her, since she had asked for them hundreds or thousands of times through the course of the previous 18 months. It is important to note at this point that *whole* bananas and apples and whole pieces of bread were used as stimulus materials. Lana rarely, however, had obtained these three foods as whole units. Typically, she obtained them in small segments, a piece at a time, by asking, PLEASE MACHINE GIVE PIECE OF BANANA/APPLE/BREAD PERIOD, as the foods in turn were available to her. (She can see the vending devices for these materials and note whether pieces are or are not available). All possible combinations of these five foods were made for half the trials administered in this experiment. The other half of the trials were comprised through all possible combinations of five foods that were familiar but unnamed to Lana; they were orange, cabbage, carrots, cucumber, and sweet potato. These foods typically were manually given to Lana in wholes, rather than pieces.

There is room for argument as to whether Lana's experience with these two types of foods was really equivalent (some vended and others not) for the purpose of the present experiment. They were chosen, however, because they approximated our ideal stimulus set and because they were the only materials that we had that were all familiar, half of which were named and half unnamed.

On half the trials the pairs consisted of identical foods; on half the trials the pairs consisted of different foods. One member of the pair was presented visually on top of the box into which Lana reached with one hand to palpate the second member of the pair haptically. Lana was significantly better (88% correct) in judging all possible combinations of the five *named* foods than she was in judging all possible combinations of the five familiar but *un*named foods (63% correct). Although more work on this question is in order, these data support the contention that naming, apart from familiarity, facilitates the execution of accurate cross-modal judgments of sameness/difference.

In the next study, cross-modal pairs were comprised by drawing one named food and pairing it with one unnamed food. The question asked was, "If but one member of a pair of stimuli has a name, is cross-modal perception facilitated more if it is the one presented haptically than if it is the one presented visually?" The answer to that question proved to be a qualified "yes," for Lana did somewhat better (84% correct) on those trials where the haptically presented stimulus was the one with the name than she did on those trials where the stimulus presented visually was the one that had the name (72% correct). The answer is a qualified "yes," however, for the difference fell short of statistical significance.

Recent Conversations

The Bowl "of Chow". On November 18, 1974, for the first time and without specific training to do so, Lana asked for a bowl specified by what it contained to be moved "behind the room," presumably to have it loaded into the vending devices. Two bowls were present, an orange bowl, which was empty, and a green bowl, which contained the monkey chow that Lana normally was given in the late afternoon.

In the following conversation it will be observed that Tim did not honor requests simply because they were correct or simply because they had been successful in earlier times. He required of her that she in some manner request that a specific bowl be moved behind the room to the area of the vending devices. It will be noted that eventually Lana specified it as a "bowl of chow," though she had not had specific training thus to identify a container by its contents:

Lana:	*? You move chow behind room.*	3:08 p.m.
Tim:	*No.*	
Lana:	*? You move into room.*	3:08 p.m.
Tim:	*No.*	
Lana:	*? You move chow behind room.*	3:09 p.m.
Tim:	*No.*	
Lana:	*? You move chow into room.*	3:09 p.m.
Tim:	*No.*	
Lana:	*? You move chow out-of room.*	3:10 p.m.
Tim:	*No.*	
Lana:	*? You move into room.*	3:11 p.m.
Tim:	*No.*	
Lana:	*? You move behind room.*	3:12 p.m.
Tim:	*No.*	
Lana:	*Bowl name-of.*	3:13 p.m.
	Bowl name-of.	3:14 p.m.
	Bowl name-of this green.	3:15 p.m.
	Bowl name-of this green.	3:16 p.m.
	? You move behind room.	3:16 p.m.
Tim:	*No.*	
Lana:	*Bowl name-of.*	3:17 p.m.
	Bowl of in.	3:17 p.m.
	Bowl of this green.	3:18 p.m.
	? You move into room.	3:19 p.m.
Tim:	*No.*	
Lana:	*? You move—.* (She depressed the wrong key and erased.)	3:20 p.m.
	Bowl name-of this.	3:20 p.m.
Tim:	*Yes.*	
Lana:	*? You move bowl behind room.*	3:21 p.m.

Tim:	*? What bowl.*	
Lana:	*Bowl name-of this which-is orange.*	3:22 p.m.
	Bowl name-of this which-is orange.	3:22 p.m.
Tim:	*Yes.* (Note: an orange bowl was present, but it did not contain chow.)	
Lana:	*? You move bowl which-is green.*	3:23 p.m.
Tim:	*No.*	
Lana:	*Bowl name-of this which-is green.*	3:24 p.m.
Tim:	*Yes.*	
Lana:	*? You move bowl of orange.*	3:25 p.m.
	? You move bowl of chow.	3:26 p.m.
Tim:	*Yes.* (Whereupon he moved the bowl of chow behind the room and put the chow into the vending device.)	
Lana:	*Please machine give piece of chow.* (Repeatedly)	3:28 p.m.

On November 22, 1974, a related conversation transpired, influenced by the fact that eventually as Lana asked for chow to be moved behind the room, Tim delivered *one* piece to the vending device.

Lana:	*? You move chow behind room.*	5:20 p.m.
Tim:	*No.*	
Lana:	*? You move chow behind room.*	5:20 p.m.
Tim:	*No.*	
Lana:	*? You move behind room.*	5:21 p.m.
Tim:	*No.*	
Lana:	*? You move chow behind.*	5:22 p.m.
Tim:	(did not respond)	
Lana:	*? You move of.*	5:22 p.m.
	? You move bowl which-is orange.	5:23 p.m.
Tim:	*Yes.* (And he moved an orange bowl behind the room; but it was not the bowl that contained the chow.)	
Lana:	*? You move chow behind room.*	5:25 p.m.
Tim:	*No.*	
Lana:	*? You move chow behind room.*	5:25 p.m.
Tim:	*Yes.* (And he carried one piece of chow and put it into the appropriate vending device.)	
Lana:	*Please machine give piece of chow.* (Whereupon she obtained that one piece.)	5:26 p.m.
	? You move chow behind room.	5:26 p.m.
Tim:	*Yes.* (And again delivered one piece to the vending device.)	
Lana:	*? You move chow behind room.*	5:27 p.m.
Tim:	*Yes.* (And again delivered one piece to the vending device.)	
	? What name-of this. (Pointing to the bowl)	
Lana:	*Bowl name-of this.*	5:29 p.m.
	? You move bowl of chow.	5:29 p.m.
Tim:	*Yes.* (And he loaded several pieces into the device.)	
Lana:	*Please machine give piece of chow.* (Repeatedly.)	5:30 p.m.

Through the course of the foregoing exchanges, Lana eventually was rewarded for asking that "a bowl of chow" rather than just "chow" or a "bowl" be moved. On November 25, 1974, it was noted that Lana had carried forward her new skill of asking that "a bowl of chow" be moved behind the room:

Lana:	*? You move bowl of chow.*	4:04 p.m.
Tim:	*Yes.* (And the vending device was loaded.)	
Lana:	*Please machine give piece of chow.* (Repeatedly.)	4:05 p.m.

That Lana has become sensitive to the maximum word length she can employ is illustrated in the foregoing exchange: When "? You move chow behind room," did not work, the phrase "bowl of chow" was introduced. Its length, however, does not allow for the addition of "behind room" just prior to the "period," for that would make for a seven-word sentence in addition to the "?" and the "period."

On November 22, 1974, in still another way Lana specified what it was that she wanted to obtain:

Tim:	*? Lana want apple.*	
Lana:	*Yes.* (Whereupon Tim went to the kitchen and got one.)	12:41 p.m.
	You give this to Lana.	12:41 p.m.
Tim:	*? Give what to Lana.*	
Lana:	*? You give this which-is red.*	12:41 p.m.
Tim:	*? This.* (Tim held up a red piece of plastic as he responded.)	
Lana:	*? You give this apple to Lana.*	12:43 p.m.
Tim:	*Yes.* (And gave her the apple.)	

Lana might have said "yes" when offered the piece of plastic. She did not, but instead, requested that the "apple" be given to her.

Drink Milk; Eat Bread. On January 9, 1975, after having learned to respond to questions posed by Tim, "? Lana want drink" and "? Lana want eat" with either an appropriate liquid or food, it was observed that Lana improved upon an expression without being required to do so:

Lana:	*? You move milk behind room.*	9:11 a.m.
Tim:	*? Lana want drink.*	
Lana:	*Yes.*	9:11 a.m.
Tim:	*? What Lana want drink.*	
Lana:	*Lana want drink milk eat.*	9:12 a.m.
	.	9:12 a.m.
	? .	9:12 a.m.
	Lana want drink milk bread.	9:13 a.m.
	Lana want drink milk eat bread.	9:13 a.m.

In her last series of expressions it is observed that she first tagged on the word *eat* and then substituted for it the word *bread*, then finally added both words in correct sequence to the other words so as to compose the sentence "Lana want drink milk eat bread." On the next day, January 10, 1975, Tim again asked: ? LANA WANT DRINK PERIOD. Lana responded: LANA WANT DRINK MILK EAT BREAD PERIOD.

Sensitivity to Sentence Length. It should be noted that the foregoing sentence uses all six of the word positions available to Lana, apart from the word or marker afforded through use of the first projector ("?," Please, Yes, and No). We have had a number of instances where Lana seemingly truncates her statement in accordance with the number of word positions available for use. On January 15, 1975, for instance, Tim was sitting on the bench with Lana in her room and drinking his cup of coffee. Without specific stimulation to do so, Lana asked, ? YOU GIVE (then pushed the key for "coffee," but it malfunctioned; and she finished the sentence—) THIS WHICH-IS BLACK PERIOD. Tim responded YES and poured a little coffee on the bench for her. (It was his impression that she did not particularly appreciate having the coffee given to her that way. She did drink it, however.) After finishing the coffee she looked into his cup and then said, ? YOU GIVE CUP OF (then pointed alternately to the key for "coffee" and the key for "this" and then pressed the latter key to end the sentence—) THIS PERIOD. Tim responded YES and gave her coffee from his cup. The suggestion is that with the "coffee" key malfunctioning, it was not possible for Lana to ask for a "cup of this which-is black" within the limitations of a six-word sentence length. To compensate for this limitation, she pointed alternately between the coffee and the "this" key so as to equate the two or to define "this" as, in fact, "coffee." This rewrite is, perhaps, properly termed linguistically, a paraphrase or ellipsis, designed to cope with removing the ambiguity as to how the next coffee was to be given to Lana—that is, in a cup, not on the bench. (Note: We plan to increase the sentence length capacity to ten words.)

Put the Milk into the Machine. On January 24, 1975, Lana extended her linguistic efforts in still another interesting manner. The time was approximately 10:30 a.m., Tim was cleaning the interior of her room, and in all probability, Lana was quite hungry, for she had not yet been fed. The following exchange transpired:

Lana:	*Tim put milk in*—(At this point she stopped for about ten minutes and looked at her various keys, stopping occasionally at "cup" and "bowl," and also "behind" and "room." It was as though she did not know what the next word should be, that word being "machine").	10:25 a.m.
Tim:	*? What give milk.* (He used her keyboard).	10:26 a.m.
Lana:	(No response).	
Tim:	*? What give milk.* (To which again Lana gave no response, quite unlike her if she "knows" the appropriate answer. At this point Tim pointed to the key for "machine," which Lana depressed, and then finished the sentence with the two words "give" and "milk," so that the jointly produced sentence read "Machine give milk." At this point Tim left Lana's room to answer an outside call. As he returned he read—).	10:26 a.m.
Lana:	*Tim put milk in machine.*	10:27 a.m.
Tim:	*Yes.* (He did so, whereupon Lana asked repeatedly for the machine to vend milk.)	10:27 a.m.

In understanding this foregoing conversation it is important to note that on previous days Lana had been working on the task of describing actions affected by either Tim or Lana with a ball relative to a bowl or a box. Specifically, on some trials, Tim would take the ball and put it either in, on, or under a bowl or a box. Her task was then to describe what he had done with the ball. On other trials the ball was given to her, and she then was to describe what she had done with the ball relative to the bowl or the box. She has become very proficient with those materials, being correct in ten successive descriptions of the relation established between the ball and the box or the bowl by either herself or by Tim. Apparently she generalized that the word "put" could be used along with the preposition "in" to other, similar situations. This probability is suggested by her very first sentence, although incomplete, which said, "Tim put milk in. . . ." Also of probable significance is the fact that with the guidance of Tim as far as what the milk should be put into (that is, the "machine"), Lana learned, and in the final analysis correctly stated that which she probably "intended" to state in the very beginning.

Prevarication? The questions are frequently asked of us, "Does Lana ever lie?" and "Does Yerkish allow for prevarication?" We have no clear evidence that Lana has lied (Heaven forbid!), but we do have evidence that at times she has been clearly obstinate.

In the following instance of January 16, 1974, she refused to give the name of a very familiar object: the orange-colored box which was part of her extremely familiar object/color set of materials. In all probability she had given the information called for at least 200 times.

Tim:	*? What name-of this which-is orange.*	
Lana:	*Can.*	10:20 a.m.
Tim:	*? What name-of this which-is orange.*	

Lana:	*Color.*	10:21 a.m.
Tim:	*? What name-of this which-is orange.*	
Lana:	*Same.*	10:22 a.m.
Tim:	*? What name-of this which-is orange.*	
Lana:	*Cup.*	10:24 a.m.
Tim:	No. (At this point Tim was exasperated and took a break. He returned five minutes later with the same question.)	
Tim:	*? What name-of this which-is orange.*	10:29 a.m.
Lana:	*No name-of this bowl.*	10:31 a.m.
	No name-of.	10:31 a.m.
	. *No name-of this which-is orange.*	10:33 a.m.
Tim:	*No.*	
	Box name-of this which-is orange.	10:34 a.m.

Despite the fact that Lana even acknowledged that the object was "orange," she would not give its name. In still another instance (Dec. 12, 1974) Lana was asked to name an item for which she had no name, a key case. After having called it a ball once, in response to repeated questioning she responded simply, NO LANA GIVE PERIOD.

Use of "More." The introduction of the word "more" is portrayed in the following exchange, which occurred on January 31, 1975. Tim was holding a can of juice and a cup as he stood at his keyboard near the doorway to Lana's room:

Lana:	*? You put juice in cup.*	3:29 p.m.
Tim:	*Yes Tim put juice in cup.* (But he did not hand the cup to Lana.)	
Lana:	*? You give juice to Lana.* (Asking that the juice be given to her.)	3:30 p.m.
Tim:	*Yes.* (He gave it to her, and Lana drank all of it; Tim retained possession of the cup.)	
Tim:	*? Lana want more juice.* (The first introduction of the word "more.")	3:31 p.m.
	? Lana want more juice.	
Lana:	*Yes Lana want more juice in . . .* (did not finish sentence.)	3:32 p.m.
Tim:	*? More juice in what.*	
Lana:	*Lana want more juice in cup.*	3:33 p.m.
Tim:	*Tim put more juice in cup.* (And he did so, but the cup of juice was not given to her.)	
Lana:	*Yes you give juice to Lana.*	3:35 p.m.
	? You give Lana.	3:36 p.m.
	? You put more juice in cup.	3:37 p.m.
Tim:	*Yes Tim put more juice in cup.* (And did so.)	
Lana:	*? You give cup of juice.*	3:38 p.m.
Tim:	*Yes.* (And Lana drank all of the juice.)	
Lana:	*? You put more juice Lana.*	3:39 p.m.
Tim:	(Ignored this statement; syntax incorrect.)	
Lana:	*? You put more juice in cup.*	3:40 p.m.
Tim:	*Yes.* (And he put more juice in the cup.)	
Lana:	*? You give juice more cup.*	3:40 p.m.
Tim:	*No.* (The syntax was incorrect.)	
Lana:	*? You give juice to Lana.*	3:41 p.m.
Tim:	*Yes.* (And he gave it to her.)	
Lana:	*? You put juice more cup.*	3:42 p.m.
Tim:	*No juice more cup.* (That is not the way to say that.)	
Lana:	*? You put more juice in cup.*	3:42 p.m.
Tim:	*Yes Tim put more juice in cup.* (He put more juice in the cup, but the cup was not given to her.)	
Lana:	*? You give more juice to—*	3:43 p.m.
	? You give juice more.	3:43 p.m.
	? You give juice more.	3:44 p.m.
	? You put juice in machine.	3:44 p.m.

Tim:	*No.*	
Lana:	*? You put juice in cup.*	3:44 p.m.
Tim:	*Juice in cup.* (The cup was full, as more juice had been put in the cup as a result of a prior request.)	
Lana:	*? You give more juice to.*	3:45 p.m.
	? You give juice to Lana.	3:46 p.m.
Tim:	*Yes.* (And it was given to her to drink.)	

On February 3, 1975, Lana had her next session with the word "more."

Lana:	*Please you give cup of juice.*	5:00 p.m.
Tim:	*Yes.* (And gave her a cup of juice, which she emptied.)	
Lana:	*? You put coke in cup.* (No coke was present.)	5:00 p.m.
Tim:	*No coke.*	
Lana:	*? You put more juice in cup.*	5:01 p.m.
Tim:	*Yes.*	
Lana:	*? You put juice of.*	5:02 p.m.
	? You put.	
	? You give juice to Lana.	5:02 p.m.
Tim:	*Yes.* (Whereupon he gave her the juice to drink, though he kept possession of the cup.)	
Lana:	*? You give cup.*	5:03 p.m.
	? You give cup of juice.	5:03 p.m.
Tim:	*Yes.* (And he gave her the cup of juice to drink.)	
Lana:	*? You put more of.*	5:04 p.m.
	? You put more juice in cup.	5:05 p.m.
Tim:	*Yes.* (With the cup empty, then Tim put more juice into it as specifically requested by Lana.)	

On February 4, 1975, for the first time Lana asked for "more" of something to be put into the machine, another instance of her generalizing word usage appropriately. The time was in the morning, and she had had her first ration of milk through the machine and one piece of bread. It is important to note and to remember that during the following episode there was a pitcher of milk and a piece of bread in clear view near the vending devices "behind the room."

Lana:	*? You put bread in.*	9:31 a.m.
	Please machine give milk. (Whereupon Lana probably got a few drops of milk though the device was essentially empty.)	9:31 a.m.
	Please machine give milk.	9:32 a.m.
	? You put more bread in machine.	9:33 a.m.
Tim:	*Yes.* (And he did so, whereupon Lana asked repeatedly—)	
Lana:	*Please machine give piece of bread.*	9:34 a.m.
	Please machine give piece of bread.	
Lana:	*? You move into room.*	9:37 a.m.
Tim:	*No.*	
	? Lana want drink.	
Lana:	*Yes Lana want drink.*	9:38 a.m.
	? You move more bread in machine.	9:38 a.m.
Tim:	*No move more bread in machine.* (Incorrect syntax; also, there was no bread readily available to honor her request.)	
Tim:	*? You want drink.*	
Lana:	*Yes Lana want drink milk.*	9:39 a.m.
	? You move milk behind room.	
Tim:	*Milk behind room.* (Note the pitcher of milk had been there all this time.)	
Lana:	*Yes.* (Apparently acknowledging that it was.)	9:39 a.m.
	? You move. (Erased.)	9:39 a.m.

? You put more milk in machine.   9:40 a.m.
Tim: *Yes.* (Whereupon he put "more" milk into the machine. Lana then
         asked for it repeatedly from the machine.)

From this point on, Lana has become highly reliable in asking for "more" of
either milk or bread after she has already had her initial ration, e.g., only as the
vending devices once loaded become empty. Although this usage does not provide
any basis for concluding that Lana has a total comprehension as to what the word
"more" means in a relational sense, it does provide a basis for concluding that "more"
is something above and beyond the initial amount rationed to her on a given day or
within a given session of a day.

DISCUSSION

Without question, the specific training that was given Lana equipped her with
certain fundamentals for linguistic-type communication. That fact notwithstanding,
she acquired the most important, indeed critical, skills without the benefit of training
procedures implemented specifically to cultivate them. The record is also clear with
reference to her demonstrated ability to transfer information and to abstract from the
specific to the general.

In summary, Lana learned how to read the lexigrams. Without specific training to
do so, she perceptually equated the lexigram-facsimiles produced on the projectors
with the lexigrams embossed on the surfaces of the keys. Of all of the matters that
concerned us, none was greater than the one that she might never attend to and read
the projected images and the serial orders thereof as portrayed in the rows of
projectors—a requisite for communication with her. She developed sentence-
completion skills on her own, completing valid sentence beginnings and erasing
(rejecting) invalid ones initiated by the experimenter.

In terms of problem-solving efforts, Lana has used sentences specifically taught
her in ways not intended, for example, to ask the technicians to move behind the
room in the instances of equipment malfunction. More importantly, she has
composed new sentences that were quite appropriate to the problem as defined by the
context. For instance, from having learned that she could ask persons to move either
their own bodies or hers about in space, she generalized that she might ask for food
to be moved from one point to another.

With regard to naming-skills, the initial training was arduous; however, from that
training came forth a readiness to learn the names of other things—foods, drinks,
and objects—for which she had worked through the use of stock sentences taught her
by instrumental conditioning procedures. Through the course of naming-training she
came to use pronominal references—the word "this" as a referent for unnamed
objects, although that was not intended to be one of the benefits of that training.
Furthermore, she became facile in learning the names of newly presented objects/
events, for example, when she spontaneously named the projected image (slide) after
just having observed Tim request PLEASE MACHINE MAKE SLIDE PERIOD
through use of his keyboard. Not only has she requested that names be given for
unnamed objects, but she has assigned names to things and has specified things she
wanted by indicating what she would do with them if obtained, or where they were
located.

She also, and again without specific training to do so, introduced her own name
as the indirect object.

It bears restating that it was Lana who initiated the phenomenon of conversation
and the instrumental use of her language to solve problems of various types. Also,

she came to use the word "no" in protestation, whereas it has been taught to her specifically as one of two responses, "yes" or "no," in response to being questioned as to whether the door of her room or the window to the outdoors were open or closed.

Perhaps the most important observation is that Lana's language skills allowed us to learn that she could readily identify (give names of) familiar objects haptically sensed and to judge visual and haptic stimuli for their sameness/difference; she was able to perceive cross-modally and judge stimuli without the benefit of extensive training to do so. This finding, perhaps more than any other, supports the contention that the chimpanzee normally perceives its world in a manner quite similar to man. Thus, the perceptual world of the chimpanzee is probably highly integrated and coordinated.

We believe that the Lana Language Project has served to demonstrate that computer science can be incorporated both meaningfully and productively into research that bears upon our initial question, "Is the ape capable of human-type language skills?" Currently (March 1, 1975) Lana has a functional vocabulary of 80 words; as a rule, all keys are in an "active" state at all times. Although expansion of the vocabulary is surely an important dimension of the project, we have been primarily concerned that Lana acquire what we believe to be the conceptual use of words and combinations as they are introduced. Our experience has been that the acquisition of new words by Lana is a relatively simple matter. It is their interactional use with other words that is the challenge. Each of the word keys has been used hundreds of times correctly in sentences that now tax the length-of-sentence capacity of the system. One should not assume, of course, that she "understands" the meanings of each and every one of those words in the same way that we do (or as English equivalents!). The various conversations with Lana that have been recounted in this paper do serve to support the conclusion, however, that she must have conceptual meanings of many of them; otherwise, her productivity in conversations would not run as consistently as it does with regard to the topic of the moment.

Although we will never be able to understand absolutely the how and why of what Lana has mastered, it remains true that her data can serve to evaluate certain alternate views of language. It is our considered opinion, indeed, belief, that Lana has acquired skills that are very much involved in at least the rudiments of human-type linguistic communication. Lana has surpassed by several orders of magnitude the level of competence we initially held for her, or any chimpanzee, as we commenced this study program.

To the degree that Lana has excelled, we believe that we have support for the definition of language as cast at the beginning of this article: the foundations of language are to be found in the nature and processes of intelligence. Man is facile in language because of his high intelligence. Whereas the chimpanzee does not have intelligence sufficient to generate language-type communication systems, it is clear that it has sufficient intelligence to support covert language and to benefit from certain types of language-type training programs instituted by man.

We suspect that in the evolution of the higher primates (chimpanzees included), the basis for the eventual emergence of language-type communication in man was a type of intelligence sensitive to ordering, cataloguing, and eventually, through reasoning, to the interrelating of the attributes of things and events of the environment as perceived. We believe that intelligence inherently has those processing functions and that it is those functions which provide the readiness for the acquisition of language-type communication when it is as high as it is in man. In chimpanzee, intelligence is sufficient only to allow for rudimentary language-type communication, and then only if given special impetus through human intervention. The chimpanzee does not possess any genetically dictated biological template specific to language-type communication, not unless one wants to assume the improbable—that at one point in their history the chimpanzee did have language skills, but that they have now become vestigial and, in general, nonfunctional.

We believe that language projects with chimpanzees succeed because they have the intelligence level sufficient for the covert idiosyncratic generation of symbols. The generation of those symbols and the interactions of them are, we believe, the basic processes of language. The language-training projects serve primarily (though not *simply*) as the occasions by which, through various means, man and ape come to agree upon the symbolic referents of various stimuli/signals/signs/lexigrams/words. The *similarities* of their intellects allow them to do so, despite the fact that their respective *levels* of intelligence differ profoundly.[25,26]

Questions as to Lana's limits or the chimpanzee's limits for language-type skills should remain open for the foreseeable future. It would be unwise for anyone to conclude at this point in time that the ape is or is not incapable of mastering a given aspect of language skill.

Should these perspectives prove wrong, it still remains probably true that ways have been devised whereby at least a significant subset of mentally retarded human children can be assisted in the acquisition of language processes and studied to the end that we will better understand the essence of their language difficulties.

ACKNOWLEDGMENTS

We thank Mayvin Sinclair and Judy Sizemore for preparation of the manuscript. At the time of this paper, the team that works on the Lana Language Project consists of the senior authors of this paper: Professor Harold Warner, Professor Ernst von Glasersfeld, and Mr. Pier Pisani, co-investigators; Mr. Charles Bell, electronics technician; Professor Josephine V. Brown, consultant; and Mr. Michael Haberman, Ms. Shelley Pogue, and Ms. Gwen Dooley, behavior technicians. (April 14, 1975). Also, the continued interest and support of Dr. Geoffrey H. Bourne, Director of the Yerkes Regional Primate Center, is sincerely appreciated.

REFERENCES

1. GARDNER, B. T. & R. A. GARDNER. 1971. Two-way communication with an infant chimpanzee. *In* Behavior of Nonhuman Primates. A. M. Schrier & F. Stollnitz, Eds. Vol. **4**: 117–184. Academic Press, New York, N.Y.
2. PREMACK, D. 1971. On the assessment of language competence in the chimpanzee. *In* Behavior of Nonhuman Primates. A. M. Schrier & F. Stollnitz, Eds. Vol. **4**: 185–228. Academic Press. New York, N.Y.
3. FOUTS, R. 1973. Acquisition and testing of gestural signs in four young chimpanzees. Science **180**: 978–980.
4. RUMBAUGH, D. M., T. V. GILL & E. C. VON GLASERSFELD. 1973. Reading and sentence completion by a chimpanzee (*Pan*). Science 182: 731–733.
5. SALZINGER, K. Animal communication. *In* Comparative Psychology: a Modern Survey. D. A. Dewsbury & D. A. Rethlingshafer, Eds.: 161–198. McGraw-Hill Inc. New York, N.Y.
6. LIEBERMAN, P., D. H. KLATT & W. A. WILSON. 1969. Vocal tract limitations on the vowel repertoires of rhesus monkey and other nonhuman primates. Science 164: 1185–1187.
7. HEWES, G. W. 1973. Primate communication and the gestural origin of language. Current Anthropol. **14**(1–2): 5–24.
8. HOCKETT, C. 1960. The origin of speech. Scientific American 203: 88–96.
9. ALTMANN, S. A. 1967. The structure of primate social communication. *In* Social

Communication Among Primates. S. A. Altmann, Ed.: 325–362. The University of Chicago Press. Chicago, Ill.

10. CHERRY, C. 1961. On Human Communication: a Review, a Survey, and a Criticism. Science Editions. New York, N.Y.

11. STOKOE, W. C., D. CASTERLINE, & C. G. CRONEBERG. 1965. A dictionary of American sign language. Gallaudet College Press. Washington, D. C.

12. SEBEOK, T. A., A. S. HAYES & M. C. BATESON. 1964. In Approaches to Semiotics. Mouton. The Hague, The Netherlands.

13. WARNER, H., C. L. BELL, D. M. RUMBAUGH & T. V. GILL. 1975. Computer-controlled teaching instrumentation for linguistic studies with the great apes. IEEE Trans. Computers. In press.

14. BROWN, R. 1970. The first sentences of child and chimpanzee. In Selected Psycholinguistic Papers. R. Brown, Ed. Macmillan. New York, N.Y.

15. GARDNER, R. A. & B. T. GARDNER. 1969. Teaching sign language to a chimpanzee. Science 165: 664–672.

16. FOUTS, R. 1974. Language: origins, definitions and chimpanzees. J. Human Evolution 3: 475–482.

17. RUMBAUGH, D. M., E. C. VON GLASERSFELD, H. WARNER, P. PISANI, T. V. GILL, J. V. BROWN & C. L. BELL. 1973. A computer-controlled language training system for investigating the language skills of young apes. Behav. Res. Meth. Instrumentation 5(5): 385–392.

18. VON GLASERSFELD, E. C. & P. P. PISANI. 1970. The multistore parser for hierarchical syntactic structures. Commun. Assoc. Computing Machinery 13: 74–82.

19. VON GLASERSFELD, E. C. 1975. The Yerkish language for nonhuman primates. Am. J. Computational Linguistics. Microfiche 12.

20. LANCASTER, J. B. 1968. Primate communication systems and the emergence of human language. In Primates. P. C. Jay, Ed.: 439–457. Holt Rinehart & Winston. New York, N.Y.

21. GILL, T. V. & D. M. RUMBAUGH. 1974. Mastery of naming skills by a chimpanzee. Journal of Human Evolution. 3: 483–492.

22. DAVENPORT, R. K. & C. M. ROGERS. 1971. Perception of photographs by apes. Behaviour 39: 2–4.

23. GILL, T. V., S. ESSOCK & D. M. RUMBAUGH. 1975. Color and object naming skills of a chimpanzee. Paper presented at Soc. Res. Child Devel. Denver, Colorado.

24. DAVENPORT, R. K. & C. M. ROGERS. 1970. Intermodal equivalence of stimuli in apes. Science 168: 279–280.

25. RUMBAUGH, D. M. 1971. Evidence of qualitative differences in learning processes among primates. J. Comp. Physiol. Psychol. 76(2): 250–255.

26. RUMBAUGH, D. M. & T. V. GILL. 1972. The learning skills of great apes. J. Human Evolution 2: 171–179.

REFERENT COMMUNICATION IN SCHIZOPHRENIA:
THE PERSEVERATIVE-CHAINING MODEL*

Bertram D. Cohen

Rutgers Medical School
College of Medicine and Dentistry of New Jersey
Piscataway, New Jersey 08854

Disturbances in the use of language are often among the most convincing indications of a schizophrenic psychosis. Yet, as cryptic or disorganized as schizophrenic speech may sound, it rarely (if ever) includes hard instances of agrammatism or word-finding deficits. It is a disturbance of communication, rather than of language *per se;* its most dependable feature is that listeners find the patient's referents too elusive to grasp. Thus, measures of "communicability" are among the most effective discriminators of schizophrenic speech samples, such measures being clearly superior to measures of style, structure, or thematic content.[1] Accordingly, the emphasis in this paper is on disturbances of the referential process, itself: the process through which a speaker selects his utterances so as to make it possible for his listeners to know what he is talking about. I will also have something to say about the listener's process; that is, how the listener uses the speaker's utterance as a basis for identifying the speaker's referent.

Putting the issue this way requires that we have some grasp of the *normal* referent-communication process, one that would permit investigators to pinpoint components of the process as possible "loci" of schizophrenic disturbances. Previous investigators in this field have rarely paid much attention to the need for an explicit conception of normal referent communication, perhaps on the assumption that normal processes are so obvious that they can be taken for granted. In order to provide background for our own conception of normal and pathological referent communication, I will first review briefly the major approaches to schizophrenic language and thought and the normal referent communication processes that they imply.

A productive place to start is Bleuler's[2] 65-year-old analysis of schizophrenia as a cognitive disorder. Bleuler's theory dealt with "ideas" and "associations"—which were, of course, the popular concepts of the eighteenth and nineteenth century psychology. Ideas were psychological representations of objects and events, and associations were the relational "threads" that connected ideas. For Bleuler, associations came in two main kinds: *logical* and *autistic.* Bleuler believed that logical associations are the dominant forms of association in the normal adult. They occur more frequently than autistic associations and are, in effect, models of reality. Thus, if one's associations are predominantly logical, one is not likely to combine ideas in a bizarre, delusional, or incoherent manner. Autistic associations, by contrast, give rise to combinations of ideas that are likely to be analytically or empirically false. For Bleuler's normal adult, autistic associations are, in effect, held in check by the logical associations and intrude into thought—and through thought into speech—only during moments of high emotional stress.

With the onset of schizophrenia, the single crucial change was, for Bleuler, the "loosening" of the associations, a psychopathological process that he assumed to

*This work has been supported in part by NSF grant GS-40265. The research has been part of a program of studies on referential processes conducted in productive collaboration with my long-time friend Professor Seymour Rosenberg of Rutgers University.

attack principally the logical associations, with the result that the autistic associations are permitted freer access to expression.

Bleuler's theory can be viewed as a *hierarchic model* or as a *control model*. From the hierarchic viewpoint, the emphasis is on changes in the schizophrenic speaker's hierarchically ordered *repertoire* of associations insofar as the relative strengths of autistic associations have been increased. From the control point of view, the emphasis is, instead, on the schizophrenic speaker's loss of organizational control over his thought process; that is, the loosening of the logical associations diminishes the speaker's power to control associative *selection*. Under these conditions, one's thoughts become autistic in the sense that they are determined by fortuitous contiguities in experience or by partial or inessential similarities among ideas. It is important to note that the control model permits the same associations to be logical in one context but autistic in another. The control model emphasizes failure in a mechanism that selects contextually appropriate associations, whereas the hierarchic model emphasizes pathological changes in the repertoire, itself.

Contemporary "interference theories"[3] of schizophrenic deficit appear to be of the hierarchic type. These twentieth century conceptions speak of "responses" in place of ideas, and associations are seen as relations among responses (or between responses and stimuli). Broen and Storms,[4] for example, proposed a theory in which responses that are for the normal adult low in frequency of occurrence and contextually inappropriate, accrue larger relative strengths in the associative repertoires of schizophrenic patients and are therefore more likely to intrude into thought and language.

A difficulty with such hierarchic theories is that they equate the appropriateness of a given association with its relative dominance in the associative repertoire from which it is selected. Such a theory would require the normal adult to possess as many repertoires as there are contexts if he is to speak or think "appropriately." Aside from questions of parsimony, this type of conception also fails to consider the large diversity of situations in which an unusual association to a referent is recognized (by nonschizophrenics) not only as appropriate, but even as astute, witty, or creative.

In contrast to the Broen-Storms theory is the Chapmans'[5] dominant-response hypothesis. Whereas the Broen-Storms theory views schizophrenic performance in terms of the increased strengths of normally weak responses, the Chapmans view the schizophrenic patient as someone whose verbal behavior is unduly influenced by what are normally the *strongest* responses in his associative repertoire. This type of interference-by-dominant-associations conception is reminiscent of the theory proposed 35 years earlier by Kurt Goldstein[6] in which schizophrenic "concreteness" was seen as an inability to shift one's attention from some single, salient feature of a referent object, regardless of that feature's pertinence to the context in which it is perceived or communicated.

The Chapman and Goldstein theories are variations on a control model in the sense that they posit deficits in the patient's ability to resist interference from strong but inappropriate associations, meanings, or descriptions of a referent object. Presumably, normal adults are able to neutralize the power of such salient or dominant responses in order to scan their repertoires for responses that are more pertinent to the momentary context. But how do normals manage this? These theories may specify a normal outcome, but are silent about the process through which this outcome is achieved.

Sullivan[7] is quite unusual among theorists in this field in that, although lacking precision and detail, he did propose, explicitly, a conception of the normal speaker's referential process and then attempted to explain schizophrenic communication in terms of certain disturbances in the normal process. He postulated a self-editing process whereby a normal speaker pretests his utterances against an implicit "fantastic auditor" before saying them aloud to listeners. Insofar as this inner listener is an accurate representation of the speaker's real listener, the pretest helps the speaker edit out utterances that might prove too cryptic, misleading, or unacceptable to his actual listener. Schizophrenic speech, according to Sullivan, occurs either when the speaker fails to pretest his utterances altogether or when he pretests them against an invalid fantastic auditor; that is, one that fails to represent the actual listener realistically.

Although brief, I hope my reference to Bleuler and more recent investigators highlights the two principal ways in which disorders of referent communication are explained: disorders in the speaker's *repertoire* of associations, meanings, or descriptions of his referent, and disorders in the *selection* mechanism through which the speaker edits out contextually inappropriate (cryptic, ambiguous, or misleading) responses before they intrude into overt speech.

In the following sections I will (1) describe and illustrate an experimental paradigm for studying referent communication, (2) outline a theoretical model that accounts for behavior in these experimental situations and incorporates both repertoire *and* selection (self-editing) components, and (3) examine a number of studies designed to analyze schizophrenic speaker disturbances in terms of the model.

Experimental Paradigm

Our basic experimental situation has involved the presentation of an explicit set of stimulus objects to a speaker, with one of the objects designated as his referent. The speaker's task is to provide a verbal response so that his listener can pick out the referent from the set of objects. The listener's task is to identify the referent from the stimulus set on the basis of the speaker's response.

In early studies we used words as the referent and nonreferent objects. Speakers were shown pairs of words and instructed to provide a third word, one that neither looked nor sounded like either of the words in the stimulus pair, as a "clue" (referent-response) for his listener. Although artificial, this use of single-word responses and single-word referent stimuli permitted us to take advantage of word-association norms in order to estimate certain quantitative properties of the associative repertoires from which speakers selected responses in this situation. It should be clear, however, that the use of the paradigm is limited neither to verbal stimuli nor to single-word speaker-responses; our later studies involved nonverbal referent objects and speakers' responses that consisted of continuous discourse.

The data shown in TABLE 1 were obtained in an early exploratory application of the paradigm with 18 speaker-listener pairs. The table includes the speaker-response distributions from three word-pairs. For any given word-pair, the speaker provided a clue word for a listener who was seated facing away from him in the same room. In each instance, the speaker was shown the word-pair with the referent word underlined, and the listener was shown the same word-pair but with neither word underlined. His task was to indicate to the experimenter, by pointing, his choice of the referent upon hearing the speaker's response.

We found synonym pairs to be especially instructive because many of the responses associated with the referent in such word-pairs are likely to overlap with responses to the nonreferent, thus accentuating a contextual factor that the speaker must confront if he is to communicate effectively; that is, if he is to avoid "overincluding" the nonreferent. The distributions of speakers' responses shown in the table are representative of results obtained for pairs of synonyms.

The content of many of the responses to these high-overlap word-pairs reflects the speaker's specific relationship to his listener. That is, the fact that speakers and listeners were self-selected pairs (in this pilot study) from the same college subculture, geographical region, and era probably made possible the effective use of such responses as *academic* and *riders* to FREEDOM: or *queer* to the referent GAY—a pejoratively toned association that would surely be less in evidence among similar college students today. Other more individualized examples are the response *Fromm* to FREEDOM by a speaker who was, at the time, enrolled in the same Psychology of Personality course as her listener; and the response *Fritz* to COMMAND by a speaker who belonged to the same fraternity as his listener, a fraternity that included a member nicknamed "Fritz, the Commander." Such responses were much less frequent when the listeners were strangers to the speaker.

TABLE 1

SPEAKER-RESPONSE FREQUENCIES AND LISTENER ERRORS IN SAMPLE PROTOCOLS
FROM EIGHTEEN SPEAKER-LISTENER PARIS
(WORD-COMMUNICATION TASK)

Freedom-Liberty*			Command-Order			Gay-Cheerful		
academic	2		general	3	(1)	queer	5	
rider(s)	2		hair	2		Ben	1	
bondage	1		allied	1		exhilarated	1	
bus	1		army	1		fairy	1	
circus	1	(1)†	chain	1		happy	1	
democracy	1		cigarette	1		homo	1	
four	1		direct	1	(1)	homosexual	1	
Fromm	1		exclamation	1		joyful	1	
jail	1	(1)	force	1		light	1	
land	1		Fritz	1		liquor	1	
nondetermined	1		hunger	1		lively	1	(1)
sexual	1		military	1		Paris	1	
slave	1		official	1		party	1	
slavery	1		short	1		wild	1	
speech	1	(1)	tell	1				
unchained	1							

*The first word in each pair was the referent.
† Number of responses that led to listener errors are shown in parentheses.

Although, as indicated, a number of the speaker responses reflected special features of the interpersonal relationships between speakers and listeners, it was also clear that the speakers' repertoires of associations to any given referent were similar enough to those of other "normal adults" in the same general linguistic community to be adequate to communicate most (if not all) of the 149 referents that were used in this exploratory study. In fact, Rosenberg and Cohen[8] later confirmed the hypothesis that all but a very small proportion of the speakers' responses to the referents in these word-pairs can also be found in word-association distributions obtained using the referent words alone in standard free word-association tests. There is, however, an important difference between the speaker-response distributions and those obtained from free word-association; the proportions of responses of any given "type" are often drastically changed. This is because the speaker's selection of a response from his repertoire of associations to the referent takes into account the associative strengths of the response-word both to the referent and to the nonreferent. Thus, a response that is a strong associate of the referent is not likely to show up as a popular speaker-response if it is also a high-frequency associate of the nonreferent. By contrast, a weak or unusual associate of the referent might be used given that the speaker happens to "think of it" and that its relation to the nonreferent is even more tenuous. From the listener's side, the results suggested that the listeners' choices also were functions of the relative associative strengths linking the speaker's response to referent and nonreferent; listeners' errors were more likely to occur when these differences were small or actually favored the nonreferent, as sometimes happened.

On the basis of these observations we constructed and then tested formal models of speaker and listener processes in which quantitative parameters were estimated from large-group word-association and speaker-response norms. Mathematical versions of these models have been published.[8,9] Further tests and extensions of the theory have been made with a variety of nonverbal referent stimulus displays, including facial expression photographs,[10] snowflake designs,[11] fictitious animal drawings[12] in studies of young children, and Munsell colors[13] in our later studies of schizophrenia.[14,15]

THEORY OF REFERENT-COMMUNICATION PROCESSES

The speaker process, as shown in the diagram, is assumed to consist of a two-stage process in which the stages are termed *sampling* and *comparison*. When confronted with a display containing referent and nonreferent objects, the model assumes that the speaker begins by sampling a response from his repertoire of linguistic units associated with the referent. (The "units" may be names, descriptions, meanings, word-associations, and so on, depending upon the demands of the particular setting.) The speaker's repertoire usually contains many possible responses to any given referent, and the probability that any given response will be sampled is proportional to the strength of its association with the referent alone. For example, when single-word referent and nonreferent stimulus displays were used, it was shown that the probability with which a speaker-response is sampled can be estimated by its relative frequency as a free word-associate of the referent.[8] However, having sampled a response, the speaker does not necessarily emit it; the probability of emission depends, instead, on the second, or comparison, stage which follows the sampling stage (FIGURE 1).

In the second stage, the speaker implicitly compares the associative strengths of his sampled response to referent and nonreferent objects. The conditional probability that the speaker will emit (or reject) the sampled response is determined by its relative associative strength to referent and nonreferent stimuli. The stronger the association with the referent, relative to the nonreferent, the higher the probability that the speaker will emit the sampled response in order to communicate the referent. If, instead, its associative strength to a nonreferent is similar to, or larger than, its association with the referent, the sampled response will more probably be rejected and the entire two-stage cycle repeated. That is, the speaker again samples, compares, and either emits or recycles-and-repeats the two-stage process. Ultimately, a response is sampled, "passes" the comparison-stage test, and is expressed, thus terminating the speaker's referential process.

The process for the listener is considered to be essentially similar to the speaker's comparison-stage in that, given the speaker's emitted response, the probability that the listener will correctly choose the referent is also determined by the relative associative strengths of the speaker's response to referent and nonreferent objects.

This correspondence between speaker- and listener-comparison highlights the speaker's comparison-stage as a self-editing function in which the speaker implicitly takes the role of listener in order to pretest the communicability of his utterances prior to their emission (or rejection) in interpersonal communication. It is important, therefore, that speaker and listener share substantial portions of their referent-response repertoires if accurate and fluent referent communication is to be maintained.

Our conception of the speaker's comparison stage as a self-editing function in which the speaker implicitly projects himself into the listener's role has antecedents not only in Sullivan's[7] "fantastic auditor" construct, but also Piaget's[16] conception of socialized (nonegocentric) speech, Mead's[17] "generalized other," and Vygotsky's[18] theory of the process through which inner speech is transformed into external speech.

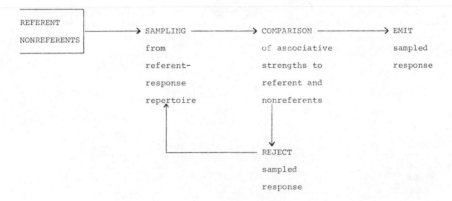

FIGURE 1. Diagram of the two-stage normal speaker's referential process.

EXPERIMENTS WITH SCHIZOPHRENIC PATIENTS

In our first study (Cohen & Camhi, 1967[19]) 72 hospitalized schizophrenic patients were assigned randomly to speaker or listener roles in the word communication task, as were the same number of normal hospital employees.† Each of the speakers was shown a list of word-pairs and asked to provide clue-words that would later be delivered to an individual listener. The design was such that four speaker-listener groups were assembled: (1) schizophrenic speakers with schizophrenic listeners, (2) schizophrenic speakers with normal listeners, (3) normal speakers with schizophrenic listeners, and (4) normal speakers with normal listeners.

The results, given in TABLE 2, are for communication accuracy, the average proportion correct referent choices by the 18 listeners in each of the four speaker-listener combination groups.

---

† In each experiment to be reviewed, the schizophrenic and control groups were comparable in age, education, and gender, and, unless otherwise stated, patients were under maintenance dosages of tranquillizing medication.

These results indicated that (1) the schizophrenics were inferior to normals in the speaker role; (2) there was no significant difference between the schizophrenics and normals in the listener role; and (3) there were no special interactions between speaker- and listener-diagnosis; for example, schizophrenic speakers achieved no better accuracy in communication with schizophrenic than with normal listeners.

How might one account for the specific schizophrenic deficit in the speaker role? In terms of the theory, one could attribute a speaker deficit to the sampling stage of the two-stage speaker-process on the assumption that the associative repertoires from which schizophrenic patients' sample are deviant, a hypothesis that is consistent with the findings of many studies of free word-association in schizophrenia.[3] However, if deviant associative repertoires were crucial to the schizophrenic speaker deficit, one would also expect a schizophrenic listener deficit because listeners' choices are determined by the same associative strengths that determine speakers' sampling probabilities. Therefore, the failure of the findings to indicate a schizophrenic listener deficit tends to contradict the hypothesis that schizophrenic speakers' deficits are due to deviant sampling repertoires.

An alternative interpretation implicates the speaker's comparison stage as the locus of the schizophrenic deficit. If schizophrenics are unable to make the requisite comparison of associative strengths, their self-editing decisions would be faulty,

TABLE 2

COMMUNICATION ACCURACY: AVERAGE PROPORTION CORRECT REFERENT CHOICES IN EACH SPEAKER-LISTENER GROUP*

| | Listeners | |
Speakers	Schizophrenic	Normal
Schizophrenic	0.66	0.67
Normal	0.72	0.74

*From Cohen & Camhi.[19]

leading to the emission of poor speaker-responses. Here, too, however, the relative adequacy of the schizophrenic listeners' performance suggests that the speakers' abilities to make these comparative judgements were also intact, since the listener's comparison process is formally identical to the speaker's comparison stage.

Another way to implicate the speaker's comparison (or self-editing) stage derives from the conception of the speaker role as a two-stage process in which comparison is combined with sampling, and, in contrast, the listener role is a one-stage process involving comparison only, the sampling having been accomplished for the listener by his speaker. Thus, faulty integration of the comparison stage with the sampling stage rather than faulty comparison, *per se,* might be responsible for the schizophrenic speaker deficit. This hypothesis was tested in two follow-up studies.

In one of these experiments, Nachmani and Cohen (1969)[20] used recall and recognition tasks as analogs of the speaker and listener roles in referent communication. This analogy was based on the Rosenberg-Cohen[8] theory that recall involves a two-stage process similar to the speaker model and recognition, a one-stage process similar to the listener model; and the results of the experiment were indeed parallel to the Cohen-Camhi speaker and listener results; schizophrenic patients were inferior to controls (nonpsychotic psychiatric patients) on the recall, but not on the recognition tests. These findings were interpreted as support for the hypothesis that faulty self-editing is responsible for schizophrenic deficits whether in recall or in speaker-communication tasks.

Further evidence of the culpability of the speaker's self-editing stage was provided by the results of a second experiment, by Lisman & Cohen (1972),[21] in which a word-association task was used as an analog of the speaker role. Lisman and Cohen reasoned that the occurrence of deviant word-associations by schizophrenic subjects, compared to normals, could be explained by either a one-stage or a two-stage model of the process through which individuals find and emit responses in (free response) word-association tests. The one-stage model involves only a sampling stage, and deviant performance by schizophrenics is attributed to deviant associative (sampling) repertoires. According to the two-stage model, the process starts with a sampling stage in which the subject samples a potential response from his repertoire of word-associates of the stimulus word; then, in a self-editing stage, the sampled response is compared with criteria of appropriateness supplied by the subject himself as in free word-association, or by an experimenter, as in controlled word-association (Rothberg, 1967).[22] The outcome is a decision to emit or reject the sampled response (and then resample, etc.), depending upon how appropriate it is to the relevant criterion. Thus, deviant word-associations can occur despite the presence of a nondeviant repertoire, the deviancy attributable instead to faulty self-editing during the two-stage process.

In the Lisman-Cohen experiment, schizophrenic and normal subjects were administered word-association tests under standard and controlled conditions. In the controlled condition, the subjects were to respond with a word they believed other people would *not* be likely to think of as an associate of the stimulus word. The point of these instructions was to pit the self-editing stage against the tendency of the sampling stage to favor common—but now inappropriate—associations.

The results showed that the normals were much better able than the schizophrenics to edit out common responses under the controlled instructions. In fact, the patients' word-associations under this condition were *more common* than the normals', although they were more deviant under the standard word-association conditions. The results confirmed predictions from the two-stage model and clearly favored a faulty self-editing hypothesis in contrast to one that posits a deviant sampling repertoire as the basis for schizophrenic responses in word-association tasks.

The evidence reviewed so far tends strongly to implicate the self-editing stage as the locus of the schizophrenic speaker deficit. Aside from the original Cohen-Camhi experiment, however, the follow-up studies described above were only indirectly related to referent communication. Accordingly, an experiment involving the direct use of a referent-communication task was designed (Cohen et al.[14]) in which the demands placed on the speaker's self-editing function were systematically manipulated. Also, the experiment involved communication via continuous discourse. This permitted a more detailed analysis of the speaker disturbance than was possible in any of the prior studies where the subjects had been limited to single-word utterances.

The stimulus materials were sets of Munsell color discs that were presented to individual speakers with one of the discs in a given display designated as the speaker's referent. The sets of colors varied in hue similarity (and number), the point being thus to manipulate the self-editing requirements of the displays; since colors similar in hue tend to evoke overlapping descriptions, the more similar (and numerous) the displays, the more rigorous the self-editing requirements placed on the speaker.

The speakers were 24 acute, nonparanoid schizophrenics not on medication at the time of the experiment and 24 normal hospital employees. In order to measure

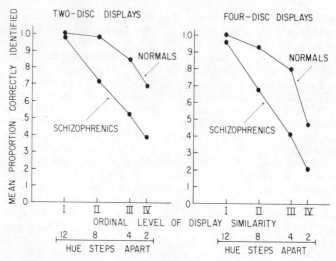

FIGURE 2. Communication accuracy: mean proportion of referents correctly identified by the listener panel. (By permission of the publisher of J. Abnorm. Psychol.[14])

communication accuracy, a panel of 24 normal listeners who had not served in the speaker role were given, via audio-tape recordings, the speakers' color-descriptions together with the appropriate stimulus displays. The communication accuracy results are shown in FIGURE 2.

It is apparent that both groups of speakers achieved progressively poorer communication accuracy with increases in the self-editing requirements of the displays and that this drop-off was clearly much sharper for the schizophrenics (who showed little or no deficit when display similarity was minimal). These results confirmed the hypothesis that schizophrenic speakers suffer from a self-editing deficit. Further analyses of the speakers' responses were then made with the aim of specifying the nature of this malfunction.

Three different models of the self-editing malfunction were considered. I will outline and then evaluate each of them in turn by reference to certain quantitative properties of the speakers' responses.

The first hypothesis, termed the *Tower of Babel Model*, reconsiders the notion that schizophrenic speakers base their comparison-stage decisions on idiosyncratic associative strengths, at least in situations in which culturally dominant responses (the common color names in this experiment) are inadequate. This model is similar to Sullivan's conception that schizophrenic speech lacks "consensual validity" insofar as the patient pretests his utterances against an idiosyncratic, rather than a socially representative, "fantastic auditor." The fantastic auditor functions for normals as an internal representation of cultural referent-response norms. If the schizophrenic speaker pretests his responses, instead, against idiosyncratic referent-response norms, he may go through the same two-stage response-selection process as do normals but nevertheless fail to communicate accurately to other persons. However, his message should be meaningful to himself; that is, if he served as listener to his own speaker responses he should have no more difficulty in identifying his referents than would a normal speaker who was asked to identify *his* own referents on the basis of his (the normal's) speaker-role descriptions. A strong case could be made for the Tower of

Babel Model if instead of the imparied communication accuracy scores found when the listener panel was used, the patients showed levels of accuracy equal to the normals when each speaker served as his own listener.

This hypothesis was tested by placing each speaker in the listener role and feeding back to him his own speaker-role descriptions a week after he had served in the speaker role.

The self-accuracy findings shown in FIGURE 3 disconfirm the Tower of Babel Model. The results were similar to those obtained with the independent listener panel. That is, the schizophrenic speaker deficit was found even when the speakers served as their own listeners.

The second hypothesis is called the *Impulsive Speaker Model*. It asserts that schizophrenic speakers fail to self-edit altogether. In Sullivan's terms, the patient functions without a "fantastic auditor" to modulate his utterances prior to their overt expression. In our terms, the patient samples from a nondeviant repertoire and emits responses without going through a self-editing stage. Such a truncated one-stage (sampling, only) model implies that the speaker's descriptions of a referent will be independent of the contextual constraints provided by the nonreferents from which it is to be distinguished. Thus, if the speaker samples the common color name—the most probable referent description in this experiment—he will emit it regardless of its "overinclusion" of the nonreferent. This will produce a steep drop-off in communication accuracy (to self or others) with increases in display similarity, a prediction that is consistent with the results shown in FIGURES 2 and 3.

The Impulsive Model also has implications for two other properties of the speaker's responses: utterance length and response time. Normal speakers usually increase the lengths of their color descriptions as display similarity increases.[23] This is because the typically short common color name will not distinguish the referent color under high or even moderate levels of display similarity and will probably be replaced by longer and more elaborate forms of description, if the speaker intends to communicate accurately to listeners. In addition to utterance length, normal speakers

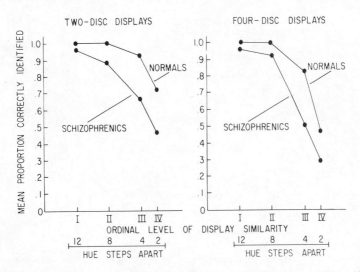

FIGURE 3. Communication accuracy: mean proportion of referents correctly identified by the speaker himself. (By permission of the publisher of J. Abnorm. Psychol.[14])

will also increase their response times (the time between the presentation of a display and the initiation of a description) as display similarity increases. This is because the more similar the colors, the more likely will the speaker need to recycle a number of times before sampling a discription that "passes" the self-editing stage and is emitted.

In contrast to these expectations for normal (two-stage process) speakers, Impulsive Model speakers should show no such progressive similarity-induced increases either in utterance length or response time, since their referent descriptions are not influenced by a self-editing stage.

The results for utterance length and response time were as shown in FIGURES 4 and 5. Clearly, the data disconfirm the Impulsive Speaker Model as an explanation of these patients' self-editing impairments. Not only do the findings show no evidence of insensitivity to the display similarity variable, but instead, the patients' progressive increases in both measures *exceeded* those of the normal speakers. Possibly, the patients were trying harder to communicate but succeeding less.

The third hypothesis is termed the *Perseverative Speaker Model.* According to this model, the speaker samples from a nondeviant repertoire and engages in normal editing-stage activity, but continually resamples the same inadequate response after each rejection of it. Ultimately, because of the probabilistic nature of the comparison stage, the response is emitted. Looked at in terms of this model, the schizophrenic speaker's "fantastic auditor" might be depicted as accurate but impotent; his vetos are astute, but he cannot make them stick.

This implicit perseveration hypothesis is related to the "disattention deficit" conception proposed by Cromwell and Dokecki,[24] who viewed schizophrenic patients as deficient in the ability to "disattend from" a stimulus after having attended to it. In the present context, this is analogous to a speaker's inability to ignore a sampled-and-rejected response.

The data needed to evaluate the Perseverative Speaker Model are those already presented in FIGURES 2–5. The Perseverative Model entails the same predictions as the Impulsive Model with respect to communication accuracy (FIGURES 2 and 3) and utterance length (FIGURE 4) but is different with respect to response time (FIGURE 5).

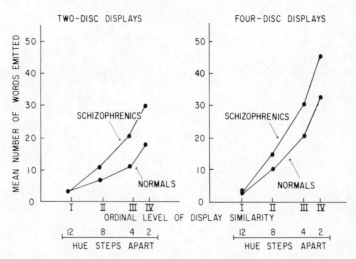

FIGURE 4. Mean length of a description. (By permission of the publisher of J. Abnorm. Psychol.[14])

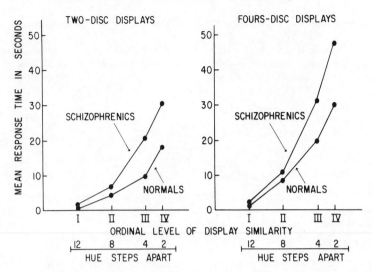

FIGURE 5. Mean time between the presentation of a display and the initiation of description. (By permission of the publisher of J. Abnorm. Psychol.[14])

For communication accuracy, the Perseverative Model calls for the same progressively steeper-than-normal decrements with increasing display similarity, as did the Impulsive Model. That is, since according to both models, the common color description is the one most likely to be sampled and (ultimately) emitted, regardless of the nonreferents in the display, the predictions from both models are consistent with the sharp drops in schizophrenic communication accuracy shown in FIGURES 2 and 3.

A second prediction from this common feature of the Impulsive and Perseverative Models, the emission of the initially sampled response regardless of the nonreferents in the display, is that utterance lengths will not change with increases in display similarity. The findings (FIGURE 4) clearly disconfirmed this prediction from the Perseverative Model for the same reasons given above for the Impulsive Model; the schizophrenic speakers gave progressively even longer descriptions than the normals, with increases in display similarity.

Because of its inclusion of an active (even if ineffectual) self-editing stage, the Perseverative Model, in contrast to the Impulsive Model, predicts progressive increments in response time with increases in display similarity, a prediction that is quite consistent with the results shown in FIGURE 5. With respect to response time, therefore, the Perseverative Model is superior to the Impulsive Model as an account of these schizophrenic speakers' self-editing problems and, were it not for their exaggerated increments in utterance length, the Perseverative Model would account adequately for all findings.

What is the source of the schizophrenic speakers' abnormally protracted descriptions? At this juncture it will prove helpful to examine some examples‡ from the

‡ Additional speaker protocols can be obtained by writing to the author.

speaker-response protocols of both groups with an eye to the composition of the longer schizophrenic descriptions.

The following descriptions were typical of those produced under conditions of minimal challenge to the speakers' self-editing stage—a two-disc, low-similarity display in which the referent, a purple blue, was 12 Farnsworth-Munsell hue steps from a red nonreferent.

> Normal Speaker 1: "Purple."
> Normal Speaker 2: "Purple."
> Normal Speaker 3: "This is purple blue."
>
> Schizophrenic Speaker 1: "Blue."
> Schizophrenic Speaker 2: "Purple."
> Schizophrenic Speaker 3: "The bluer."

The appropriateness of the schizophrenic responses and their comparability to the normal responses is consistent with either the Impulsive or the Perseverative Models. Both predict that the common color names will be the most likely to be given by the schizophrenics. At the same time, these responses are highly acceptable to normal speakers in this low-similarity situation.

By contrast, the following examples, produced by the same normal and schizophrenic speakers, were typical of those given under conditions in which the speaker's self-editing stage was subjected to much more rigorous challenge. These were descriptions of a red referent in a display containing a highly similar (slightly yellower) nonreferent two hue steps distant.

> Normal Speaker 1: "Both are salmon colored. This one, however, has more pink."
> Normal Speaker 2: "My God this is hard. They are both about the same except that this one might be a little redder."
> Normal Speaker 3: "They both are either the color of canned salmon or clay. This one here is the pinker one."
>
> Schizophrenic Speaker 1: "A fish swims. You call it a salmon. You cook it. You put it in a can. You open the can. You look at it in this color. Salmon fish."
> Schizophrenic Speaker 2: "This is the stupid color of a shit ass bowl of salmon. Mix it with mayonnaise. Then it gets tasty. Leave it alone and puke all over the fuckin' place. Puke fish."
> Schizophrenic Speaker 3: "Make-up. Pancake make-up. You put it on your face and they think guys run after you. Wait a second! I don't put it on my face and guys don't run after me. Girls put it on them"

The examples bear out the impression that the normal and schizophrenic protocols became increasingly different both in length and in content as display similarity was increased. As the self-editing demands increased, both groups complained about the difficulty of the discriminations required. The normals' comments, however, remained pertinent to the task, and their utterances retained the character of coherent color-descriptions even for the most challenging displays. One frequent normal-speaker tendency was to describe a nonreferent in order to exclude it; another was first to express a common color-name—for example, "salmon"—and then, after noting its overinclusive character, shift to other units of description that particularized the referent disc; for example, ". . . more pink" or ". . . a little redder."

Although initial units of the schizophrenics' descriptions often consisted of the same overinclusive common response to the referent as the normals', later units appeared to be drawn instead from associations to prior components of the strings resulting in chains of loosely connected elements rather than coherent descriptions. Perhaps the single most distinctive feature of the schizophrenics' long utterances was this tendency to disconnect from the referent. The objective referents (the discs) were replaced by references mediated through a bewildering variety of intraverbal associations. In addition, the content of the patients' utterances reflected feelings of frustration in the face of difficult challenges to their self-editing capabilities. The normals' difficulty-comments were more specific and were usually followed by a separate attempt at description. The patients were more prone to react with implicit anger which then "colored" their descriptions. For example, one patient, after commenting on the sameness of the colors in a high-similarity display, warned the listener "not to be fooled," then alluded to the referent as "full of tricks" and to the nonreferents as "liars" and "punks" who are "scared shit" and "yellow."

Whether they were associations to prior words or to feelings, these *responses,* rather than the referents, came to serve as the major source of the schizophrenics' verbal excess. An adequate model of the schizophrenic speaker deficit would need to include this switch in the source from which the speaker samples new responses.

The Perseverative-Chaining Model

This model is identical to the Perseverative Model but with the addition of a two-stage "chaining" process. The chaining process begins immediately after the initially sampled—and implicitly perseverated—response has either been emitted or terminated without express verbalization. In either case, in the chaining process, the speaker (1) samples each new response from a repertoire of verbalizations associated with a just prior response rather than with the referent, (2) expresses the sampled-but-rejected responses overtly, and (3) continues to sample and reject in this overt fashion until a response passes the probabilistic self-editing stage and the patient stops talking.

The implicit perseverative process accounts for the schizophrenics' increments in response latency and the overt chaining process accounts for the abnormal increments in utterance length, both under conditions requiring increasingly rigorous self-editing. The key assumption with regard to the perseverative process is the schizophrenic's inability to reject a sampled response, or, at least, to make the rejection stick. As mentioned earlier, this is analogous to the "disattention deficit" posited by Cromwell and Dokecki.[24] It is also tempting to relate it to a possible habituation deficit in schizophrenia at a level that may implicate neurophysiological processes.[25] The key assumption of the chaining process, that each successive component of a schizophrenic utterance is more likely to be sampled from the patient's associations to a just prior response in the string rather than from the referent—is consistent with Salzinger's[1] "immediacy hypothesis." Also, the role of the dominant response—the response most likely to be sampled, but rejected in high-similarity displays—is consistent with the influence accorded dominant responses by the Chapmans.[5] Finally, the hypothesized tendency to escape from the perseverative response via tangential interresponse associations is (perhaps too loosely) reminiscent of Mednick's[27] theory of bizarre thought generation in schizophrenia. As an interesting related touch, I am tempted to refer here to Auster's[28] review of Louis Wolfson's extraordinary account in French of his radical attempt to escape from aversive perseverative responses by disconnecting entirely from the English language, his mother tongue.

Referent Communication in Chronic Schizophrenia

The findings leading to the construction of the Perseverative-Chaining Model were obtained from acute, first admission, nonparanoid schizophrenics. It is possible that changes occur in the referential functions with increasing chronicity of schizophrenia. Cohen *et al.*[14] pointed out that the perseverative and chaining tendencies indicated by their patient group might be specific to the psychopathology of the early stages of schizophrenia during which the patient still persists in the struggle to communicate effectively. In later stages of the disorder, referent communication might be better described by the Impulsive Speaker Model insofar as long-term patients might be more prone to express, with no (or minimal) attempts to self-edit, sampled but inappropriate responses, once they have learned to anticipate the futility of their attempts to reject them.

In a recent study, Kantorowitz[15] administered a variation of the color-description task to 30 long-term patients selected from the wards of a custodial Veterans Administration hospital. Fifteen were classified as reactive schizophrenics and 15 as process schizophrenics on the basis of Phillips Scale ratings. The length of hospitalization varied from about six to nine years for the reactive, and seven to ten years for the process patients. Kantorowitz also tested 15 normal hospital employees.

As anticipated, both groups of patients showed poorer communication accuracy than the normals as measured by the referent choices of a (normal) listener panel. However, in contrast to the acute patients seen in the previous color-description study, both groups of long-term patients showed little change in response to increases in display similarity either in their response latencies or in their utterance lengths. Compared to the process group, the reactives did show somewhat sharper increments in response latency and utterance length with increased display similarity, but the difference was nonsignificant. One interesting finding was that the combined patient groups showed significantly *faster* speaker-response times (overall) than the normals.

Qualitatively, the patients' descriptions rarely went beyond common color names or phrases, even for the high-similarity displays. This fact, together with the relative speed of response shown by the patients, suggests that their referent communication process conforms ot the Impulsive Speaker Model.

One further finding of interest emerged when the patients were divided into two equal N groups on the basis of clinical judgments of the prevalence of paranoid vs. nonparanoid features in their current clinical status: At either of the two levels of similarity used in this study, the paranoids' utterance lengths were significantly shorter than the nonparanoids. No other differences between these two groups were found.

This paranoid-nonparanoid difference may represent a difference in style that is manifest in situations where the patient is likely to sample responses that are contextually or interpersonally inappropriate but difficult to reject and replace with responses that are more appropriate. The paranoids' terseness is consistent with a generalized pattern of suspicious, self-guarded behavior; the nonparanoids' verbosity would seem, instead, to represent a superficially more open style, one in which the patient maintains a semblance of verbal contact with listeners.

It is, of course, not possible to make very strong inferences from a comparison of the acute[14] and chronic[15] color-description studies, since they differed in many ways other than the patients' lengths of hospitalization. We are inclined, however, to regard chronic schizophrenia as a condition that develops as the patients gradually (or suddenly) yield more and more to the "pull" of referent stimuli rather than continue the struggle to edit out sampled but inappropriate responses. As this process develops, contextual cues become less effective as determinants of thought and speech; and perhaps as a means of dealing with this handicap, chronic schizophrenic patients learn to avoid situations that are likely to involve novel or ambiguous interpersonal circumstances.[26]

CONCLUSIONS

The research summarized in this paper attests to the usefulness of an explicit conception of normal referential processes as a basis for the study of referent communication pathology. The two-stage model of the normal speaker process provided a theoretical basis for distinguishing empirically between hierarchical and control models of disordered referent communication in schizophrenia. The results, taken as a whole, clearly favored some form of control model and indicated that a fundamental deficit in schizophrenia is the inability to reject a sampled response, a problem that different patients may adapt to differently, depending upon the stage of illness and other sources of heterogeneity in schizophrenia. As tentative as the Perseverative-Chaining and Impulsive Speaker Models are as representations of early- and later-term patients' attempts to deal with—or surrender to—the fundamental deficit, these models seem to me to accord with clinical experience and to have implications for research in other areas of schizophrenic deficit, particularly conceptual thinking and social behavior.

REFERENCES

1. SALZINGER, K. 1973. Schizophrenia: Behavioral Aspects. John Wiley & Sons. New York, N.Y.
2. BLEULER, E. 1950. Dementia-Praecox and the Group of Schizophrenias. International Universities Press. New York, N.Y. (Originally published in 1911.)
3. BUSS, A. H. 1966. Psychopathology. John Wiley & Sons. New York, N.Y.
4. BROEN, W. E. & L. H. STORMS. 1966. Lawful disorganization: The process underlying a schizophrenic syndrone. Psychol. Rev. **74:** 265–279.
5. CHAPMAN, L. & J. CHAPMAN. 1973. Disordered Thought in Schizophrenia. Appleton-Century-Crafts. New York (particularly Ch. 6).
6. GOLDSTEIN, K. 1944. Methodological approach to the study of schizophrenic thought disorder. In Language and Thought in Schizophrenia. J. S. Kassanin, Ed. University of California Press, Berkeley, California.
7. SULLIVAN, H. S. 1944. The language of schizophrenia. In Language and Thought in Schizophrenia. J. S. Kasanin, Ed. University of California Press, Berkeley, California.
8. ROSENBERG, S. & B. D. COHEN. 1966. Referential processes of speakers and listeners. Psychol. Rev. **73:** 208–231.
9. ROSENBERG, S. & B. D. COHEN. 1964. Speakers' and listeners' processes in a word-communication task. Science. **145:** 1201–1203.
10. ROSENBERG, S. & A. GORDON. 1968. Identification of facial expressions from affective descriptions: A probabilistic choice analysis of referential ambiguity. Journal of Personality and Social Psychology. **10:** 157–166.
11. ROSENBERG, S. & B. MARKHAM. 1971. Choice behavior in a referentially ambiguous task. J. Pers. Soc. Psychol. **17:** 99–106.
12. ROSENBERG, S. 1972. The development of referential skills in children. In Language of the Mentally Retarded. R. L. Schiefelbusch, Ed. University Park Press. Baltimore, Md.
13. FARNSWORTH, D. 1957. The Farnsworth-Munsell 100 Hue Test for the Examination of Color Discrimination. Manual. Munsell Color Co. Baltimore, Md.
14. COHEN, B. D., G. NACHMANI & S. ROSENBERG. 1974. Referent communication disturbances in acute schizophrenia. J. Abnorm. Psychol. **83:** 1–13.
15. KANTOROWITZ, D. 1974. Referent communication in chronic schizophrenics. Master's thesis. Rutgers University. New Brunswick, N.J. Unpublished.
16. PIAGET, J. 1926. The Language and Thought of the Child. Harcourt Brace Jovanovich Inc. New York, N.Y.
17. MEAD, G. H. 1934. Mind, Self, and Society. University of Chicago Press. Chicago, Ill.

18. VYGOTSKY, L. S. 1962. Thought and Speech. The M.I.T. Press. Cambridge, Mass.
19. COHEN B. D. & J. CAMHI. 1967. Schizophrenic performance in a word-communication task. J. Abnorm. Psychol. **72:** 240–246.
20. NACHMANI, G. & B. D. COHEN. 1969. Recall and recognition free learning in schizophrenics. J. Abnorm. Psychol. **74:** 511–516.
21. LISMAN, S. A. & B. D. COHEN. 1972. Self-editing deficits in schizophrenia. J. Abnorm. Psychol. **79:** 181–188.
22. ROTHBERG, M. 1967. The effect of "social" instructions on word-association behavior. J. Verb. Learning Verb. Behav. **6:** 298–300.
23. KRAUSS, R. M. & S. WEINHEIMER. 1967. Effect of referent similarity and communication mode on verbal encoding. J. Verb. Learning Verb. Behav. **6:** 359–363.
24. CROMWELL, R. L. & P. R. DOKECKI. 1968. Schizophrenic language: a disattention interpretation. *In* Developments in Applied Psycholinguistics Research. S. Rosenberg & J. H. Koplin, Eds. Macmillan. New York, N.Y.
25. VENABLES, P. 1973. Input regulation and psychopathology. *In* Psychopathology: Contributions from the Social, Behavioral, and Biological Sciences. M. Hammer, K. Salzinger & S. Sutton, Eds. John Wiley. New York, N.Y.
26. CROMWELL, R. 1972. Strategies for studying schizophrenic behavior. Psychopharmacologia **24:** 121–146.
27. MEDNICK, S. A. 1958. A learning theory approach to research in schizophrenia. Psychol. Bull. **55:** 316–327.
28. AUSTER, P. 1975. One-man language. New York Review of Books. February **6:** 30–31. (Review of Wolfson, L. 1974. Le Schizo et les Langues. Gallimard. Paris, France.)

PSYCHOLOGY AND THE SOCIAL ORDER

Joseph Church

Department of Psychology
Brooklyn College of the City University of New York
Brooklyn, New York 11210

The psychologist who wishes to put forth a program of radical social change that includes recommendations in such alien domains as the law, economics, and constitutional revision, is driven to elaborate justifications. The first justification is that thinking in these realms is laced through and supported by numerous assumptions about the nature of human nature. Most such assumptions are erroneous, but they are so widely and tenaciously held that they have come to form a cultural mythology. Myths about human nature shade into myths about the nature of nonhuman reality, such as the economic ideal of perpetual growth, which collides head on with the fact of limited planetary resources. A second justification is that contemporary psychological thought is approaching a point where we can reconcile our myth-making propensities with our capacities for reality testing and for rationality. A third justification is that fields like the law and economics are portrayed by their practitioners as arcane realms accessible only to the initiate. To reinforce this portrayal, the experts speak an exotic language of priestly mumbo jumbo designed to mystify and awe the masses. Stripped of the jargon, the myths, and the mysteries, however, the important governing principles in these fields are quite easily accessible to anyone of reasonably sound mind who takes the trouble to study them. Which leads us to a fourth justification, namely that progress in any field may depend on the insights of the outsider, the interested amateur who may perceive relationships hidden to those inside the system. Occasionally, of course, the amateur can benefit from the ideas of the maverick, iconoclastic professional, as I hope I have learned from the writings of John Kenneth Galbraith. Pure amateurism is not always a handicap, however. One of the great social documents of all times, the United States Constitution, was written by people with very few formal credentials in social and political philosophy.

Our social system rests to a frightening degree on the pervasive myth of social darwinism, a pseudohistorical, pseudobiological rationalization of the status quo (almost any status quo). Even amid pious pronouncements that all men are created equal we find written into the Constitution the assumption that some men are more equal than others: the propertied are more equal than the poor, women are less equal than men, whites are more equal than blacks or redskins, the young are less equal than the old. In our own day, we are told that our biology makes us aggressive and warlike, that biologically fixed differences make inequality inevitable between rich and poor, men and women, black and white. Some people, we are informed, are driven to lives of crimes by their faulty genetic make-up. These propositions issue from the mouthes of learned men decked out with titles, degrees, diplomas, and documentary proof of wisdom. The behavior of the "best and the brightest" might make one wonder if education is not a sure path to lunacy.

Our family life is founded on the myths that enduring monogamous love is the norm, that parenthood is psychologically rewarding for all stable adults, that any departure from the standard heterosexual pairing is depraved, that the roles of male and female, husband and wife, father and mother, are self-evident givens, and that the way to prepare young people for competence and responsibility is to keep them in extended bondage to school and family.

Our laws are founded on the myths that the state displays paternalistic benevolence towards its citizens, that criminal behavior can be explained in terms of warped character, that people are turned away from criminal acts by the threat or actuality of punishment, and that we can have equal justice despite blatant social and economic inequalities. The laws, the police, and the courts have evolved, even if unconsciously, into a system that protects the prosperous and the powerful against depredations by the deprived and embittered. Our supposedly secular system of laws embodies the religious morality of the Judeo-Christian tradition, including some of the more repressive features of our Puritan heritage.

Our economy is clothed in a mythology so complex as to defy coherent description. We have, for instance, the myth of free enterprise, which says that government meddling in the "natural" processes of economics can only lead to disaster. The easily established fact, of course, is that government and business have lived symbiotically from the early days of the republic. We have the myth that a capitalist economy can thrive only on waste and war. This myth was initially propagated by the communist philosopher Rosa Luxemburg, but it has been incorporated into our sustaining ideology. We have the mirror-image myths of scarcity and abundance. The scarcity myth, which has broad social implications, justifies the unequal distribution of wealth: since there is not enough to go around, wealth must be differentially distributed according to the worthiness or deservingness of different segments of the population. The abundance myth supports the dream of an ever-expanding economy: when the total pie gets big enough, even those with only a tiny piece of the whole will live in luxury. Needless to say, this myth goes hand in hand with the one that tells us that fulfillment lies in the gluttonous consumption of the economy's products. It should be emphasized that this does not imply simple materialism. In addition to its material manufactures, the economy stands ready to sell good health, sexual potency, physical beauty, art and music and literature, intellectual enhancement, and spiritual salvation. God and Mammon coexist as comfortably as each coexists with the Crown.

In the field of government we are just beginning to awaken from the myth of democracy, of government of, by, and for the People. The myth of the presidency is in a bad way, and a few disgruntled souls have started to question the myth that the states are rational, useful political units. The states have long fed on the myth that rural life and people are by nature virtuous, whereas cities and their people are steeped in iniquity. The residents of New York City and other big cities do not have to be told about the practical consequences of this particular myth. Norman Mailer and Jimmy Breslin wanted to solve New York City's problems by forming a fifty-first state, but their thinking, too, was warped by the myth of the states.

One would assume that the popular view of present-day psychology is defined by the utterances of certain highly visible and audible spokesmen for psychology and allied fields. On one side are the biology-minded, those who give us man the aggressor, the naked ape, biologically fixed sex differences, the constitutional criminal, the genetically fated schizophrenic, and genetically determined intellectual differences among races and social classes. Then we have the lonely antiphonal voice of B. F. Skinner, singing the power of environment as embodied in operant conditioning. This leaves out of account, of course, the images of man being beamed by the remnants of the psychoanalytic persuasion, by the twilight-zone oracles of alpha, psi, zen, and encounter, and by those who tell parents how to give their children superior personalities and intellects. One would do as well, I suspect, to derive a theory of human nature from the behavior of characters in soap operas.

Whatever the popular image of psychology, the main body of the discipline shows signs of an emerging synthesis and consensus. This is admittedly an eclectic consensus, with strands drawn from psychoanalysis, learning theory, the Gestalt tradition, the developmentalism of Piaget and Werner, the humanist movement, and from neighboring fields like zoology and anthropology. For all its disparate origins, this synthetic vision is beginning to take on a remarkably human quality. It is not a patchwork monster fabricated by a committee of jostling, rivalrous Frankensteins. It is a vision of a quite credible person, a biological organism permeated by culture, a creature simultaneously insightful and obtuse, self-controlling and externally determined, loving and hostile, arrogant and vulnerable, forthright and devious, logical and superstitious, brave and fearful, trusting and paranoid, idealistic and cynical, inventive and tradition-bound, and so on through all the inconsistencies, anomalies, ambiguities, and paradoxes of the human condition.

It is a difficult notion to state concisely, but people live and act in a psychological life space that is a strange amalgam of reality and delusion. The history of science is largely a chronicle of humankind's attempt to battle free of suffocating myth and superstition, to struggle into the fresh air of objectivity and reasoned judgment. Our progress has been by no means uniform, if only because the quest after truth all too often gets entangled with the personal vanity, greed, and ambition of the fallible human beings who cast themselves in the role of scientist. Even without these complications, the scientific enterprise has a hard time keeping its bearings. Psychology, as we know, in its attempt to dispel the fog of supernaturalism that surrounded early thinking about people, overshot into barren, scientistic reductionism. In attempting to redress the balance, other psychologists have dragged us too far back into mysticism. But we are gradually learning to see the human creature whole, in meaningful if sometimes irrational congress with its material, human, institutional, and ideological surroundings.

We are coming to understand that the key to diversity lies in patterns of development, the shaping of biologically unique specimens by the action of direct and socially mediated feedback, learning from imitation and observation of models, and also from autonomous discovery and problem solving. We are coming to appreciate the subtle yet potent influence of language in forming our characters and outlooks. Without buying the entire Whorfian package, we can recognize that a given cultural orientation has its own special vocabulary, syntax, and logic, and that statements made in the dialect of a particular world view may abound in vital implications invisible and inaudible to speakers of other dialects. At one extreme, we can inhabit a primitive symbolic universe of tradition, supernatural entities and forces, unquestionable axioms of conduct, and intense adherence to ritual forms. At the other extreme, we have come to know the hyperrational, emotionless symbolic universe of the technologist, technocrat, and military strategist, those who claim to know how to but prefer not to wonder why; this universe is realistic, pragmatic, hard-nosed, laboriously prosaic, and rich in numbers and formulas. If one can get a computer to do one's talking, so much the better. This, as we know, is a linguistic universe of what the General Semanticists call empty abstractions, in which bloodless symbols replace and obliterate the messy actualities of biology, behavior, and values. It is, ultimately, the realm of what C. Wright Mills called "crackpot realism," a realm in which the reasoning is impeccably logical and the premises monstrously, pathologically false.

We can also recognize the kind of symbolic universe in which we can find probabilistic order without losing sight of the richness, intensity, and variety of the phenomena we are describing. The psychologist is rediscovering herself and himself as an empathic instrument of observation and analysis. Without abandoning our commitment to empiricism and statistical validation, we are learning to practice the skills of the novelist and the critic. Like the novelist, the psychologist must resonate to his subjects, while, like the critic, he maintains a cool analytical distance from his own resonances. Even in the role of objective observer, the psychologist can react to his subject as a sentient human organism rather than a specimen wriggling on the point of a pin.

I think, then, that the message of an organismic, ecological developmental psychology is that there are many human natures, shaped in diverse patterns by lifetime encounters with things, people, situations, institutions, ideas, and ideologies, codified in implicit and explicit cultures and the linguistic forms that embody them. We know that there are cultures and languages that stifle and imprison human possibilities, and others that hold the promise of liberation. We could debate endlessly about our own preferred versions of human nature, but I read history, for all the calamities and regressions, as saying that the human impulse is toward liberation. I feel sure that we could get consensus that we want our own children to be loving, bright, well-informed, imaginative, articulate, humorous, generous, trustful, compassionate, serious, brave, and capable of sensuality.

We are rapidly learning how to rear such children. There are, however, doubters, those who fear that people with these qualities would be unfit for survival in our savage society. It seems to me that the answer is not to raise up yet another generation of savages but, rather, to design new social institutions that will nourish and fortify the human qualities most of us esteem. The realists will object once more that a nation of loving human beings would be a nation of softies, easy prey for its implacable enemies abroad. There are two answers to this argument. The first, and weaker, is that even loving people can be roused to enraged self-defense when attacked. The second, and stronger, argument is that the reciprocal paranoia of international relations is for the most part a manufactured paranoia. It suits the ruling classes—on both sides—very well to keep the masses churning with xeno-phobia. The universal myth of the enemy justifies policies and programs and restraints and manipulations that would be intolerable in a rational world. We might remind ourselves that our annual death budget is mounting to $100 billion even as the GNP shrivels, our currency deteriorates, and unemployment transforms erstwhile customers into needy supplicants and, increasingly, desperate thieves.

Let us turn, then, from these general considerations to some of the specific measures we might take in the interests of a sane social order. Two things need to be said. First, this is only a sampling of the ideas I will propose in my book. Second, my proposals are not meant to be final prescriptions for the future. They are offered as a framework for discussion and debate. I have no pretensions to the role of messiah; I am happy to play the part of simple catalyst. My suggestions apply to the four interconnected domains of child rearing and education, economics, the law, and a new Constitution.

In the domain of child rearing and education, we need to get away from the myth that our mating, marrying, and reproducing should be subject to tight regulation by government. There are, of course, some easily defined areas in which the common interest can take precedence over individual impulse. We have a collective interest in population control, and while compulsory contraception or abortion would be incompatible with a humane society, the state can at least be enjoined against rewarding fecundity, as through income-tax deductions, and punishing infertility, as in proscriptions against homosexuality or intercourse with animals. A sensibly run state needs good statistics, and it can legitimately require that the birth or adoption of a child be recorded. Also, I think we would all agree that the authorities should intervene when there is serious neglect or abuse of children, although even here informal mechanisms of community control might work better than any legal procedure we can devise. Beyond these minimal restraints, how people choose to arrange their private lives should be nobody's business but their own. As we shall see in a moment, freedom from official regulation can impose some reciprocal obligations on the family.

A first obvious implication of this way of thinking is that people should be free to experiment with all kinds of family groupings. It seems to be the case that people with permanent or semipermanent partners fare better physically and psychologically than those who live alone, but this carries no presumption that people who elect to live alone should be penalized or stigmatized. Neither does it suggest that the conventional family is the ideal arrangement for those who want to share their lives. People should be free, at their own risk, to try communal marriages, open marriages, polygyny or polyandry, one-parent parenthood (either through adoption or by finding a temporary partner willing to bear or sire a child), homosexual or bisexual groupings, or whatever other combinations promise satisfaction. Those who wish to formalize their marriages with religious or secular ceremonies (the phrasing of the wedding vows gets complicated when there are more than two spouses) or with binding contracts should of course be free to do so, but equally of course they should not be required by law to do so. Most of us share an intuition that there should be legal criteria for adoption; unfortunately, though, I have found it impossible to frame a satisfactory set of criteria, and it may be that adopted children can be protected from unfit parents only after the fact, through laws dealing with neglect and abuse.

Another, less palatable, corollary to the noninterference principle needs to be put in context. I believe that all citizens of an advanced, humane, reasonably affluent society are entitled, as a matter of fundamental right, to a decent share of the necessities of life. In a modern society, these necessities go far beyond the basics of food, clothing, and shelter. They include such things as a ration of free energy (the Cuban experience indicates that unrationed access leads to waste), free mass transportation, and free access to the electronic media and the entertainment and information they carry. The necessities further include a full range of health services, psychological and educational services included. Now comes the hard part: what citizens are not entitled to is custodial, residential care for their flawed children. There are two considerations here. It seems that all publicly funded custodial institutions tend to become snake pits. On the basis of the continuing exposés of conditions at Willowbrook and Creedmore, as well as my prior knowledge of a number of other institutions, I incline to the dangerous thought that euthanasia might be preferable. Since I most decidedly do not favor euthanasia, I feel that damaged children can be helped best by remedial services delivered on an outpatient basis in the community, subject to general scrutiny. The second consideration is that we should use every means possible to impress upon people that parenthood is a serious business, not to be undertaken frivolously, and that parents have to be responsible for their offspring, whole or maimed. High-risk parents who gamble on having a child will have to be aware that they cannot simply dump their lost bets on society as a whole. Needless to say, the available health services should include birth control information and devices, genetic counseling, antenatal diagnosis for high-risk parents, and abortion for those who want it. A third consideration in this way of thinking is that it helps counter the myth that organically impaired children are foredoomed to blighted lives. In fact, flawed children reared lovingly in normal settings stand a good chance of developing well.

A further implication of this principle is that the state may not compel parents to send their children to school. The basic idea here is that schools have to be so good that parents want to send their children to them. In general, we need a radical overhauling of our thinking and practice with regard to schools, schooling, and education.

Another institution ripe for close scrutiny is the familiar phenomenon of psychological adolescence. L. J. Stone and I[1] have long argued that institutionalized adolescence is a cultural invention that does not work very well, and I am all for disinventing it. Adolescence is supported by a complex of habits, attitudes, customs, and beliefs, and we have to begin by asking how much psychological sense this condition of life makes. It is also supported by a network of laws, ostensibly designed to protect young people from their own immaturity, which may in fact infantilize them or expose them to abuse. For instance, child labor laws may shield young people from exploitation, but such laws can also keep them from getting useful experience and from earning needed money. A major problem of the young people I know is achieving independence from their parents, which most of them find impossible as long as they are in economic bondage. It would make better sense to have laws that protect the welfare of all workers, and not just the young. Juvenile-offender status deprives the youthful criminal of full responsibility for his misdeeds, and it may also deprive him of due process and subject him to more severe penalties than adult offenders. Laws restricting the sexual behavior of young people can offer them no real protection: such laws only help reinforce our Puritan-Victorian anxiety about sex.

What I propose is, simply, that anyone past puberty should be free to declare himself or herself an adult. I realize that abolishing the institution of adolescence will not magically banish the young person's immaturities, but being on one's own produces much more rapid learning than does being kept dependent and subservient. I know, too, that many youngsters would find the prospect of abrupt, total emancipation quite terrifying, and I propose a number of optional courses that young people might follow into full independence. One such option is a voluntary youth corps, offering the young person on-the-job training in a variety of skills. I have tried to work out the details so that the young person could learn to accept reasonable discipline, make and fulfill commitments, and still be a self-determining adult. The young person's options would not include, however, a return to the parental nest. Obviously, youngsters and their parents could cheat on such a prohibition, but the pressures ought to be in the direction of autonomy. One vital ingredient in the young person's liberation would be a national living-allowance program, for which the self-proclaimed adult would immediately become eligible. At all ages, psychological independence seems to be closely tied to economic independence, and we need a system in which people cannot be coerced by the threat of destitution into doing things that they do not want to do. The secret to getting economically secure people to perform society's more revolting tasks is to reward them handsomely, offering a change, if only temporarily, from subsistence to luxury. In general, the people who do the hardest, nastiest, most dangerous jobs should be entitled to a higher standard of material living than those with jobs high in psychic rewards, like being a college professor.

I hope it is clear that one cannot think about how to rear and educate children without becoming entangled in considerations of economics and law and encountering the iron grip of conventional thought. Economic thinking in turn is hobbled by mythical assumptions: the mirror-image myths of scarcity and abundance, the myth of the perpetually growing economy, the mythical will-o'-the-wisp of full employment, the myth of free enterprise, of the discipline of the marketplace, and of the necessity for war and waste as economic stimulants.

Most of my economic recommendations are consonant with those of John Kenneth Galbraith,[2] although there are divergences that I shall mention shortly. What we agree on most fundamentally is that, even in an ecologically responsible society, we should be able to guarantee all our citizens a decent material standard of living. We are able to produce more than enough of the essentials to go around, so what we need is mechanisms for a better distribution of wealth. Like Herbert Gans,[3] Galbraith and I do not envision absolute economic equality; but there is no reason whatsoever that people should have to live in want and misery in the midst of plenty. Galbraith and I offer somewhat different mixes of socialism and private enterprise, but in both systems socialism plays an important part. Galbraith, for instance, would nationalize giant corporations as a way of controlling them. My solution to the problem of the giants is simpler: oblige them to offer only goods of superior quality. An end to planned obsolescence and the replacement market it generates will, I feel confident, quickly trim the giants to size. Some of our familiar conveniences, like cars and appliances, would rise in initial cost, but this would be compensated for by long life. In fact, recent legislation dealing with warranties is a valuable step in the direction of raising quality.

Galbraith clings to the view that full employment will solve our economic woes, whereas I am convinced that a more rational economy will entail considerable idleness. There is much useful work to be done, growing crops to fight famine, rebuilding the cities and providing good housing for all, building and renewing mass transit facilities, providing health services, and so forth, and these will absorb great quantities of people-power. On the other hand, if we deflate the automotive and related industries, shrink our runaway military establishment to a sensible size, disband useless bureaucracies, and otherwise act to reduce waste, I think we will find ourselves with a lot of unemployed people. I hope I am wrong, but we have to be prepared to support those who lack regular employment and, in addition, to offer them satisfying life styles outside or on the fringes of the economy. It should be possible for some portion of the chronically unemployed to escape boredom by becoming artists, composers, poets, playwrights, actors and actresses, scholars and scientists, or political theorists or activists. Some, of course, will invent their own diversions, and others will settle for planned recreation. Some will dream up new business ventures and others will move in and out of the economy to pick up extra cash.

Economic thinking nowadays has to take account of global forces. As things are going, we may be relieved of further decision making by the Middle-Eastern potentates who are in a fair way of buying up the country. We have to think of ways to feed both ourselves and as many of the world's people as possible. The ghost of Thomas Malthus is abroad in the planet, reminding us in sepulchral tones that food production can never keep up with unfettered baby production, and that we are going to have to make some excruciatingly painful choices. Countries with desirable raw materials but limited food supplies are going to drive some very hard bargains indeed. Some poor countries may still be willing to accept glittering fleets of warplanes in exchange for their dwindling resources, but I think the realization will soon dawn that the one truly valuable commodity we can offer is food. Those countries without resources to barter for our foodstuffs are in danger of being caught in a crushing and perhaps lethal squeeze. I hope we will find ways to transcend economics and inject a measure of humanitarianism into our food policies. We have the further conflict that we should be doing everything in our power to expand production of food, including synthetic foods, and at the same time changing our agricultural practices to avoid ecological devastation.

Moving on to the domain of law, we need to relinquish the myth that equates immorality and criminality, the myth that punishment is the proper response to wrongdoing, and the myth that we have a system of impartial, equal justice. Everybody wants to reduce crime, but people are only now beginning to take seriously that a first step to reducing crime might be to expunge a number of laws from the books. People are noticing that the police are kept busy trying to enforce unenforceable laws merely clogging the courts and jails with a miscellany of miscreants who shouldn't be there, to the neglect of crimes that really count. Most of these unenforceable laws breed secondary crime and corrupt the enforcers. Following John Stuart Mill, a great many people, including me, feel that we should stop legislating in the domain of private morality and repeal laws against what have come to be known as "victimless crimes." I would change the label to "abuse of the self," both to avoid any implication of criminality and at the same time make explicit that the individual may be doing himself or herself an injury. The abuses of the self against which a paternalistic state should no longer attempt to shelter its childlike citizens include forms of suicide that threaten no physical harm to others, consenting sex of whatever variety (a case can be made for regulating prostitution, but not for forbidding it), gambling, and drug use. Prohibition had some important lessons to teach us, but people have been slow to learn them. People hooked on gambling, drugs, or alcohol should of course have access to whatever voluntary treatment will get them unhooked, but the contented addict should be left undisturbed.

With such "crimes" wiped off the books, the police and the courts should have abundant time and energy for dealing with real crimes, those that do injury to other people, their persons, property, or state of mind. To decriminalize abuse of the self would deprive organized crime of major sources of revenue; it might encourage the Mafia to go completely straight, although there would still be possibilities for abuse in loan-sharking and in doing society's dirty work, such as refuse removal and burying the dead. We might even find ourselves free to give some attention to crime in high places like corporate board rooms and government offices. I would go so far as to propose a double standard of law, whereby powerful people who abuse the public trust would have fewer legal safeguards and be subject to much harsher sanctions than ordinary wrongdoers.

Mill's dictum against legislating morality has a second, less often discussed meaning. There is pretty good agreement that it is permissible for the state to prohibit bad behavior directed against others, but there should also be agreement that the state may not coerce good behavior. That is, proscriptive laws, which forbid criminal acts, are legitimate, whereas prescriptive laws, which ordain virtuous behavior, are not. This principle fits in well with observations that a wide variety of animals resist coercion, even when it entails doing things that the animal, left to its own devices, might find pleasurable. It does not require elaborate investigation to discover, for instance, that high school and college students detest and evade compulsory physical education, although, on their own, these same students engage in numerous healthful physical activities. According to this principle, military conscription and compulsory schooling should be taboo. There are, however, three areas where I believe that the collective good should take precedence over the principle. These are providing census information, paying personal income tax (our present unjust system begs to be violated, and I will propose a better one), and serving on juries. Jury duty can be made far more equitable than it is now. For one thing, we can end the system of exemptions that frees women and other categories of people from the obligation to serve. Secondly, we can end the present time-consuming process of jury selection: jurors should be assigned to a case strictly by lot, and be excused only if they have some link to one or more of the principals.

Let me digress and say a word for random selection as an answer to many social problems. Indeed, the draft was meant to operate by lot, which is the only fair system, but in fact, the introduction of special considerations shifted the burden of service for the most part to the poor and powerless. Currently, there is fervent debate about affirmative action and the possibility of quotas for ending discrimination. I feel that the debate is misguided. Those who advocate quotas ignore demonstrable differences in competence for various social roles and occupations. The opponents of quotas, however, err in thinking that these demonstrable differences permit a rank-ordering of candidates or applicants for an opening. In fact, the best we can do, if my experience in accepting graduate students and hiring colleagues is typical, is classify people as probably qualified and almost certainly unqualified. Measures to raise the qualifications of the unqualified are certainly needed, but that is a separate issue. How we might proceed right now, pending utopia, is to select appointees by lot from the pool of the probably qualified. This spares us the painful task of making impossible judgments about the relative merits of individuals and blunts the complaints of those who feel that they have been unjustly discriminated against. The unsuccessful candidate will inevitably feel that he or she is better qualified than those chosen, but there will be no grounds for hurt or resentment at having been misjudged.

To return to the topic of law and order, I favor doing away with both old-fashioned ways of treating convicted criminals, like incarcerating them, and new-fangled ones like behavior modification or drugs. A few incorrigibly bad actors would almost certainly have to be locked away, but very few, and imprisonment should be a measure of last resort. Some convicts might be in need of psychotherapy, in which case behavior modification could have a role, but the gloomy or at best ambiguous assessments that I have been reading of behavioral techniques applied to real life should make us skeptical. What I favor trying is supervised probation with courses of constructive action made available to the criminal. There are three guiding themes. The first is identification: to protect others, the convict should be made to wear a distinctive emblem signaling both that he is under sentence and the serious-ness of his crime. If this causes shame, all right; shaming is an ancient and often effective technique of social control. The two other themes are restitution and rehabilitation. Full restitution is not always possible, as when somebody has been maimed or killed, but we can do only what we can. I define rehabilitation very modestly to mean simply that the criminal must not commit any more crimes. He or she is free to be a loathsome person, as long as he or she refrains from criminal acts. Except for these constraints, the criminal would be encouraged to live as normal a life as possible, with his case reviewed periodically until he is adjudged rehabilitated.

No person charged with a crime could be excused from trial or acquitted by reason of insanity. The court's first duty is to ascertain, in keeping with the usual rules, whether the accused person did or did not commit the crime. Only after conviction could the person's psychological condition be taken into account in planning treatment. The psychotic criminal might be required to have psychiatric treatment, but only if it could be shown that such treatment would actually contribute to rehabilitation. But if psychotic criminals must be held accountable for their misdeeds, noncriminal psychotics must be treated as normal unless they voluntarily seek help. Psychosis alone cannot be grounds for incarceration. The mental health profession's track record in predicting who will or will not be a menace to his fellow man is too poor to permit people to be locked up on a professional's say-so. Only conviction on a criminal charge would justify treating psychotics differently from other people.

Let us turn now to the design for a new constitution. Thinking in this area is cramped by a number of myths, of which I should like to emphasize two. One is the myth that we need a President who will embody all our sacred principles and provide strong leadership in solving national problems. What we need is not strong leader-ship but a new set of constitutional principles to guide national policy. The performance of our recent string of imperial presidents should inspire little confidence that we can reform or redeem so ill-conceived an institution. Alexander Hamilton, arguing in support of the office, assured his fellows that the president could never take on the trappings of a monarch; he was dead wrong. The second myth is that the states are God-given, immutable, rational political entities that help protect us from an over-concentration of federal power. There are good historical reasons why we are an assemblage of states, but history should not blind us to the absurdity of what the states have become.

This is not to disparage our present Constitution. It is an altogether remarkable document that, along with its twenty-five amendments, is still reasonably serviceable. We can, however, do considerably better. The late twentieth-century world is radically different from the late eighteenth-century world, and we need a charter that preserves our best traditions while spelling out principles that recognize modern realities.

The new constitution, then, has two chief aims. First, it seeks to democratize political processes to the utmost, and second, to make explicit a set of principles to replace the impulse-ridden expediency that seems to prevail in governmental decision making. Thus, the constitution should set forth the principles of economic organization that will ensure a fair share of the national wealth to every citizen. The constitution should state principles of law, including both accepted conventions, like the presumption of innocence, that have no Constitutional status, and principles that have evolved through judicial interpretations, like the right to be represented by an attorney from the moment of arrest. The constitution should define our foreign policy, including principles of nonexpansion and nonaggression. And, of course, the constitution should spell out the structure of government. In the course of this spelling out, it must make clear that government exists only for the convenience of the citizenry, that it must adhere to constitutional principles, and that new policies may be adopted only with the consent of the electorate. Most of all, the new constitution has to expand and strengthen the rights of free, law-abiding citizens as originally set forth in the Bill of Rights. The Bill of Rights was an afterthought: in a new constitution, the rights of citizens should form the heart of the document.

Without a president, the responsibility for running the country would rest with the congress and whatever administrative structures it found useful. Without states, we need a new design for a congress. I propose a bicameral legislature, to consist of a house of geographical representatives, much like our present House, and a house of delegates representing various interest groups without regard to geography. Dwight Macdonald too has proposed doing away with the states as political entities (some people might want to preserve them as sentimental entities, although I find it hard to understand why), suggesting instead a system of regions made up of groups of states. My idea is rather different. I would favor a system consisting of metropolitan areas and rural regions, each to govern its own internal affairs in keeping with constitutional principles, and each being represented in the geographical house according to the number of voters. Representation in both chambers would be on the basis of one congressman for each 400,000 voters—not inhabitants, but voters. All adults would be free to vote, but only those who chose to vote would be represented. The boundaries of regions and areas would be defined by a combination of demographic logic and voter identification. Within a metropolitan area, we could have geographical representation at the national level either according to districts, as we have now, or through representatives-at-large from the entire area. I would favor the latter as a way to minimize gerrymandering.

I cannot conceive of a rational scheme of special-interest groups, so I would favor allowing them to form spontaneously and to shift as people's concerns shift: labor, students, women, blacks, industrialists, homosexuals, motorists, food faddists, antivivisectionists, farmers, whatever. Any group or coalition that could rally 400,000 voters would be entitled to a delegate. Obviously, each individual is potentially a member of many groups; for any one election, however, the voter would have to declare a single affiliation. This calls for a more complicated but more democratic election process than we now have, with preferential ballots and runoff elections as needed; computerized voting should help.

The power of the voters would be further enhanced by the rights of referendum, as already suggested, and of initiative and recall. But the electorate, like the congress, would be restrained from wild-eyed impulses by constitutional principle, with the courts as final arbiters. Note that nobody has yet come up with a set of principles so cleverly worked out that conflicts would never arise. For instance, we have the recurring friction between the need for a free press and the impartial administration of justice. I would propose a further principle, then, that when principles are in conflict the court must sometimes make a judgment ad hoc, on the merits of the particular case, but without thereby setting a precedent. The important thing is that the voters know what is going on and have a chance to express their feelings at the ballot box or computer console. Public opinion polls, letters to the editor, and paid advertisements in leading newspapers cannot substitute for a public debate followed by a democratic vote.

I offer alternatives not with any expectation that my views will prevail, but in hopes that I can provoke people to reexamine their assumptions and values, think, argue, and look for escapes from the apocalyptic future that all too many people see as inevitable. There are alternatives to apocalypse. Totalitarianism is one. But the democratic alternative requires that we break loose from the prison of cultural givens and see what other possibilities remain to be explored. The crackpot realists have had their day; perhaps it is time to make room for some crackpot idealists.

REFERENCES

1. STONE, L. J. & J. CHURCH 1973. Childhood and Adolescence. 3rd edit. Random House. New York, N.Y.
2. GALBRAITH, J. K. 1973. Economics and the Public Purpose. Houghton Mifflin. Boston, Mass.
3. GANS, H. J. 1973. More Equality. Pantheon. New York, N.Y.

DATE DUE

	261-2500		Printed in USA